Cookie Rojas

ALSO BY LOU HERNÁNDEZ

The Cobalt Moon's Fury (Austin Macauley, 2020)

The Curse of the Cobalt Moon (Austin Macauley, 2019)

Bobby Maduro and the Cuban Sugar Kings (McFarland, 2019)

Manager of Giants: The Tactics, Temper and True Record of John McGraw (McFarland, 2018)

The 1933 New York Giants: Bill Terry's Unexpected World Champions (McFarland, 2017)

Chronology of Latin Americans in Baseball, 1871–2015 (McFarland, 2016)

Baseball's Great Hispanic Pitchers: Seventeen Aces from the Major, Negro and Latin American Leagues (McFarland, 2015)

Memories of Winter Ball: Interviews with Players in the Latin American Winter Leagues of the 1950s (McFarland, 2013)

The Rise of the Latin American Baseball Leagues, 1947–1961: Cuba, the Dominican Republic, Mexico, Nicaragua, Panama, Puerto Rico and Venezuela (McFarland, 2011)

Cookie Rojas
A Baseball Life

Lou Hernández

McFarland & Company, Inc., Publishers
Jefferson, North Carolina

ISBN (print) 978-1-4766-9457-3
ISBN (ebook) 978-1-4766-5279-5

LIBRARY OF CONGRESS AND BRITISH LIBRARY
CATALOGUING DATA ARE AVAILABLE

Library of Congress Control Number 2024019119

© 2024 Lou Hernández. All rights reserved

No part of this book may be reproduced or transmitted in any form or by any means, electronic or mechanical, including photocopying or recording, or by any information storage and retrieval system, without permission in writing from the publisher.

Front cover: Kansas City Royals second baseman Cookie Rojas (National Baseball Hall of Fame Library, Cooperstown, New York)

Printed in the United States of America

*McFarland & Company, Inc., Publishers
Box 611, Jefferson, North Carolina 28640
www.mcfarlandpub.com*

For all those players and their families
whose love for baseball sustained them
through their long journey.

Acknowledgments

The subject of this book and his family were very giving of their time to participate in this book project. Without such a commitment, the end result would not have been possible.

The author is grateful for the opportunity to speak to Candida Rojas, the Rojas children, José Padilla, Jorge Maduro and Armando Mendez.

All quotes attributed to Cookie Rojas and wife Candida, except where otherwise noted, came from personal sit-down or phone interviews and conversations conducted by the author with the subjects between November 2021 and June 2023.

All WAR and other analytic numbers are from baseballreference.com. There was no official statistic for saves prior to the 1969 season. Those have been retroactively compiled.

Table of Contents

Acknowledgments	vi
Preface	1
Introduction	5
One—Minor League Zenith	7
Two—Forced Exile	31
Three—Enough to Make Billy Penn Cry	47
Four—Major League All-Star	76
Five—All-Time Phillie	100
Six—Happy to Be a Royal	116
Seven—Playoff Disappointment and Bowing Out	142
Eight—From the Coaching Lines and Beyond to Contented Retirement	160
Chapter Notes	183
Bibliography	195
Index	199

Preface

Fewer than 12,000 players had held the privilege and distinction of playing in the major leagues when Octavio Rojas debuted at professional baseball's highest level in 1962. Today, more than 60 years later, expansion and increased roster limits have swelled the total to well over 22,000. A relative few had as lengthy a major league career or stayed in baseball in different capacities after retiring as a player as long as Rojas. The 16-year big league veteran's dedication and commitment to the sport he loved is best reflected by the life he led following his active service, which kept him associated with the game in various dugout, scouting and broadcast positions for another 39 years.

After retiring as a player in 1977, Rojas coached in the major leagues for 14½ years with four different clubs. In between, Rojas managed the California Angels in 1988. Another 11 interspersed years were dedicated to scouting. He spent his final 14 years in the game in the Spanish-language broadcast booth of the Miami Marlins as a color analyst.

To be sure, the former infielder was an "old school" player—no matter how diminished that phrase has become in today's baseball lexicon. Most of his generation of hit-and-run, sacrifice-them-over, hit-behind-the-runner athletes were. "I would hit .400 today," Rojas boasted, when asked his opinion of the ubiquitous defensive shifting of the current era (pre–2023). "I'd bet my life on it. The way I could bunt. I'd bunt the heck out of the ball every time up if they tried that nonsense [with me]." Rojas, a right-handed batter, struck out only 489 times in 6,309 at-bats, a testament to his skill with the lumber.

Rojas also contended, "I think it's easier to reach the major leagues now than when I played," referring to the number of big league franchises in existence today—30 as opposed to the 20 when he broke in and vastly fewer minor league teams.

Like some others his age, Rojas is not a fan of the quantitative data that drive defensive positioning, pitching changes, and at-bats, but he understands that it is an inherent part of the game's strategy now. "I would like to see the numbers balanced more with personal experience," he stated, alluding to relying more on the "eye test" or a manager's memory (neither probably as accurate or productive as new-age numbers crunching).

Who were the best players Rojas saw? "I've played against Hall of Famers and with Hall of Famers. Willie Mays, number one player. Barry Bonds could do it all, Roberto Clemente." Today's game: "Trout." Best pitchers? "Koufax, Gibson, incredible slider. Breaking ball pitchers gave me the most trouble."

Two major league franchises, Kansas City and Philadelphia, have honored Rojas with enshrinement in their Halls of Fame.

As a rookie in 1962, Rojas was one of the 18 players who inaugurated Dodger Stadium, now the majors' third-oldest playing facility. Eleven years later, he was one of the first nine players to take the field in the American League's first synthetic turf stadium in Kansas City.

Thanks to his longevity, Rojas has witnessed first-hand the game's transformation and progress. "Baseball has changed.... When I started in organized ball, there was a manager and two coaches, one for the pitchers," said the man who played, coached, managed, or broadcast in seven decades. "Now with so many more coaches, you would think the fundamentals would have improved, but the opposite has taken place. Baseball today is only about home runs and pitching velocity. Defense has suffered terribly."

Rojas was a five-time All-Star. A nose-to-the-grindstone type of ballplayer, Rojas was easy to root for and cheer on. "Because of my glasses, I looked like a schoolteacher. They called me 'Professor' a lot. I was very serious on the field, and that made people think I was older." Blessed with defensive versatility, he evolved into a very likable player, complete with an appealing nickname. "Cookie" Rojas became a favorite among hometown followers while at the same time earning the respect and admiration of his peers.

His playing career traversed a low run-scoring environment, and Rojas was the rather small, prototypical middle infielder that teams of his era built their first line of defense around. Light hitting, and generously listed at 5'10" and 160 pounds, the Havana, Cuba, native was someone the average fan could relate to. Rojas was a reflection of themselves—hard-working and driven to succeed.

Known mostly as a second baseman (his 1,446 games rank in the top 50 all-time among second sackers), Rojas was one of the rare players to take turns at every position on the major league diamond. "[Manager]

Gene Mauch believed in platooning. Being able to play different positions helped me get more playing time. That's what I most wanted—to play."

During Jim Bunning's Father's Day perfect game in 1964, Rojas was asked to hold the line at shortstop (five innings, three putouts) and left field (four innings). In 1967, in his sixth major-league season, after having defended every spot on the baseball field but one, Rojas broke that last barrier by hurling an inning from the mound in a lopsided Phillies loss to the Giants. Of those few multi-dimensional individuals to play all nine positions in baseball history, Rojas is the only one to make the All-Star Game as a representative from both leagues, and in 1972, he became the first Hispanic player to homer in one for the American League. (National Leaguers Tony Pérez and Roberto Clemente had gone deep in 1967 and 1971, respectively.)

Even as his defensive positions changed, his glove did not. Rojas never deviated from his regular infielder's glove when he played first base or caught, two positions generally associated with specialty gloves. In 2019, he donated his reliable, nine-position glove to the National Baseball Hall of Fame in Cooperstown. "I thought the glove would be better served in the Hall of Fame than on some stand or shelf in my house."

Rojas and his wife Candida have retired to Naples, Florida. They boast a rare off-the-field achievement: more than six decades of marriage. Their special union produced four children (all boys), 14 grandchildren, and nine great-grandchildren.

Introduction

I first met Cookie Rojas in October of 2021, when he was recognized by the city of Doral, Florida, for his baseball achievements in a ceremony inside the city hall council chambers.

"I wanted to be a baseball player since I was ten years old," he told everyone present. Afterward, I spent time with him and his wife at his home on several occasions and spoke to him on many more. Whenever I was at his home, I noticed stacked—somewhere on a side table—correspondence from fans requesting an autograph, often accompanied by various editions of his baseball cards. Part of one afternoon was spent on his backyard patio, which abuts one of the greens of the 18-hole golf course on which his home is situated.

Now in his mid–80s, Rojas sometimes struggles to recall the details of his career. It's to be expected, regardless of age, when one's career has been so long and so diverse. Otherwise, he—as well as his gracious wife—maintains a robust physical presence and pleasant demeanor. Candida, who looks much younger than her years, is clearly Rojas' go-to person on many different things, especially names and dates.

"You have to be able to cope with failure," the former ballplayer told me, almost at random, one afternoon. "If you can't cope with failure, you'll never be successful in baseball. Players today don't know how to deal with failure, in my opinion."

My mind immediately popped back to 1964 and the ignominious collapse of the Philadelphia Phillies, a team of which he was a fundamental part. Two years shy of the 60th anniversary of the disastrous occurrence for southeastern Pennsylvania, Rojas was unfazed when I broached the subject. "It was like swimming in a long, long lake ... and then you drown," he answered, as if in a prepared statement. "It was not just the fact that we lost ten games in a row toward the end of the season. It's that the Cincinnati Reds won nine games and St. Louis Cardinals won eight games in a row at the same *exact* time. If those parallel occurrences had not happened, we would have backed into the pennant even with our losing streak and given Philadelphia fans what they were expecting and deserved—a World Series appearance."

His father, who was a hospital administrator, wanted Rojas to become a doctor. "I could never have gone into that type of medical profession. I couldn't stand the sight of blood." Rojas instead became the professional baseball player he dreamed of becoming, surmounting forced exile from his native country and separation from his immediate family. "I felt such a love for the game that playing it helped overcome the harsh reality of not being able to return to Cuba."

Apparently impressed with my book about Bobby Maduro and his Cuban Sugar Kings (a team for which Rojas played), the octogenarian reached out to me to help him share his life story.

It is one worth telling, I think, for those fans who saw him play and for those who didn't.

ONE

Minor League Zenith

In March of 1939, as the clouds of war were gathering on the not-too-distant horizon over parts of Europe, the United States continued to struggle in its progress against the economic ravages of the Great Depression. A labor report issued a few years later by the National Bureau of Economic Research listed nine million people as unemployed in the United States, about one-sixth of the total labor force. "In effect," read the missive, "we were operating in 1939 with a working force that excluded not only some two million of those who had been employed in 1929, but also excluded the net additions contributed by a growing population to the available labor supply (an increase in some 10 million in population between 1929 and 1939)."[1]

"The Dow did not return to 1929 levels until nearly a decade after [President Franklin] Roosevelt's death," wrote Amity Shlaes, award-winning author and expert on economic history. "The goodwill of the New Dealers, and there was enormous goodwill, could not excuse such consequence."[2] Shlaes questioned whether Roosevelt's massive works programs did more harm than good by creating only temporary jobs and therefore prolonging the nation's economic woes. Unemployment never fell below 10 percent under Roosevelt until the Second World War, she pointed out, when "it was a period of a power struggle between two sectors of the economy, both containing a mix of evil and virtue. The public sector and private sector competed relentlessly for advantage. At the beginning, in the 1920s, the private sector ruled. By the end, when World War II began, it was the public sector that was dominant."[3]

As it has been through the course of human history, undaunted by economic or political headwinds, young couples everywhere made plans to start a family or expand an existing one. On March 6, 1939, Octavio Gregorio Rojas Muñiz and Estela Rivas Solay became parents for the second time in Havana, Cuba, with the birth of their son, Octavio Victor Rojas. A daughter, Roxana, had preceded him.

"I was raised in two places," said Cookie Rojas, sitting at his breakfast table, the bright Florida sun illuminating his age-worn face. "One, in el Vedado in el Edificio América. Our apartment was three blocks away from the CMQ radio station building. When I was about nine years old, I began becoming interested in baseball. We played on the streets, which were narrow, with balls made of rolled-up cigar cartons, with a small rock inside. You couldn't run, you had to walk to the designated bases space. We swung at the 'ball' with our fists, and then threw it at the runner. If you struck him with the 'ball,' he was out."

Home life for the young Rojas was not without familial turbulence, however. "My parents divorced when I was young," he relayed. "When I was nine or ten, I went to live with my father in a two-bedroom apartment on Infanta Street in the San Lázaro neighborhood of Havana."

> I could still walk to my school, Colegio La Luz, in my old neighborhood of Vedado. It was there I received a scholarship to play [baseball] in the 13- to 15-year age group. My father was one of the coaches at my school. His primary job was as a medical supply supervisor at Calixto García Hospital. The next level up was the 16–18, which was the equivalent of high schoolers. It was great. Our team played and practiced on the grounds of the old Havana Biltmore. [Rival schools] La Salle and Maristas were our opponents.
>
> When my father remarried, we moved to another neighborhood—la Vibora.[4] I used to bounce and field rubber balls off the walls of a rooftop behind our building. I was first noticed, believe it or not, by a man who was a taxi driver by trade. He started a baseball team called la Rosa Cubana and asked me to play. It was my first venture into organized type of baseball playing. We traveled outside of Havana to play. I was named the best juvenile player in Cuba. I still have the certificate I was awarded.
>
> I even played amateur ball for one year. I tried out for Vedado Tennis Club first, but they didn't have room for me. It was suggested I try out for club Fortuna in Guanabacoa, which was another neighborhood, or municipality as they call it now, of Havana. Pepito Otero was the manager. I made the team. To be able to put on the uniform of Fortuna and play for the amateur championship of the island was a great experience.

While the teenage Rojas was obviously taken with playing baseball, his prospects for making a future within the game were dim, at least in the eyes of those who were supposedly in the know. "All the scouts in Cuba," said Rojas, "including the scouts of the [Cuban] Sugar Kings, all had their doubts about me; my fielding, my hitting, everything raised concerns. Armando Llanos was a scout for the Sugar Kings, but *he* believed in me. He said, 'Rojita will make it.' He called me 'Rojita.' It was thanks to him that I signed my first contract." Rojas was signed professionally by Llanos at 16. Inking Rojas was an example of Sugar Kings team owner Bobby Maduro's desire to cultivate native talent.

"I think Bobby Maduro should be in the U.S. Hall of Fame," opined Rojas. "He was an architect, engineer ... electrician, plumber—he did everything rolled up into one. He did everything for the benefit of baseball in that great stadium of his that we were able to enjoy for at least a few years." Rojas was referring to the multiple roles Maduro held throughout his career in baseball as a stadium builder, team executive and owner, scout, MLB administrator, and international league founder.

A "working agreement" had been signed between the Cincinnati Reds and the Triple A Cuban Sugar Kings in 1955. The player development pact was spearheaded by Gabe Paul, Reds general manager and repeat visitor to Cuba. This alliance guided the young Rojas' subsequent baseball journey.

In 1956, Rojas was propelled away from Cuba at the tender age of 17, following his contract commitment. "In those days, the minor leagues were very prevalent," Rojas recalled. "Starting at Class D and up to Triple A. Each level had its own leagues. My first contract was for $125 a month, with $1.50 meal money [per diem]." Not surprisingly, Rojas started at the rock bottom minor league stanchion of the Class D Florida State League with the West Palm Beach Sun Chiefs.

To underscore the grassroots appeal of the game during that time, Rojas reported to the Dobbins, Georgia, army barracks because of an overload of personnel. "We slept in triple bunk beds," Rojas remembered. "And there were at least 400 players initially. So many that they pinned numbers to their uniforms; I remember men wearing numbers 215, 218. We ate our meals in a huge mess hall. Every morning we checked the big bulletin board for our names. If your name was listed, you were still on the team. If it wasn't there, you were gone."

Unlike some fledgling Hispanic players of the era who pursued a baseball career in the United States, Rojas did not have to confront the harsh racial realities of the segregated American South. Rojas' skin tone and acquired application of English facilitated his integration abroad.[5] "We were taught English at Colegio La Luz every afternoon, so I was able to defend myself with the language here," he revealed. "I served as interpreter for many Latin players during those first few years in the States."

Rojas made the Sun Chiefs and, despite his age, accrued the most plate appearances (541) on the team and most hits (131). Rojas finished second in extra-base hits to teammate and future big-league manager Dave Bristol (31 to 26). The youngster topped Bristol for most bases stolen, 28 to 20.

Another Cuban on the Sun Chiefs, José Padilla, participated in the most games for the club with 134 out of 139 played by the team. "I played for Duluth [Northern League] and Olean [PONY League] in my first year in organized ball," Padilla stated from his current home in South Miami.

> The next year [1956] I was assigned to West Palm Beach. Cookie and another Cuban player, Luis Boullón, were on the team. They were both rookies. Cookie was a very intelligent player. Good with the bat, good with the glove. Cookie Rojas and Tony Taylor were, in my opinion, the two best Cuban second baseman. Tony might have been a little better because he was faster and had more power than Cookie. I played shortstop for West Palm Beach. Cookie and I set a double play record in the league, if I'm not mistaken. Dave Bristol was our third baseman.[6]

A native of the capital like Rojas and also with acceptable skin pigmentation, Padilla was four years older than his keystone partner. "I played amateur baseball [in Cuba], most recently with club Artesano," said a still physically active Padilla, who has spent the past 20-plus years of retirement involved in coach-pitch Little League, an age level above T-ball.

> My name started getting into the newspapers. Then a man named Daniel Parra came to my house. Parra was a scout for Milwaukee, and he offered a $5,000 bonus if I would sign with the Braves. That was a huge amount of money. My father told him we'd think about it. Fermín Guerra came to my house right afterward and told me that Bobby Maduro wanted to see me. Everybody knew who he was. The next day I went to El Cerro [Gran Stadium].
>
> Maduro had an office there. I remember Paul Miller was there, he was Maduro's right-hand man. He was an impressive person, spoke Spanish better than most of us. [Before becoming general manager of the Sugar Kings, Paul Miller was the treasurer of the Cuban Winter League.] Bobby told me, "I can't match the bonus Milwaukee is offering, but I can give you a minor league contract of $350 a month to go play in the U.S. minor leagues and arrange for you to be placed on the roster reserve list of Marianao [Tigers, of the Cuban Winter League]."
>
> Well, I knew that in the United States, you had to pay income tax on your earnings. So, I asked Bobby if he would cover the amount of income tax I would have to pay. He said, "of course."
>
> I wasn't interested in money. I was interested in playing in the Cuban Winter League. Can you imagine? As a result, I got to go on the field with Minnie Miñoso, Julio Bécquer, players I admired so much. Tony Taylor was on the reserve list with me. Bobby Maduro became like a second father. His name was synonymous with his team.
>
> Armando Llanos, Napoleón Reyes, Tony Pacheco, Regino Otero were all

part of the organization. Maduro was a hands-on owner, spent a lot of time on the field. We stayed friends in exile, before he died.

The Sugar Kings had a saying, almost like a jingle, *"Un paso más y llegamos."* ["One more step and we arrive," referencing the desired franchise goal of scaling upward from Triple A to the majors.] Communism prevented Cuba from placing the first international franchise in the major leagues.[7]

Padilla never made the major leagues. By his own admission, "I was pretty agile, was a good fielder, had a good arm, but I did not hit enough. The long season seemed to wear me down. I've been 62 years without returning to Cuba. I was able to get my wife, who was pregnant, and mother and father out at the same time. For that I am eternally grateful to the Chicago White Sox organization. I was with the Sox minor league affiliate in Sarasota when they helped facilitate visa issuances for them. They were able to fly directly to the United States.... Soon after that, you had to go through Mexico to bring out your family, if you were able."[8]

Padilla parted ways with Rojas when Rojas, Bristol, and first baseman Charles Tulner were promoted one level by the Sun Chiefs, in 1957, to the Northern League. "I got my first taste of what cold weather was like, playing for the Wausau Lumberjacks," said Rojas, flinching at the recollection. "I was unprepared. All I had were thin sweaters. But I had to play where I was sent. It was now my livelihood."

Joining him in Wausau were five other Cuban athletes, one Dominican, Alfredo Contón, and Venezuelan Teodoro Obregón. Two of Rojas' compatriots were Afro-Cuban players who would make the major leagues: 20-year-old Andrés Antonio "Tony" González and 23-year-old Cristobál "Minnie" Mendoza. The increased Latin American diversity was a direct result of the talent pipeline in place between the Cincinnati Reds and Bobby Maduro, as all the Hispanic prospects were under the Reds' control. Prior to reaching the big leagues, González and Mendoza would don Cuban Sugar Kings uniforms. Right-hander Andrés Ayón (before settling in Mexico and pitching for more than a dozen years there) and catcher Alberto Alvarez made the Sugar Kings squad but advanced no higher. The fifth Cuban in the bunch, pitcher Reinaldo Alonso, and Contón also ended up as career minor leaguers. So did infielder Obregón, who was elected to the Venezuelan Baseball Hall of Fame in 2010.

The 1957 Wausau Lumberjacks placed sixth in an eight-team league with a record of 52–69.

The 1958 Savannah Redlegs also finished sixth (and last) in the South Atlantic League—with Cookie Rojas as a new member. The 19-year-old Rojas had been elevated from Class C to the Class A League in the cradle of the Deep South. The league had been integrated five years earlier through rostered players Henry Aaron, Félix Mantilla, and Horace Garner on the Jacksonville Braves and Elbert "Al" Israel and Fleming Reedy on the Savannah Indians. "It was a quality league, but you could tell the differences in attitudes toward Latin or Black players," stated Rojas. "In general, I don't remember a great deal of antagonism from the fans toward Latin or Black players. It was more attitude. There's always one loudmouth every now and then, of course, but I don't recall any incident, nothing that elicited an actual confrontation."

Again, as with Wausau, an abundance of players from Cuba stocked the Savannah team. Eight Cubans, including Rojas, played for Savannah over the course of the season. Some were better than others, which was a cause for concern for the club's field director, but not in a way one would think. "If Havana starts making eyes at Savannah second baseman Cookie Rojas, manager Bob Wellman may go to Cuba and start a revolution of his own," alerted one mid-season report. The reference alludes to the armed insurrection currently underway on the island, headed by guerrilla insurgent Fidel Castro, who gained international attention from a series of *New York Times* articles the previous year.

> Wellman, who has already lost two Cuban stars to the Havana club, is thinking of posting a guard on Rojas to prevent a further raid by Savannah's "Big Brother" in the Cincinnati farm organization.
>
> Rojas, hero of Savannah's Monday night victory over the South Atlantic League All-Stars, drilled a three-run homer last night in the Redlegs' come-from-behind 6–5 victory over Macon.[9]

Rojas smacked another four-bagger on August 15, the only run of the game in a pitching duel between Macon's Frank White and Candido Andrade, the Redlegs' top winner on the year with 15.

As far as diversity was concerned, the 1958 Savannah Redlegs showed a significant improvement over the prior year's team, when only two men of color played regularly for the club: 18-year-old Leo Cárdenas and 19-year-old Curt Flood, both of whom enjoyed standout seasons. Pitcher Bill Powell, an African American like Flood, suited up for only three games with the team. The veteran posted a 2–0 record in his brief stint.

Cárdenas, an Afro-Cuban who was a few months older than Rojas, had an early career that paralleled his fellow citizen. A shortstop, Cárdenas was signed at 16 and began his professional indoctrination a year later with the Tucson Cowboys in the Class C Arizona-Mexico League in 1956. Cárdenas was bumped up two levels to Savannah in 1957, where he became teammates with Flood and, for a short time, Powell.

A Society for American Baseball Research biography of Flood described some of what the player experienced in back-to-back seasons in two Southern baseball leagues.

> [In 1956 at High Point–Thomasville of the Class B Carolina League] Flood could not stay in the same accommodations as his white teammates; he could not eat in restaurants with his teammates and was forced instead to go to the back door for "service" or to wait on the team bus until a teammate brought him food. He could not use the restroom in the gas stations where the team bus stopped; instead the bus would stop on some deserted stretch of highway where Curt could disembark and "wet the rear wheel." Fans around the league expressed their displeasure at the appearance of a black man on the diamond as well. His teammates and manager weren't any more supportive. [In 1957 at Savannah] Flood endured many of the same indignities he had suffered at High Point–Thomasville, if not more.[10]

With a great deal of grit, Flood fought back the only way he could— with stellar play on the diamond; he was called to the big leagues in 1958. The same year, Cárdenas and Rojas, both 19, shined for Savannah. The teenagers paced the Georgia club in several offensive categories, while absorbing a share of the defensive hard knocks that are common to many young infielders. Rojas, playing second base, led the Redlegs in plate appearances (587), AB (527), and hits (134). With the same presumed grit as Flood, Cárdenas appeared in the most games (141), tallied the most runs (76), and collected the most doubles (29) on the team. The shortstop committed 36 errors (.950 fielding percentage). Rojas was charged with 25 errors in 125 games (.964 fielding percentage).

The following season, Savannah infielders Cárdenas and Rojas were named to the 1959 roster of the Cuban Sugar Kings. With three years of minor league experience, both Cárdenas and Rojas made the jump to the minor leagues' highest level (AAA). Cárdenas maintained his upward trek with the Sugar Kings, playing in every regular and post-season game at shortstop. Rojas, meanwhile, shared the second base chores with Elio Chacón, the Sugar Kings' second baseman for the past two seasons. Rojas battled a physical setback, which limited his playing time to 99 games (82 at second base), plus three more games in the post-season. "I hurt my back in 1959," remembered Rojas. (Newsprint reports of the day identified another cause of distress as well.)

The Cuban Sugar Kings

The Cuban Sugar Kings came into existence in 1954 as part of a sweeping reorganization that made the International League a far-reaching, three-nation operation from Canada to Cuba. Along with the Richmond Virginians, the Sugar Kings were approved as new associates in an expanded circuit of eight teams. "Havana is a great sports city," proclaimed IL president Frank Shaughnessy, "and we can give the fans there just about the same class of baseball that they see in the Cuban Winter League."[11]

From Cuba's perspective, it was all made possible by one man. Roberto "Bobby" Maduro was the son of a wealthy sugar and insurance magnate who became eminently successful in his own right in the world of business and commerce, including transportation and cattle-raising. Maduro had an immense love for baseball from a young age and carried it into adulthood. Getting involved with the sport in the mid–1940s, while in his late 20s, Maduro's dedication to promoting the game internationally from the 1950s through the 1970s was unrivaled. He headed Havana-based clubs in the Cuban Winter League and several teams in the U.S. minor leagues, particularly the Sugar Kings, which helped brand Caribbean baseball in the eyes of North American fans for the first time.

Maduro initially applied for membership in the International League under the territorial rights of the Havana Cubans franchise he had purchased in 1953. The team had been successfully based for years in the lower-level Florida International League. (The Havana Cubans were the first team to fly regularly as a means of travel in organized baseball.) The franchise was purposely folded by Maduro to make way for his broader plan.

Professional baseball in Cuba had long been integrated, but due to segregation laws in Florida, the Havana Cubans retained an all–Caucasian composition. In the more tolerant International League, the Cuban Sugar Kings, under Maduro, promoted a diverse lineup of multiracial players from its inception in 1954. Men of color, from all over Latin America and the United States, played for the Sugar Kings throughout their eventually short but significant franchise history.

Maduro smartly wanted a new team identity for his debuting AAA franchise. He retained "Cubans" as the new official name and adopted the nickname of "Sugar Kings." He stressed in the naming that the team would project a representation of the entire country and its baseball fans and not just the ardent followers in the capital.[12]

Maduro's teams had, for several years, difficulty gaining traction in the top echelon circuit, and in 1959 the club again began poorly as a potential repeat of the trend. However, a four-city road excursion in mid–May that included an eight-game winning streak dramatically turned things around. Overcoming a rough start of 11–19 and a last-place station, "the Sugar Kings returned home June 1, ending the road trip with an 11–3 record that levitated them into the pennant race."[13] Road games for the Cubans took them all along the Eastern Seaboard of the United States, from as far south as Miami (Marlins) to the northern trans-border reaches of Montreal (Royals) and Toronto (Maple Leafs).

For the Sugar Kings' new second baseman, as his team's product on the field improved, he was dealt a setback. "Rojas contracted jaundice in mid–July," divulged one team chronicle, "giving Chacón back his old job."[14]

Rojas missed an eventful, if not pivotal, occurrence in the history of the franchise during his convalescence. In Havana, on the evening of July 25, with the Rochester Red Wings as opponents, the teams took up a previously suspended game and played it to its nine-inning completion—a 1–0 Sugar Kings victory hurled by Ted Wieand, the club's top pitcher.

The regularly scheduled game commenced thereafter and stretched into extra innings, broaching the start of a new calendar day. An eyewitness described what occurred as the clock struck 12: "Promptly at midnight, rockets in the background behind the stadium signaled the start of Cuba's first July 26 celebration. The Cuban anthem played and everyone rose to sing. At the same time, weapons inside and outside the ballpark began firing."[15] The new, 24-hour commencement marked the July 26 (1953) anniversary date of the beginning of the Cuban Revolution, which had victoriously culminated on the first day of the current calendar year. The armed uprising and subsequent social upheaval left all public venues in the capital with a standing military presence. The spontaneous and irresponsible celebrations, in and around Gran Stadium, the Havana home of the Sugar Kings and Cuban Winter League, caused the game to be delayed.

A short time later, more gunfire erupted. A spent bullet struck the Red Wings' third base coach along the plastic lining of his cloth cap, knocking him to the ground. The strike left a noticeable hole in the coach's cap. Luckily, he was not seriously injured. An umpire felt a bullet just miss hitting his face as he rendered aid. Another stray projectile left a noticeable tear in infielder Leo Cárdenas' uniform sleeve. The game was then halted for good by the umpires. The Red Wings refused to take the field the next day and left Havana.

Fortunately for Maduro's team, the abandoned games marked the end of the Sugar Kings' homestand, avoiding potential bad publicity if the next scheduled club had also balked at taking the Gran Stadium field.

Cookie and Candy set off on their honeymoon in Pinar del Rio, Cuba, in February 1960 (courtesy Cookie Rojas).

The Havana squad won 12 out of 16 games during their home stay and moved squarely into playoff contention. The franchise was seeking its second first-division finish. In their maiden season of 1954, the club tied for fourth place but was eliminated in a one-game playoff. In 1955, the team improved to take third place uncontested, its sole first-division placement, but was knocked out in the first round of playoffs.

Rojas rejoined the club in Rochester on August 4. Batting .263 prior to his illness, he finished the season at .233, no doubt weakened by its probable lingering effects. The same month, International League President Frank Shaughnessy visited the Cuban capital and "let it be known that he found nothing in the city to consider stopping any future trips of IL teams."[16]

Managed by Pedro "Preston" Gómez, the Sugar Kings went 69–54 in their final 123 games to finish in third place (80–73–1) and qualify for a post-season berth. "Preston Gómez and Gene Mauch taught me everything I know about baseball," Rojas often reiterated to the author. "I always saw Gómez during the season and after the season and in the winter leagues. Preston was one of the smartest people I ever met in baseball. Every chance we had, we would sit down and talk baseball."

The Sugar Kings' roster of 26 players (with 10 or more games played) included 21 former or future major leaguers. Twelve of the 21 were Hispanic and the rest from the United States. On the strength of their pitching, the Cubans beat the second-place Columbus Jets (84–70–2) four straight games in the first round of the Shaughnessy playoffs, and then defeated the upstart Richmond Virginians (76–78) in six contests to win the International League championship. The league champion Buffalo Bisons (89–64) had been upended in a big, five-game series upset by the fourth-place Virginians in the first round. The playoff victories earned the Sugar Kings the right to meet the American Association's repeat champion Minneapolis Millers in the annual Triple A championship clash.

The playoff winners from two of the three highest-ranked minor leagues had squared off for more than 40 years in a post-playoff championship to decide the best minor league team in North America. The American Association, with its collection of midwestern teams, annually provided a championship representative to confront the International League's best team standing. The best-of-seven interleague confrontation was referred to as the Junior World Series. (It should be mentioned that the third top circuit, the Pacific Coast League, held an "open" classification grade that some considered slightly above Triple A, though not recognized as such by organized baseball.)

The first two games of the Triple A league championship, played in Minneapolis on September 27 and 28, were conducted under weather conditions bad enough to force league officials to move the remainder of the seven-game series to Havana. The competing clubs split the pair of games in the North.

Clearly, the Cuban capital rolled out the welcome wagon as the series shifted venues, based on this report from Havana: "Sirens squalled, auto horns blared, a band played both national anthems and fans cheered as Havana welcomed home its Sugar Kings and said hello to the Minneapolis Millers. A cheering throng greeted the teams at the airport."[17]

Knowing there would be no more travel dates, the fan favorites won the first two contests on home soil and took a commanding 3–1 series lead. But the Millers, managed by Gene Mauch, fought back with consecutive victories to extend the engagement to Game Seven. On October 6, with a highly partisan crowd of 24,990 cheering on, the Sugar Kings won a thrillingly climactic game, 3–2, scoring in the bottom of the ninth inning. Outfielder Danny Morejón, who tallied the Sugar Kings' second and tying run in the eighth inning, bounced a single up the middle, scoring winning pitcher Raúl Sánchez from second base with the deciding run.

An apparently still-debilitated Rojas was a non-factor in the series, as he had been in the playoff rounds. The infielder pinch-hit three times without result over the course of the seven final games, as Elio Chacón played every defensive inning at second base.

"It was incredible," recalled Rojas of the championship victory. "Fans were cordoned off on the field. Everyone was having a boisterous time, even with the armed soldiers present, it was a fan's delight. Danny Morejón rolls the ball up the middle, and Raúl Sánchez dives head-first into home with the winning run."

Jorge Maduro, Bobby's oldest surviving son, easily recollected the joyous atmosphere. Twelve years old then, Jorge recalled, "there were so many people on the field. I got separated from my father. I ended up in center field. But one of my father's people found me and brought me to the clubhouse. I vividly remember Preston Gomez celebrating with [coach] Reinaldo Cordeiro."[18]

Shortly following the championship celebrations, the winter circuit wrapped up roster selections that included 24 major leaguers, half of whom were Cuban natives. Additionally, "a history-making Caribbean winter ball venture with plans to televise 26 Cuban Winter League games to major markets in the United States enthusiastically preceded the start of the 1959–60 campaign."[19]

The big-market stations included WOR in New York, WBKB in Chicago, and Los Angeles' KTTC. The cities of San Francisco, Salt Lake City, Houston, Milwaukee, Pittsburgh, and Richmond rounded out the metropolitan centers with the most expected winter baseball interest that would receive selected broadcasts delayed and condensed to 90 minutes. Added monetary perks of $8,000 would be distributed to all the players in the four-team circuit, with the bulk of it ($5,000) going to the victors of the final game of the season between the first- and second-place clubs, which would be the broadcast finale. Rosters were set at 19 men per team, excluding rookies who had less than 45 days of big-league experience. The television company also offered bonuses of $1,000 for each player to slug a grand slam home run and a bonanza of $10,000 for the hurler who tossed a no-hitter. No one collected on the latter prize, but the home run bonus was breached during the first week of the campaign, when Francisco "Panchón" Herrera of Habana (Lions) swatted a game-deciding jackpot wallop in the ninth inning, providing a 5–2 victory over Cienfuegos (Elephants), October 13.

Based on this unique sponsorship deal, things, on the surface, appeared very promising for solidifying, for years and years to come, the hand-in-hand baseball partnership existing between the United States and Cuba, developed from both country's historic ties and common interests. With respect to the underlying political unrest that had gripped the country for several years, it had seemingly been quelled with grand promise on the first day of 1959 with the establishment of a new revolutionary government. Its guerrilla leader, Fidel Castro, in accented English, told the BBC, months earlier in a live interview on January 10, 1959, that free elections would come to Cuba "in less than 18 months, maybe one year."[20]

Contrastingly, "less than two weeks into power, the new [government] cabinet revised two constitutional articles to allow both the confiscation of property without trial and the application of the death penalty. These measures cleared the way for the government to eliminate not only the old political games, but also the old political class."[21]

Revoked International League Franchise and Collapse of the Cuban Winter League

The Cuban Winter League opened its season October 8, 32 days after the Sugar Kings' crowning victory, with Gran Stadium and its fans no doubt still basking in the residual triumph of that special evening.

Two Minneapolis Millers, perhaps their sensibilities more grounded through the experience of defeat, would later remember a more sobering outlook from the prior month. "We had been warned not to leave the hotel between games," recalled Hall of Famer Carl Yastrzemski, the Millers' second baseman in the championship face-off. "It was like a revolution in the street, even though it wasn't violent. But with the guns and noise it was just scary." The prevalence of weapons also was a cause for concern for Millers pitcher Ted Bowsfield. "In some ways nobody minded losing the game in that country under those conditions," said Bowsfield. "We were just happy to get it over and to get out of town with our hides. During every game we could hear shots being fired, and we never knew what was going on."[22]

Concurrently, for the 20-year-old Rojas there was not only the exhilarating and permanent mark of being part of a Triple A championship club, but also the resumé-boosting bid for his talents by the Cienfuegos Elephants of the CWL. "All the Sugar Kings players were placed on a reserve list from which the four winter league clubs could choose," explained Rojas. "I was chosen by Cienfuegos. I did not play much that winter [1959–60], until later in the season." With his placement with the Elephants, Rojas began, according to him, a more than two-decade-long playing career in the Caribbean basin winter leagues.

The Cienfuegos Elephants were a powerful team, posting an all-time high in wins in the league with a 48–24 record. Bolstered by multiple major league players, the club earned the circuit championship in convincing fashion (12 games over the second-place Marianao Tigers). While Cienfuegos seemed assured of capturing the pennant in the final month of the season, the Cuban Winter League began displaying troubling signs of instability, notably at its highest levels. In January, league president Arturo Bengochea resigned and other members of the circuit's board of directors quit. Alfredo Pequeño was named provisional league president.

The same month as the 1960 Caribbean Series, the nascent totalitarian regime in Cuba began usurping civil liberties at one of its most fundamental levels. "February saw the government seizure of newspapers," detailed Pulitzer Prize–winning author Ada Ferrer, "including *El Mundo* and *El Pais* ... the latter of which ran into trouble when it decided to print a prominent priest's denunciation of Mikoyan's visit to Cuba."[23] Anastas Mikoyan was the deputy prime minister of the Soviet Union who had arrived in Cuba on February 4, 1960. (Months later, in May, Cuba's oldest newspaper, *Diario de la Marina*, was forced to shut.)

Around the same time as the appropriations of the first newspapers, in Panama City, the Cuban pennant-winning club swept through the culmination spectacle of the winter baseball campaigns of Latin America with an undefeated record of 6–0 against champion clubs from Panama, Puerto Rico, and Venezuela, in what turned out to be the last of the 12 original Caribbean Series played between 1949 and 1960. Rojas (three for seven in the series) homered in the unblemished team's 10–7 clinching victory over the host Marlboro Smokers on February 15. It was the 12th and last game played, and Rojas' seventh-inning blast was the final home run hit in the popular double-round robin tournament, involving these four national teams. The following year's competition was to be held in Havana as part of the event's annual rotation, but growing international political hostilities between the United States and Cuba put asunder those plans.

Two weeks after the Caribbean Series, Rojas embarked on a personal journey of dual commitment and devotion with the woman who has become his more than six-decades-long spouse and mother of his children. Candida Rosa Boullón García attended the same Catholic academy as Cookie Rojas, but their acquaintance was nothing out of the ordinary. "We knew each other from school but were not close," said Candida. "I got close to Cookie through his father, who was baseball coach. Cookie signed so young at 16, during his first year away, I would often sit next to his father during recess or other free time and ask him how Cookie was doing, and I began developing feelings for Cookie as a result."

Nine months younger than her budding beau, Candida, born

December 7, 1939, was the only daughter of Luis Roberto Boullón and Caridad García González. A brother, Luis Boullón, Jr., rounded out her family. He briefly played minor league baseball.

Candida explained that it wasn't until she continued her education abroad that she entertained the prospect of delving into a more serious relationship with the person she would eventually marry: "I went away to school in the United States, to the University of Michigan. At La Luz we had our courses in Spanish in the morning. In the afternoon everything was in English, so I knew English and got better at it at the University of Michigan. I stayed in Ann Arbor at a cousin's house with his wife."

> It was while in Michigan that I got Cookie's address; he was at Savannah at the time and we began to correspond, and that's how our courtship began to blossom. When Cookie and I returned to Cuba we began dating—chaperoned dating. My mother always went with us. My mother, my entire family, loved Cookie. So much so that they would side with him more than me on things!
>
> Cookie proposed to me at the end of 1959 at my house. He schemed with my grandmother with putting the engagement ring in the refrigerator where anyone would see it if they opened the door. So they sent me to fetch something from the fridge. I opened the door and there was the ring. We married two and half months later.
>
> In those days you had to marry under civil law first, which we did, February 27. The next day we tied the blessed knot at Iglesia del Carmelo. We honeymooned at Cabañas in Pinar Del Rio [eastern Cuban province].

With little travel burden, Rojas had time to enjoy his honeymoon and be ready to report to the Sugar Kings' training camp in March. All the same, Rojas and his country's fortunes changed dramatically during the next 12 months.

On April 20, 1960, the Cuban Sugar Kings opened their seventh season at Gran Stadium. Pre-game ceremonies included a police marching band flying American, Canadian, and Cuban flags. League president Frank Shaughnessy presented Bobby Maduro with the Governor's Cup for winning the most recent league championship. Premium boxes of cigars were presented to each member of the opposing Rochester Red Wings team by a Sugar Kings counterpart. The man most responsible for the political hostilities between the United States and Cuba threw out the first pitch. Arriving late and delaying the game 47 minutes, the self-appointed premier of Cuba, Fidel Castro, tossed the ball to Sugar Kings catcher José "Joe" Azcué, who would break into the major leagues with Cincinnati later that summer. The Red Wings' Luke Easter homered off Luis Arroyo in the top of the tenth inning to decide the game,

4–3, and spoil the first game festivities for the local fans, numbering 12,045 for the contest. The newlywed Rojas, at 21, was the primary second baseman for new manager Tony Castaño's team.

A young Rojas strikes a batting pose as a member of the Cuban Sugar Kings, ca. 1959 or 1960. One of Gran Stadium's lighting stanchions is visible in the background (SABR-Rucker Archive).

Three days earlier, a column by Rochester sportswriter George Beahon disclosed that the IL's southernmost team would be moved after the completion of its 13-day, season-opening homestand. The newspaperman qualified his report by stating that league officials would not confirm or deny the story. The biggest problem was not getting other clubs to play in Havana, Beahon wrote, but getting the Sugar Kings out of the country for road games. The sports scribe, however, did not elaborate on the latter point. But it indicated a lack of cooperation from Cuban authorities, arising from the social reforms that were transgressing more and more on the personal mobility of their citizenry. "There have been reports circulating in government circles during the past week that all non-diplomatic travel by Cuban citizens might be banned within the next month," elaborated a concurrent news item.[24]

The visiting Red Wings inflicted a season-opening three-game sweep of the Cuban team, which set the tone for an underperforming start to the new campaign for the Sugar Kings that lasted well past its opening home series. Castaño's club (6–8) closed the homestand on May 2 with a doubleheader split against the Toronto Maple Leafs. The twin games were pushed back a day to a previously scheduled travel day when all sporting events on tap for Sunday, May 1, were postponed, so as not to interfere with May Day (International Worker's Day) celebrations ordered throughout the island. The International League was helpless in the matter. On that final day of the homestand, Cuba restored diplomatic ties with the Soviet Union, which the island had broken off in 1952.

The country's increasingly suffocating social reforms spread to the financial sector. Squeezed were the pocketbooks of Cubans from all walks of life, including those individuals of high net worth. Not spared was Bobby Maduro. "The Sugar Kings seven rivals are carrying the Havana team on credit," alerted one U.S. columnist. "So tight is the financial grip in Cuba, the Havana club is not even able to provide cash for daily 'meal money' when the Sugar Kings are on road trips in the United States and Canada." The home club provides the funds and charges it against the account. "We draw none of the money due us at the gate for games in Havana," a league general manager explained. "In turn we do not pay the Sugar Kings their share for visits to our park. With all other clubs, there is a settlement after each series."[25]

The stricter financial circumstances must have been extremely injurious to Maduro's pride. He had always been considered the most generous of league owners. In 1954, his team's first year in the league, in a goodwill gesture, he covered the airfare costs of all the other clubs' travel trips into Cuba. By the end of June, Maduro was not only forced to resort to scrimping for meal money for players, he also had to search for solutions to larger operational concerns. "Representatives of the Sugar Kings baseball team dropped a small bombshell by asking for a loan of $20,000 at the International League meeting here today," disclosed *Buffalo News* writer Cy Kritzer. "Havana wants $7,000 to pay salaries of American players on the team and $13,000 to help finance the club for the rest of the year."[26]

Yet things for Maduro, and many others, soon became worse. On July 6, U.S. president Dwight D. Eisenhower cut off Washington's guaranteed quota purchase of the island's sugar harvest, a substantial source of income annually for Cuba. The action came in response to Castro's nationalizing of Shell, Texaco and Standard Oil, after the companies had refused to refine Soviet oil now being exported to Cuba (one of the end results of the Russian deputy secretary's visit in February). Perhaps not coincidentally and provoked by the high stakes tit-for-tat being played out on the international stage, on July 7, Shaughnessy announced that he was relocating Bobby Maduro's franchise to the U.S. state of New Jersey. Shaughnessy inconsiderately announced to the press, from his Montreal office, the relocation plans *before* advising Maduro the same day. The decision inflicted a crushing blow to Maduro's major league aspirations. But economic considerations from poor attendance and mounting tensions between the U.S. and Cuba due to the monocrat Castro's incessant anti–American declarations had made the situation untenable for the league. It feared for the safety of its players. "It was a warlike atmosphere," recounted Beahon half a century afterward. "The Cubans weren't even trying to hide their antagonism."[27]

A "lone wolf" scenario, in which an incited fan by Castro's rhetoric could have caused a tragedy, was one the league did not want to risk. On its editorial page, *The Sporting News* made an effort to explain it to the average fan.

> The International League had a tough decision to make recently, one with which it had been wrestling for almost a year. The Havana franchise was moved to the United States. Certainly, there was a measure of reluctance in making the move out of respect to Roberto Maduro, the franchise owner and one of the most dedicated men in the minor leagues. It is unfortunate that Maduro was scarcely consulted on the move. In the final analysis, however, the transfer would have had to be accomplished over his protest. Ever since a Rochester player escaped serious injury by roistering Cuban soldiers at the ballpark a year ago.
>
> Now as conditions between our two countries have been strained to the breaking point, there seemed but little choice but to move the club.[28]

With their next scheduled home date, Friday, July 15, the Sugar Kings were playing a series in Columbus, Ohio, when the news broke. The team split a doubleheader with the Jets on the July 7 announcement date. Maduro called the pronouncement "completely outrageous," and "for me it means bankruptcy and the loss of a holding of $400,000."[29]

In name only, the Cuban franchise traveled to Richmond, Virginia, to begin their next series on July 8. In the third game of the set, July 10, Miguel Angel "Mike" Cuéllar seven-hit the Virginians, 7–1, at Parker Field. Rojas had one of the Sugar Kings' 11 hits to back their southpaw pitcher's keen effort. It was the last time a Cuban professional sports team played outside the country through the remainder of the century and into the next.

The next day, July 11, the *Cincinnati Enquirer* reported that the parent Reds team would operate the "revoked International League franchise," adding that "Shaughnessy said that a telegraphic poll of the league's board of directors had approved the transfer of the club and all that remained to be settled were final details for the use of Roosevelt Stadium in Jersey City and an equitable settlement with Maduro."[30]

Following Cuéllar's win, the team flew to Miami. Howie Nunn, a first-year right-hander with the team, took the mound at Miami Stadium on July 11 and blanked the Marlins, 3–0. In U.S. newspapers the succeeding day, International League standings and box scores reflected *Jersey City* instead of *Cubans* (or *Havana*), and the team henceforth was known as the Jersey City Jerseys. Silk patches with *Jersey City* lettering were provisionally sown over the team's *Cubanos* uniform chest lettering, and a white "J" stitched over the red "C" of the players' caps. After being shut out twice in a row following Nunn's whitewash, the Jerseys gained a split in their four-game series with Miami with a 7–3 win in the final game on July 14. The club hit three home runs, including one by Rojas.

The transferred squad had left Havana following a Sunday, June 26, doubleheader against Rochester. The first game, scheduled for seven innings, was won, 6–5, by the home team on a two-run, walk-off home run by Félix Torres in the seventh. (Often in doubleheaders in minor and winter leagues, one game was scheduled for seven innings.) Rogelio "Borrego" Alvarez, who had gone deep earlier in the contest, was on base. Torres, a native of Puerto Rico, clubbed what turned into the last home run hit by a Sugar Kings—and International League—player in Cuba. The homerless nightcap was called a 3–3 tie after nine innings due to curfew. It was scheduled to be replayed in its entirety on the next visit by the Red Wings to Havana—a visit that never came. In a complete game, Raúl Sánchez threw what became the last pitch by a Sugar Kings hurler on native soil to batterymate Joe Azcué. Red Wings pitcher Tom Hurd relieved Bobby Tiefenauer in the final inning, closing out the game with catcher Chris Cannizzaro, thus tossing the final pitch in International league history in Cuba.[31] Official attendance was logged at 1,098.

The eight o'clock start time for the twin bill had been delayed almost 90 minutes because of an electrical power outage, caused by an ammunition dump explosion in the vicinity, which killed one and injured hundreds more—according to government reports. The same reports categorized the occurrence as an accident, but it mirrored, albeit on a larger scale, recent shows of discontent in the city by denizens who were feeling more and more deceived by the more and more authoritarian Castro's political turns.

Back in the States, there was still a question of loyalty that had to be resolved with a significant segment of the Jerseys' roster. "We had a reunion with the Cuban players," said Rojas. "I was the translator for Gabe Paul. Castaño decided to leave because of his family's business, but no one else left." Including Rojas, nine Cuban nationals opted to stay with their team: Borrego Alvarez, Andrés Ayón, Joe Azcué, Mike Cuéllar, Enrique "Hank" Izquierdo, Danny Morejón, Orlando Peña, and Raúl

Sánchez. Trainer Luis Navarro was the only other Cuban to leave the squad.

Alvarez, the team's slugging first baseman, recalled in an interview 45 years afterward another incentive that helped drive the decision and the prevailing sentiment that the rupture would be a short one: "Gabe Paul took a few of us aside and gave us money; I don't remember how much. We figured, 'Well, two months and we'll be back in Cuba anyway,' so we stayed."[32]

Following the Miami series, instead of making the short flight to Havana as the schedule originally dictated, the uprooted franchise flew north. The team's relocation began with a new manager. Tony Castaño, who had a financial interest in a grocery store in Havana, returned to Cuba. (He later defected to the United States.) Former Hispanic major league pioneer Napoleon "Nap" Reyes, who managed the club in 1957 and 1958, was named the new skipper.

The Cuban manager's first game was the team's initial home contest, played at Roosevelt Stadium in Jersey City on July 15. Although the team arrived from Miami in the early morning hours of the same day, the city fathers honored the players with a mid-afternoon motorcade parade, Reyes on display in the lead car, a white convertible. Riding with Reyes was a Jersey City commissioner and two players—Peña and Izquierdo—along with Miss Jersey City, Delphine Lisk. Peña took the loss (8–3), in relief, in that evening's "inaugural" game against the Columbus Jets. Less than one-third of Roosevelt Stadium's 24,500-seat capacity was occupied.

Candida Rojas remembers the disruption of the time period well. "The Sugar Kings were forced to move because of...." She paused, with a tilt of the head, in the manner of many Cubans from her generation, reflexively reluctant to say the name everyone knows but is loath to dignify through enunciation. "I went with Cookie to New Jersey. That first trip began a long trajectory of following Cookie wherever he played. We stayed at the Jack Tar Hotel in Jersey City. I remember Mrs. [Orlando] Peña, Hank Izquierdo's wife and Mike Cuéllar's wife, God rest his soul. We all lived on the same floor of the hotel and supported one another. We were always together when the husbands were away. Our favorite activity was buying paint-by-numbers kits and spending long hours painting and seeing whose rendering would come out best."

Her husband easily recalled the communal experience as well. "In 1960, in New Jersey, we stayed at a hotel. I can't remember the name, but one floor had all the Cuban players and their families. At lunch or dinner, we'd knock on each other's doors. Our wives would yell out, 'Oye, who wants frijoles? I've got some extra potatoes, if anybody wants.... My wife just made flan ... come and get a slice before it's all gone....' It was like that all the time."

The former Sugar Kings franchise concluded their tempestuous season in Jersey City with a record of 76–77–2, missing playoff consideration by two wins. Reyes did an admirable job steering the squad under what had to be difficult circumstances. Following his acceptance of the job, he had been called a traitor and branded an enemy of the state by Cuba's new official newspaper, *La Revolución*. In the initial days at the helm in New Jersey, Reyes had been assigned 24-hour protection by local authorities.

Winning 100 games, in a complete reversal of last season's basement placement, the Toronto Maple Leafs finished head and shoulders above the league. The Canadian team breezed through the playoff rounds to win the Governor's Trophy, but they were defeated in the Junior World Series by the Louisville Colonels.

A resentful Bobby Maduro did not accompany his team to the States. He stayed in Cuba, where "news media refuse to report results of Jersey City games" and "standings and scores have been dropped right out of government-controlled newspapers."[33] He put Paul Miller in charge of the club. Maduro's position stemmed from the fact that he thought sports and politics should not mix, rather, should be viewed and treated independently of each other.

In September, Maduro was witness to the nationalization of the largest American financial institutions, Chase Manhattan Bank among them. New York University professor Ada Ferrer itemized the additional actions occurring before Maduro's eyes: "In October, the government—now targeting Cuban-owned property—expropriated 105 sugar mills, 18 distilleries, 8 railroad companies, department stores, hotels, casinos, pharmacies, and more. By the end of the month, the government had seized approximately 550 U.S. and domestic properties, including nearly all remaining nonresidential property in Cuba."[34]

In retaliation, as later chronicled by international correspondent and *Washington Post* editorial board member David E. Hoffman, "Eisenhower announced a complete ban on exports, October 13, except for medicine and food, a trade embargo that would remain in place for decades. In response, Cuba took over 382 large private enterprises, including all the banks, and nationalized another 166 U.S. enterprises, including Woolworth's; Sears, Roebuck; General Electric; Westinghouse; and Coca-Cola, as well as hotels and insurance companies."[35] Of passing interest, insurance, finance and transportation were the leading business holdings of Bobby Maduro and his patriarchal father, Salomón.

The 1960–1961 Cuban Winter League season began play on

October 15, and without North American players for the first time in four decades. Baseball Commissioner Ford Frick had announced the ban five weeks earlier. The exclusion did not apply to Cuban major leaguers.

Two weeks into the season, Cookie Rojas was traded to the Almendares Scorpions for two U.S. minor league Cuban players, infielders José César (Macon) and Hernan Valdés (Charlotte). Not long after the trade, a United Press International dispatch from November 3 denoted a bleak picture of an almost previously unthinkable situation:

> Dwindling attendance is threatening the possible collapse of the Cuban League. The gate decline is attributed in part to the ban imposed on U.S. players this winter. To offset the drop in receipts, the players voluntarily met here, November 2, to accept salary reductions. Minnie Miñoso, veteran White Sox outfielder, earned an estimated $2,500 playing winter ball, but is expected to draw only $400 this season. A league official said an average daily attendance of 4,500 is needed to break even. Recent gates frequently have been around 1,000.[36]

A glance away from the sports pages made it easy to identify the intrusive distractions surrounding the league. More than halfway through the season, on January 2, 1961, no games were played as "Fidel staged a massive display of armaments Cuba had purchased from the nations of the Eastern Bloc, primarily Czechoslovakia and the Soviet Union, including tanks, rocket launchers, and antiaircraft guns." In his obligatory speech, the bearded, fatigue-clad orator "attacked the enemies of the revolution as *gusanos*, or worms. The crowd perked up at every mention. Castro then ordered the U.S. embassy staff cut from 87 to just eleven persons within forty-eight hours. 'Kick them out!' he shouted. The crowd answered, 'Kick them out!'"[37]

It's clear from this event and from other historical transcripts of the time that a majority of the Cuban people were fully behind their new supreme leader and thus were his biggest enablers.

Rojas' time with Almendares was short-lived. "I was traded to Habana soon afterward," he stated. "Miguel Angel [González, owner/manager], I think, gave up two players to get me."

On January 3, 1961, President Eisenhower severed diplomatic relations with Cuba, joining six other hemispheric countries that had previously done the same: Dominican Republic, Guatemala, Haiti, Nicaragua, Paraguay, and Peru. "There is a limit to what the United States in self-respect can endure," read a portion of the president's declaration. "Our friendship with the Cuban people is not affected. It is my hope and my conviction that in the not-too-distant future it will be possible for the historic friendship between us once again to find its reflections in normal relations of every sort. Meanwhile our sympathies go out to the Cuban people now suffering under the yoke of a dictator."[38]

On the baseball front, for dozens of major league–caliber Cuban signees, the news could not but arouse concern, as one South Florida newspaper outlined: "The rupture of U.S. Cuban relations last week threw a cloud over the future participation of Cubans in organized baseball in the States. It has been the practice of [major league] clubs to make visa requests on behalf of their players via the State Department. General Felipe Guerra Matos, Cuban sports director, already has announced there will be no restrictions imposed on Cuban players requesting exit permits to play abroad."[39]

Despite the terrible, home-country purloining of his team and with surely the foundations of the world he had known all his life cracking beneath him, the owner of the former Cuban Sugar Kings somehow remained upbeat. "Bobby Maduro, Cuban baseball executive," read part of the same report, "is optimistic that no obstacles will placed before local players going to the United States. 'This is not a political matter,' he said. 'Baseball is an international sport and should be kept apart from any other consideration not related to its development.'"[40]

A week afterward, the Caribbean Professional Baseball Federation (referred to as the Confederación de Baseball Profesional del Caribe, in Spanish), issued the following change pertaining to their annual championship competition: "The Inter-American baseball series, which replaces the Caribbean Series, was scheduled today to be played in Caracas. Teams from Panama, Venezuela and Puerto Rico will participate." The organization, which was the governing body of the Latin American winter leagues, under organized baseball, added, "The Cuban League had been invited to send a representative to the Caribbean Confederation meeting but none attended."[41]

Notwithstanding the early assurances from the Cuban military sports director, Guerra Matos, Maduro's idealism suffered another blow as the majority of Cuban players would have to travel via third countries in order to reenter the United States to resume their baseball activities and would ultimately face outright extortion threats pertaining to a delayed return home.

The league soldiered on and reached a climactic ending, as all four teams finished within four games of each other. Defending champion Cienfuegos (35–31) won the pennant on the last day of the campaign, February 8. Minnesota Twins pitcher Pedro Ramos tossed the clincher with an 8–2, complete game win over Almendares (34–32). Ramos set league marks by hurling an amazing 217 innings in the four-month-long campaign and winning 16 games (an all-time record). He barely missed capturing the ERA title. A printed statistical summary identified names of players that U.S. baseball fans would come to recognize in the coming years, if they hadn't already: "While Ramos all but swept pitching honors, batting laurels were well distributed. Havana's Cookie Rojas (Jersey City) won the batting crown with a .322 average, but Julio Becquer (Angels) of Marianao led in homers (15) and RBI (50). Zoilo Versalles was runner-up in the four-bagger department. Tony Taylor (Philadelphia) ran away with base-stealing honors with 22."[42] Twenty-year-old Luis Tiant was named Rookie of the Year.

All player and team accomplishments from the championship season turned out to be bittersweet. "The politics of the time did not affect me directly only because I was so focused on playing baseball," said Rojas. "The same could not be said of so many others, including my family. Everything for me stayed more or less the same until *he* took away our games."

Not long after the circuit's final game on February 8, the Cuban Winter League, which was the second-oldest professional baseball league in the world (the U.S. National League was older), ceased to exist. On February 23, the Castro autocratic government created the National Institute of Sports, Physical Education and Recreation. It is referred to by its Spanish acronym of INDER (*Instituto Nacional de Deportes, Educación Física y Recreación*) which still prevails today as the sports arm and propaganda tool of the Cuban Communist government. A month after its inception, the INDER issued National Decree Number 936, which prohibited all professional sports on the island.

During this volatile time, and over a period of 17 months, Cookie Rojas had experienced the zenith of his minor league playing career. He was a member of the (September) 1959 Junior World Series champion Cuban Sugar Kings and the 1959–1960 Cuban Winter League and (February 1960) Caribbean Series champion Cienfuegos Elephants, and he won the last batting title in the 1960–1961 historic Cuban Winter League. "The first three were team accomplishments, and the fourth was individual, so that's last," said Rojas, in evaluating the separate achievements all these years later. "The most important, for me, was the Sugar Kings championship. Because that accomplished a special status for Cuban baseball in organized baseball. It helped legitimize Bobby Maduro's ultimate goal of having, of bringing, a major league franchise to Havana."

As if those professional triumphs weren't enough, Rojas also found time within the span to wed the love of his life and the woman destined to become his lifelong companion.

Two

Forced Exile

Shortly after winning the batting title in the Cuban Winter League, Cookie Rojas had to prepare for the 1961 U.S. minor league season. With little time to consider his upcoming 22nd birthday in March, Rojas and his wife departed Cuba, by separate means.

> For the 1961 season in Jersey City Cookie had to travel through Mexico to gain entry to the States—Tony Pérez left with him. I had kept my American student visa active and was able to leave thanks to that. I came to Miami first. I was seven months pregnant with our first child. I stayed with a distant cousin from Cookie's side of the family. It was a home at 20th Avenue and 11th Street, near the famous Tower Theater, in the area that's known today as Little Havana. I had brought two boxes of cigars with me and sold them. And with the money I opened my first bank account at the Dade Federal Bank, which was close to where I lived.

"I was on the same plane with Tony Pérez to Mexico to get our visas to come to the United States," concurred Rojas. "I roomed with him overnight in the hotel in the Mexican capital. Later, I got my grandparents, uncle, mother, stepfather, all out through Mexico, all at the same time. They stayed a week before we could finally get them across. All the connections were made through the Philadelphia Phillies organization. Then came extended family members. It was the plight of many Cubans of that era."

Although the Sugar Kings were no more, the International League stayed true to its Caribbean outreach with the relocation of the Miami Marlins to San Juan, Puerto Rico, for the 1961 campaign. Unlike its most recent franchise shift, the move had the blessing of Marlins owner Bill MacDonald. High-level baseball had been well received in South Florida with the advent of its Triple A franchise in 1956, but lately that same community enthusiasm had waned. "Fan reaction to the loss of the Marlins was mostly apathetic silence," wrote minor league historian Sam Zygner, "a sad commentary on a proud team that would ultimately lay the groundwork for professional baseball's return to the Magic City when the Florida Marlins arrived in 1993."[1] (Because of travel expenses and poor home attendance, MacDonald transferred the team to Charleston, West Virginia, only a few months into the season.)

The Jersey City Jerseys, again piloted by Nap Reyes, in their first Roosevelt Stadium season opener on April 20, defeated the Columbus Jets, 8–6. Rojas garnered two hits in four at-bats with a run scored and one knocked in. Bob Dustal picked up the win in relief of Orlando Peña. Attendance was 2,351. Rojas played in 150 of the New Jersey team's 154 games (all at second base) and established himself as a reliable player, with a .968 fielding percentage and batting a respectable .265 in 607 plate appearances.

The team, once again, failed to qualify for the post-season with a record of 70–82 and a sixth-place standing. Bobby Maduro, who had eventually abandoned Cuba (forced to leave his and his family's immense confiscated wealth and property behind), had reestablished ties with his morphed franchise. With attendance correspondingly lagging throughout the year, he made the prudent decision to move the club to Jacksonville, Florida, for the 1962 campaign.

The natural human tendency to look forward with expectations of a brighter future can sometimes cloud perspective or lead one to overlook the obvious in retrospect. That brighter future promised by Fidel Castro and his guerrilla warfare–style revolution that brought down the previous illegitimate government of imperious Cuban leader Fulgencio Batista had now all but vanished in the geopolitical eyes of many. The "one year, eighteen months" period that Castro had identified for establishment of free elections in Cuba had come and gone without a hint of it coming to pass.

On December 2, 1961, "in a televised address, Castro pronounced, 'I am a Marxist-Leninist and shall be one until the end of my life.'"[2] Cynically, it was one of the few declarations to the Cuban people that the despot, over 46 years in power, lived up to.

With the abolishment of the Cuban Winter League, native players were now faced with the continuing quandary of how to maintain and promote their higher baseball aspirations. Almost seamlessly, to a man, they turned to other baseball-loving countries in Latin America to keep those ambitions alive. Eduardo "Ed" Bauta was one of the players who received an opportunity to play and promote their skills through winter ball. A young conscript of the St. Louis Cardinals, Bauta's minor league skipper, Vern Benson, was named manager of the Santurce Crabbers of the Puerto Rican Winter League and offered Bauta the chance of impressing the Cardinals' brass by suiting up for the team.

Two—Forced Exile

To be sure, Bauta and many other countrymen were at a crossroads in their young professional lives. "Before arriving in Puerto Rico," author Thomas E. Van Hyning wrote in a profile on the Cuban player, "Bauta met with fellow players in Miami to discuss whether they should remain in the U.S. or return to Cuba. Tony Taylor led this group, which included Tony González, Cookie Rojas, Luis Tiant and Zoilo Versalles. Bauta remembered it as an emotional meeting."[3]

Rojas recalled the meeting as taking place at one of Miami's largest and most popular outdoor public places: "We had a reunion at Tropical Park. Miñoso was there. Miñoso was president of the players' association [in Cuba]. I know I speak for many when I say leaving Cuba was the hardest blow we've had to overcome. If anyone who remembers that time today would stop to think about it, they would get sick. Imagine what things would be like there now."

There was no overstating the dismal prospects the native players were facing, as substantiated by another historical account:

> Long regarded as the game's winter mecca, Cuba's capital city of Havana stands deserted this fall as far as professional baseball activity is concerned. The Cuban Winter League has fallen victim to the Fidel Castro regime. Despite threats from the Castro government to seize their properties, more than two dozen Cuban standouts passed up their annual return to their homeland following the 1961 OB season. Many are playing in other Latin American winter circuits or in the instructional leagues of this country.[4]

Taylor, a four-year major leaguer, and Versalles, a qualified rookie in 1961, with brief major league showings in 1959 and 1960, were the only members of the Tropical Park group who did not play winter ball. Taylor spent the off-season in his major league home city of Philadelphia. Versalles attempted to tune his baseball skills in the Nicaraguan Winter League but was denied the chance by his major league club, the Minnesota Twins. The 21-year-old infielder and future American League MVP spent the winter in Minneapolis instead with his expectant wife, who had recently been able to leave Cuba and join her husband. González, who had shone through as a second-year player with the Philadelphia Phillies in 1961, played over the hibernal months with the San Juan Senators. Tiant, who had pitched in Mexico's premier summer league, returned south of the border to toss from the hill for the Reynosa Oilers of the inaugural, six-team Northern Autumn League. (The 21-year-old Tiant threw a no-hitter with 16 strikeouts in his mound debut with Reynosa.)

Another future star, Tony Oliva, spent his first winter out of Cuba in the Florida Instructional League, which typically ran for two months, October to December, and consisted of six big league-sponsored clubs. Oliva had signed with the Minnesota Twins in February of 1961 and had come to the United States (via Mexico City) with a group of Cuban prospects that same spring. In his 1973 autobiography, Oliva retold the experience: "I was sad because I was leaving my family for the first time, but I figured I would come back after the season to be with them again. I had no money—we weren't allowed to take money out of the country with us—but I knew that all the expenses were to be paid. Once the season started and you were with a team, you were to get three hundred dollars a month [salary]."[5] The eventual Hall of Famer would not see his mother again until 1970, through an arranged mutual visit to Mexico. Through a similarly arranged visitation the following year in the same place, Oliva reunited with his father. This lack of freedom of movement for Cuban ballplayers was a microcosm of the plight of the Cuban nation and its government's now long-lasting, blatant disregard for Article 13 of the United Nations Universal Declaration of Human Rights (UNHR), which states that every person has the right to freely leave any country, including their own, and return to their country.

A current pitching star from Cuba, Camilo Pascual, spent several days in Windsor, Ontario, awaiting immigration approval to reenter the United States. He was scheduled to join the Twins' Instructional League club as a pitching coach, while his Twins mound mate, Pedro Ramos, also appeared as a dual coach and hurler in the rookie league. Other Cuban notables in the instructional loop were Giraldo "Chico" Ruíz and José Cardenal. Erstwhile in the Caribbean basin, in the now-joined Panama-Nicaraguan League, Panchón Herrera, Hilario "Sandy" Valdespino, Borrego Alvarez, Danny Morejón, along with pitchers Diego Seguí and Rodolfo "Rudy" Arias, all suited up for Nicaragua's Cinco Estrellas club. Cuban native Wilfredo Calviño piloted the team. Joe Azcué and Leo Posada traveled to Venezuela to perform in that country's winter baseball festivities, as did Regino "Reggie" Otero in a managerial capacity.

Preston Gómez and Napoleón Reyes found work outside of Cuba as field leaders of the Caguas-Guayama Criollos and San Juan Senators, respectively. Reyes managed Leo Cárdenas, poised to emerge as a starter and multiple-year All-Star with the Cincinnati Reds, and International League hurler Orlando Pena, hoping for a return to The Show in 1962. Also on the Senators' squad, Reyes had the pleasure of directing Miguel Angel "Mike" de la Hoz, Cleveland Indians infielder. Gómez guided Román Mejías on his Gaguas-Guayama team. Some of their Cuban opponents were Julio Gotay of the Mayagüez Indians, Dagoberto

"Bert" Cueto of the Ponce Lions, and Octavio Rojas, representing a new franchise in the league.

As did most Cuban professionals, Rojas put his career, and future, ahead of his problematic country. "John Quinn, GM of the Phillies, notified me about an opportunity to play in Puerto Rico, with Arecibo, which was an expansion team that year," said Rojas. "We reunited with my in-laws, who had established a business in Puerto Rico after fleeing Cuba. Puerto Rico welcomed us with open arms, not just me—many Cuban players and non-athletes alike, and we will always be grateful."

His wife echoed their heartfelt appreciation for the Island of Enchantment. "[That] off-season, we could not return to Cuba," said Candida. "We went to Puerto Rico, which began, which brought about, a great bond, a special love for the island that Cookie and I would both develop. Puerto Rico embraced us. We will never forget it. Cookie began playing for the Arecibo *Lobos* of the winter league. We lived in Reparto Marquez, a suburb of Arecibo."

Rojas captured several pages of note in Van Hyning's *Puerto Rico's Winter League* history. "My manager in Arecibo was Luis Rodríguez Olmo, a great player in his day, whom I'm proud of having played for, and of learning a lot from," Rojas was quoted in the 1995 publication. "Winter ball meant a lot to the careers of many players. I played 21 years of winter baseball. If it hadn't been for baseball in Cuba, Puerto Rico, and Venezuela, I might not have had a big league career."[6]

In spite of the withdrawal of Cuba, an attempt to continue the Caribbean Series was made in February of 1961 by the Caribbean Professional Baseball Federation, under the rebranded name of Inter-American Series. League executives from the remaining three prominent winter leagues joined together to present a new championship tournament. Venezuela's Valencia Industrialists defeated the Rapiños club, a native rival team from the country's western baseball league, in a one-game playoff to win the inaugural competition with a record of 5–2. The Andean country provided two championship teams, while Puerto Rico and Panama sent their winter circuit champions to compete. The winner-take-all game was decided in thrilling, walk-off manner when catcher Dick Windle homered in the bottom of the tenth inning to give Venezuelan pitching legend José "Carrao" Bracho a 2–1 victory for Valencia.

A year later, when the second Inter-American Series began, February 7, 1962, in San Juan, Otero's Caracas Lions had won the Venezuelan league championship, while the Marlboro Smokers emerged victorious in the Panama-Nicaragua circuit. The two clubs comprised half of the championship contenders, as the host country provided the other two

Rojas (center) with two unidentified men associated with the Arecibo Lobos (Wolves) of the Puerto Rican Winter League, where many Cuban players were able to continue their baseball careers, ca. 1962 or 1963. Puerto Rico welcomed many Cuban athletes and non-athletes following the Cuban Revolution (courtesy Cookie Rojas).

teams: circuit playoff champ Santurce Crabbers and the runner-up Mayagüez Indians. Santurce fortified their squad by adding Tony González and Mike de la Hoz from the rival San Juan club, and Cookie Rojas from Arecibo. Mayagüez bolstered their roster with Luis Arroyo from Ponce and Luis Tiant from the Mexico's Northern Autumn League.

Describing the splendid hitting campaign of de la Hoz that season, league archivist Van Hyning wrote: "He was a terror at the plate in four other leagues—Puerto Rico, Venezuela, Dominican Republic and Mexico. His name was at or near the top of the list of batting leaders wherever he wintered. Matty Alou and Vic Davalillo narrowly surpassed him during several batting chases, but there was none better than de la Hoz in Puerto Rico throughout 1961–62, when he won the batting crown."[7] De la Hoz was also $500 richer as the result of a bonus received from the PRWL for winning the hitting title with a .354 mark.

De la Hoz credited his batting excellence in the various Caribbean basin venues to the early competition he faced back home. "Baseball in Cuba was really top-notch when I began," he said. "You played with four teams at the same [Gran] stadium. The wind came in from center field, and sometimes a batting champion there would hit less than .320. It all depends on how good the native players are. In the late 1950s, the Puerto Rico League was a notch below Cuba, but when I played in Puerto Rico during the 1960s, they had some quality native players in the big leagues."[8]

With the competition held at Sixto Escobar Stadium, the Crabbers walked away with the Inter-American crown with a record of 8–1 in an expanded triple round robin affair. De la Hoz upped his game on the slugging side for Santurce, belting four home runs, one a grand slam. The Cuban infielder slammed a go-ahead, two-run four-bagger in the ninth inning of one game for a 3–2 road victory over Mayagüez (February 8) and a walk-off solo shot against the Indios' Luis Tiant, in the 11th inning of another, resulting in a 5–4 Crabbers victory on February 14. It was "Mighty Mike's" second long ball hit against his compatriot hurler in the series and the last professional home run hit at the venerable Escobar Stadium. According to Van Hyning, 16 Cuban players appeared on the four team's rosters.

Amazingly, Rojas, with his status of reinforcement player on the Santurce roster, had now claimed his third international team championship in four years.

First Big League Spring Training

The same month, Rojas was invited to spring training by the Cincinnati Reds for the first time. He reported to Cincinnati's training facility in Tampa, Florida. His wife, having given birth to their first child, stayed in Miami. Soon after Rojas' arrival, he sent his spouse a picture postcard from camp which, six decades later, she still maintained among many mementos and keepsakes she has collected over the decades from her husband's career.

The postcard is naturally a self-promoting one, with an aerial shot of the Causeway Inn, describing itself as the "Winter Home of the Cincinnati Redlegs [stamped in red ink on the back] 5 miles from downtown Tampa—on the causeway directly to Clearwater and the Gulf of Mexico—with 152 beautifully appointed rooms—Pool—Cabanas—Restaurant—Coffee Shop—free TV in every room—Air Conditioned and heated." Postmarked from Tampa, March 1962, with a seven-cent air mail stamp, it was addressed to *Candida Rojas 1176 SW 20 Avenue*

Apt #26 Miami 35, Fla. U.S.A. Alluding to a missed wedding anniversary together and an expression of gratitude over the birth of their first child, along with a couple's private recognition of undetailed perseverance shown by Candida, the handwritten card by Rojas reads (translated from Spanish):

> Dearest, God willing, you and everyone are well. I'm fine, thank the Lord. Many best wishes for our anniversary. What endurance you have shown. I have no complaints, on the contrary, only that I am very satisfied and happy and even more so to you for giving me a son as beautiful as Taby. Regards to everyone. Love, Cuqui.

The reference to "Taby" is to ten-month-old Octavio Jr., born May 19, 1961. Today, Tab Rojas is plant manager for a commercial cement contractor in Naples, Florida. Like all of the Rojas children, he had early professional baseball aspirations.

> I wish everyone could experience the life as a child of a major league ballplayer. It was special. To watch your dad perform in a highly specialized craft. It was exciting. It was like being on a gameshow every night.
> To get to meet such important people in the game. Stars and Hall of Famers. Lou Whitaker stands out to me. And Harmon Killebrew. What a congenial man he was. He had huge hands, I remember. Of course, Amos Otis and George Brett.
> Being the oldest and the son of a major league baseball player, you had to go through expectations, and as a result I had to grow up faster than I needed to, I feel. My Dad rarely got a chance to see me play. I think he saw me play one time in a game when I was in high school. My Mom was my biggest supporter. But looking back, I think, that helped me in the long run; it helped me forge an identity of my own and prepare for life's challenges.
> After two years of junior college, I was signed as a free agent by the Oakland A's as a first baseman/outfielder. I spent two years with Oakland, then another half-year with Baltimore. So, I had about a 2½-year minor league career. I used Tab Rojas as my professional name. It was easier than Octavio.
> When I was with Baltimore, we played an exhibition game at the Hall of Fame [Doubleday] field. I got a chance to go inside the Hall. There, I saw the lineup card of Jim Bunning's perfect game, and to see my Dad's name on it was really something special.[9]

The closing sobriquet of the postcard pertains to Rojas himself and the byproduct nickname he has carried for most of his life. "As far back as I can remember I was called Cuqui," Rojas said of his engaging nickname. "My mother never called me Octavio. She always called me Cuqui. But I was called Octavio in school." As best translated, "Cuqui" (pronounced koo-kee) means "adorable" in Spanish.

Two—Forced Exile

It's easy to surmise how the close-sounding English derivative came about. "When I went to West Palm Beach [Sun Chiefs], it became 'Cookie.'"

Rojas was part of an early arriving group at Reds camp, joining pitchers and catchers at the end of February. Entering his fourth year as a Reds coach, Reggie Otero joined the preliminary contingent of Cincinnati personnel to check in to the Causeway Inn. Like Rojas, who participated as a player, Otero had just completed managerial duties with Caracas in the Inter-American Series II. His club finished second to Santurce, posting a 5–4 record.

In one of the first spring training reports written about Rojas, sportswriter Earl Lawson sought out the Reds' Cuban coach for his impressions on Rojas. "Otero is high on Cookie Rojas, rookie second sacker who's training with the Reds this spring," wrote Lawson. "He's a very good second baseman," said Reggie, adding, "Elio Chacon is more versatile than Rojas, but Cookie is a better hitter."[10] The comparison to Chacón stemmed from his playing time as a utility infielder with the Reds the past two seasons. (The Venezuelan infielder had been selected by the New York Mets in the NL expansion draft a few months earlier.) Rojas would actually prove one of the most versatile players in MLB history.

Ten springs after this print report, a *Cincinnati Post* sports editor revealed some behind-closed-doors activity that could have altered Rojas' and another fellow rookie's careers, while bringing to light the value seen in them at the time. "In the winter preceding the 1961 baseball season, Gabriel Paul left his job as general manager of the Cincinnati Reds," penned Pat Harmon. "He took a similar job with the Houston Astros baseball club. Soon thereafter, Paul contacted William O. DeWitt, his replacement in Cincinnati, and offered to buy a couple of minor league players the Reds controlled. He was willing to pay $300,000 for Octavio (Cookie) Rojas and Giraldo (Chico) Ruíz."[11]

Dewitt declined the offer, and both players remained under Cincinnati control. Rojas, who would reach the big leagues first, played his initial exhibition game on March 11. He doubled in his first spring at-bat. Reds manager Fred Hutchinson had said he planned to give Rojas and another rookie infielder, Tommy Harper, a shot at the starting second base position, competing against the incumbent, Don Blasingame. "I'll alternate them in exhibition games," the skipper said. "They'll play every third day until one shows more promise than the others. Then we'll keep him there."[12] Harper would start the season at third base, after regular third baseman Gene Freese broke his ankle sliding in spring camp. The 21-year-old Harper was only given six games to prove his merit, however, before being optioned to the minors for the entire season. The hasty decision may have been motivated by another factor. Harper's demotion opened the way for Leo Cárdenas to become the starting shortstop when Eddie Kasko, the team's primary shortstop for the past three seasons, was shifted to third to fill the Freese vacancy. Cárdenas, a two-season utility player until then, would hold the shortstop position for the Reds for the next seven years.[13]

Early in camp, Lawson delivered interesting background briefs on Rojas for attentive fans back home. "Cookie Rojas, the Reds' rookie second baseman, has been shagging ground balls ever since he was 10 years old," wrote the longtime beat writer. "'My father hit them to me,' said Rojas. 'Go after every ball, my father would tell me. Even go after the balls you don't have a chance to stop. It will give you better range.' The young Cuban has been playing baseball, summer and winter, since 1956. He speaks English well. He has been wearing glasses since 1958, the year he played at Savannah, Ga., then a Reds farm club in the Sally League."[14]

"I was trying to score from third on a close play," elaborated Rojas on the eyeglass issue, "and in the process I collided with the knee of a heavy catcher. I suffered hemorrhages under the eyes and in the nose. The injury cleared up, but I noticed that my vision was blurring. An eye doctor recommended glasses. He said I had developed astigmatism."[15]

As was the custom for many years, the Cincinnati Reds hosted the season's first game on April 9, a full day ahead of the league's other teams. To honor the defending National League champions, the opening ceremonies had more pomp than usual. But the Reds fell flat in their first-game title defense, absorbing a 12–4 whipping by the Philadelphia Phillies. The veteran Blasingame kept his job and was the Opening Day second baseman. Rojas made the big club as a backup infielder.

The Reds flew across country to play the Los Angeles Dodgers—and the next day, Rojas made his major league debut. It occurred in the inaugural game played at Dodger Stadium, Tuesday, April 10. There were 52,564 fans in attendance. Rojas' current recollection of his initial big league game follows: "The stadium was beautiful, so clean. It was an incredible sensation to walk out on that immense field, wearing that major league uniform and seeing those players. We had the vest-uniforms, no sleeves. Fred Hutchinson was the manager and Reggie Otero was the third base coach. That was a tremendous team, Frank Robinson, Vada Pinson, the champions of 1961. 'Am I alive, I thought to myself?'"

He was alive, wearing uniform number 17, assigned to him in spring camp. Rojas followed leadoff hitter Eddie Kasko as the second batter to step in the box. He sacrificed Kasko, who had doubled for the stadium's first hit, to third. Pinson singled to bring home Kasko with the stadium's initial run. Behind pitcher Bob Purkey and two relievers, the Reds spoiled the festivities for the Dodgers and their fans, defeating them, 6–3. Although Rojas failed to get a hit in three subsequent at-bats, he impressed his manager on the defensive side of the ball. "That was a great play in the second inning when Rojas pivoted the double play," said Hutchinson. "John Roseboro really barreled into him, and he didn't budge an inch. Sure they were trying to find out something. If you move out, they'll make life miserable for you."[16] The closing portion of the comment relates to a time not long ago, prior to 21st-century rule changes, when middle infielders were subject to more aggressive sliding tactics by baserunners attempting to disrupt double play executions.

Eight days later, on April 18, the teams met in the Eastern time zone. The Reds bludgeoned the Dodgers, 14–0. Rojas missed out on the fun, but he was in the lineup the next evening against the same squad. Seeking his first big league hit, he got it. Playing second base and hitting eighth, after nine hitless major league at-bats, Rojas lashed a single to center field his first time up in the second inning. The victimized hurler was Sanford Koufax. Teammate Wally Post, on second base, was thrown out at home by center fielder Willie Davis to end the frame, denying Rojas his first big league RBI.

"Crosley Field had that incline in left field before the wall," remembered Rojas.

> Back then they did not save balls for rookies and do things like they do today. I never thought about my first hit in terms of it *being* my first hit. I wasn't thinking, wow, this is my first major league hit. I was thinking this hit is to help the team score, so the team could win. I never thought of keepsakes, certainly not as a rookie. All the opportunities I had of obtaining autographed items over the years, I ended up donating them to be auctioned for charity. I donated many items—you can't imagine—to raise money for many golf tournaments.

Future starts were not as productive for Rojas. Outhitting him, Blasingame kept his grip on second base for the Reds. At the end of July, the Reds optioned Rojas to the minor leagues, to Dallas–Fort Worth. He was recalled in September. In all, Rojas saw action in 39 games for Cincinnati. His average was .221 in 86 at-bats. He hit .241 at DFW.

Apart from the notable accomplishment of reaching the major leagues, Rojas' first season in Cincinnati can be characterized as uneventful. For his wife, who eventually joined him in the Queen City during his first big league experience, she most recalled an initiation of a different kind. "I don't remember where we stayed in Cincinnati," said Candida.

> Cookie only played a short time there. I do remember something about Cincinnati, though. My father never let me get behind the wheel of a car in Cuba. I was his baby, so, using that as a pretext for protecting me, I never learned to drive. Cookie tried teaching me one time, but I almost wrecked the car and he never let me try again. In Cincinnati, Mrs. Reggie Otero taught me how to drive. And I drove to the airport after a road trip to pick up Cookie, and he was so surprised that I was driving. That's what I remember most about Cincinnati.

Food and Grease Went Flying

Rojas returned to his adopted off-season home in the fall and another go-round in the profession to which he had committed his young life. The Puerto Rican Winter League continued its singular high brand of baseball during the 1962–1963 campaign and elevated itself in the amenities arena with the grand opening of a new baseball facility. After many years as the capital city home of San Juan and Santurce, Sixto Escobar Stadium gave way to a modern complex built in the Hato Rey district of San Juan and named after the first native player to appear in the major leagues. Hiram Bithorn Stadium, an 18,000-seat structure with a cost of $7,000,000, was packed with an overflow crowd of 18,364 (a league record) for its October 24 inaugural. Pitching into the ninth inning, Bob Veale, a Pittsburgh Pirates rookie hurling for the Ponce Lions, defeated the San Juan Senators, 6–2.

Two days hence, Rojas hit a grand slam home run in Arecibo's initial contest on October 26, and he hit safely in his first 20 games of the season. The Wolves, again managed by Luis Olmo, and with a number of Philadelphia Phillies' conscripts on its roster, defeated the visiting Mayagüez Indians, 19–10.

Interestingly, the man who recommended the Puerto Rican winter gig to Cookie Rojas ended up trading for the infielder a few days after Thanksgiving. On November 27, giving up mediocre pitcher Jim Owens in an even exchange, John Quinn obtained Rojas for his Philadelphia Phillies. The manager of the Phillies, Gene Mauch, could have been whispering in Quinn's ear. "Gene Mauch first spotted me in the International League," Rojas said. "He was manager of the Minneapolis Millers. I'm sure Mauch was behind the trade that the Phillies made to acquire me from Cincinnati. When Mauch left, I was traded, with Dick Allen, to the St. Louis Cardinals. That trade changed baseball. Later, when Mauch landed with the Angels in California, I ended up with the Angels as well.... The Reds knew what they were doing. They had a kid named Pete Rose coming up the next year."

Prior to the end of the calendar year, the newest member of the Phillies team offered his new bosses a peek into what could be described as burgeoning versatility. On December 30, Rojas was pressed into action behind the plate when Olmo's club found itself short-handed. Pitcher John Boozer, another Phillies' hopeful, teamed with Rojas to beat Santurce, 2–1.

Rojas had an exceptional winter campaign with the Wolves, so much so that the team held a night in his honor on January 19, 1963. "It was a beautiful night," recalled Candida Rojas. "What I remember most, though, is that I was pregnant and had to deal with a very rambunctious child [Taby] on the field who didn't want to cooperate with anything."

In the game that followed, Rojas collected two singles and a double. The three hits broadened a hitting clip of 10-for-15 for the infielder. Among the double-digit hit total was his second grand slam. The Wolves beat Santurce, 8–0, behind Phillies rookie pitcher Jack Hamilton and four RBI from fellow prospect Danny Cater.

Arecibo's 35–35 record was good enough to finish fourth in the league, with a qualifying slot in the post-season. Notwithstanding, the club was no match for the 42–28 pennant winners from Mayagüez, falling four games to one in the opening round of the playoffs. Rojas had a spectacular four months. He led the circuit in hits with 95 and concluded the season third in the batting race (.333) and second in runs scored to Chico Ruíz (48–46). Rojas was named as top second baseman in the sportswriters' all-star team selections (one player at each position). Luis Olmo received manager of the year honors from the same voting group.

Rojas was not asked to participate as a reinforcement player or possibly opted out of the Inter-American Series. In February 1963, the pennant and playoff champion Mayagüez Indians were joined by champion representatives from Nicaragua, Venezuela and Panama for the third edition of the competition, which went back to a double round robin format. In a competition played in Panama City, the home country's Chiriqui-Bocas Farmers bested Nicaragua's Boer Indians, 5–0, in a playoff game after both clubs finished with identical 4–2 records. Mayagüez (3–3) and Venezuela's Valencia Industrialists (1–5) were the under-performers. A fourth—and final—IAS took place a year later, as enthusiasm apparently waned without the marquee representation from the Pearl of the Antilles. (The Caribbean Series, under its original name, would be revived in 1970, with the Dominican Republic and Mexico incorporating as new country members in 1970 and 1971, respectively. The countries replaced Cuba and Panama.)

The Philadelphia Phillies trained in Clearwater, Florida. In early February 1963, it was reported that Rojas and five others, including 20-year-old pitcher Ferguson Jenkins, had come to contract terms with the team, bringing the total number of signed players to 30. No salary figures were brought to light. Gene Mauch, entering his fourth season as Phillies manager, was asked for comments on some of the green recruits. He had this to say about his newest infield addition: "Rojas can field you silly around second base. He should give Tony Taylor something to think about. I also hear his hitting has improved tremendously."[17]

The quote reinforces Rojas' growing reputation as an excellent glove man. The reference to Taylor is to the Phillies' first-string second baseman the past three seasons. In 1963, though, the 27-year-old Taylor (three years older than Rojas) would not be budged. In fact, Taylor finished with the team's second-highest Wins Above Replacement total, 4.7, behind only right fielder Johnny Callison's outstanding 8.1. (Wins Above Replacement, or WAR, is an analytic performance measure of the offensive and defensive production of a major leaguer against a replacement-level player or minor leaguer using a base rank of 0 for that minor leaguer. A position player's WAR also takes into account baserunning and games played. Pitching WAR is calculated using innings pitched and what a hurler directly controls from the mound, i.e., home runs, walks, and HBP, as well as adjusting for the runs-scoring environment associated with the parks pitched in at the time. Prior to the DH, a pitcher's offensive statistics was part of his overall WAR. A WAR of 4 is considered to be at all-star level; a 6 WAR categorizes a star player; and a WAR of 8 classifies an individual as league MVP caliber.)

The Phillies' Art Mahaffey defeated the Cincinnati Reds, 2–1, in the initial game of the 1963 season at Connie Mack Stadium, April 9. The next day, Rojas made his first appearance for his new team, displaying the Phillies' trademark oversized uniform numeral 16 on his back. (As with Cincinnati, he had no choice in the selection.) In the fifth inning, he pinch-ran for Phillies first baseman Frank Torre. The new team member reached third base but advanced no farther.

The Rojas family had a new addition themselves with the birth of second son, Miguel Angel, better known as "Mike," on April 17 in Miami. With the implementation of paternity leave nearly half a century away, Rojas played in the Phillies' scheduled game that night in Milwaukee, batting once as a pinch-hitter without success. "I was named after my godfather in Puerto Rico," Mike told the author. "I don't remember too much about him. I'm sure I met him when I was young."[18]

"Miguel Marquez was an investor in Arecibo," Candida Rojas expanded. "Cookie and I proposed that if I had a boy, Miguel and his wife would be the godparents. If it was a girl, we had another couple lined up. Both couples agreed."

The father of two obtained his first hit with his Philadelphia squad on May 11. In his fourth start, all at second base, Rojas singled his first time up, snapping an 0-for-12 beginning with the lumber. Powered by first baseman Don Demeter's five RBI, the Phillies downed the Milwaukee Braves at Connie Mack Stadium, 8–5. Rojas was otherwise not involved offensively.

The second-year player obtained his first major league game-winning hit on July 7 at Wrigley Field. As a pinch-hitter in the top of the ninth inning, the infielder singled home Rubén Amaro, who had tripled to lead off the frame. Breaking a tie score, the Phillies posted a 3–2 road win.

Later in the month, Rojas made his first foray outside of the infield cutout. He was used as an outfielder for the first time, when left fielder Tony González was ejected from a ballgame at Dodger Stadium on July 26 for disputing too strenuously his own force out at second base. Rojas handled his only chance in the outfield. He retired Dodgers outfielder Willie Davis on what was described as a backhand grab of a curving liner. Mauch said he knew Rojas could do the job in the pasture because of the number of fungoes he had hit to Rojas in practice. Prior to his seventh-inning ejection, González had driven in one of the Phillies' runs in their eventual 6–5 victory over Los Angeles.

Rojas collected his first career home run toward the end of the season on September 17. At the Polo Grounds, the part-time player connected against Mets pitcher Tracy Stallard, almost two years removed from surrendering Roger Maris' record-setting 61st long ball. The Phillies made use of the second-inning solo blast to beat the Mets, 8–6. The next day, the same two clubs played the final regularly scheduled professional baseball game at the venerated ballpark, in anticipation of the Mets playing out the remainder of their games on the road.[19] That day, September 18, in a rare start at second base, Rojas took the collar but scored one of the Phillies' runs in the 5–1 triumph over the lowly New York team. Rojas recorded the nostalgically remembered stadium's penultimate assist when he initiated a 4–6–3 double play to end the game.

Eight games above .500 but with little chance of contending for the pennant, the Phillies cosmetically improved their record in September by going 15–11.

One of the 11 losses occurred September 22 in Houston. Starter Chris Short was nursing a 1–0, ninth-inning lead at Colt Stadium. But the home club rallied for a pair of runs, both charged to Short, which saddled him with a tough 2–1 defeat. The defeat left a particularly bad taste in Gene Mauch's mouth, and he made sure any post-game dining would be literally hard to swallow when he overturned "a table full of food in the clubhouse, ruining two players' suits."[20] An irate Mauch accused his charges of playing like "Little Leaguers" as he "threw slices of watermelon and cantaloupe around the club room as well as the container of ribs and one of fried chicken."[21]

"Of course, I remember," said Rojas. "Gene kicked the table over and the food and grease went flying. It stained the clothes of two players who were already dressed. Gene had to buy them each a $200 suit."

Mauch's club (87–75) finished the season in the first division but 12 games behind the pennant-winning Dodgers.

Rojas saw action in 64 games, though many came as a pinch-runner.

Three

Enough to Make Billy Penn Cry

The Philadelphia Phillies began 1964 knowing they were a competitive team. They had ended the prior season one game out of third place and had beaten the NL champion Dodgers 11 out of 18 games. Their main shortfall, however, was pitching. The club did not have a bona fide ace. In 1963, Ray Culp and Cal McLish had paced the team in wins with 14 and 13, respectively. (The veteran McLish, sidelined with tendinitis in his pitching shoulder, would be released over the summer of 1964 after appearing in only two games.) General manager John Quinn addressed the issue when he traded for pitcher Jim Bunning in late fall.

Several factors drove the December 5, 1963, trade, which netted veteran catcher Gus Triandos along with the All-Star pitcher. Bunning had slipped to 12–13 in 1963 with an ERA of 3.88. He was at odds with Tigers manager Charlie Dressen over his pitching motion and butted heads with Tigers management as the club's union rep. Detroit received outfielder Don Demeter and reliever Jack Hamilton, addressing an outfield need while clearing the way for 22-year-old Bill Freehan to become the regular backstop. A former 20-game winner, the 32-year-old Bunning had won 118 games at this point of his eventual Hall of Fame career. "We're delighted to get him," said manager Gene Mauch. "I've always regarded Bunning as one of the best pitchers in the American League."[1] A currently non-prolific batter, Triandos was expected to back up Clay Dalrymple behind the plate.

Heading into the 1964 season, the Phillies squad that most often appeared on the field had primarily been constructed from front office trades, including their outfield: Wes Covington, Tony González, and Johnny Callison. One exception was a 22-year-old rookie from northwestern Pennsylvania named Dick Allen, who had been signed four years earlier in the amateur draft. A great deal of expectation had been placed on Allen. Turning down more than 40 athletic scholarship offers from various colleges and universities as a high school senior, he had accepted, instead, a $50,000 signing bonus from Philadelphia to play baseball. Additionally, Allen had led the International League in several slugging categories, including home runs (33), RBI (97) and triples (12), playing for the Arkansas Travelers in 1963.

Neither Bunning nor Allen would disappoint in what turned out as perhaps the most frustrating outcome for one team in a season in baseball history.

The Philadelphia club jumped off to a 10–2 start, with Bunning winning three of the games and Allen hitting .431 with six home runs and a .961 slugging mark.

Cookie Rojas made his first start of the season on May 11, against the St. Louis Cardinals, filling in for center fielder Tony González, who had an eye inflammation. Batting leadoff, Rojas collected his first two hits of the campaign and scored a run, but the Phillies fell, 3–2, at Connie Mack Stadium. The Redbirds' Julian Javier clocked a three-run home run in the seventh inning.

Two weeks later, May 26, Rojas hit a stand-up, inside-the-park home run in a 13–4 Phillies loss at Pittsburgh, in the opener of a three-game series. Coming in as a substitute in the one-sided contest, Rojas connected on a deep drive to the left-center field wall, the ball caroming away from Pirates left fielder Bob Bailey.

The following day, Mauch decided to give Tony Taylor, who was hitting in the .220s, the day off. Taylor had been obtained from the Chicago Cubs in a four-player exchange in 1960 and had been the team's regular second baseman ever since. "I am only playing because Tony got a bad start and tired out," said a deferential Rojas. "Tony is still the greatest. He pulls for me when I am in there. How do I know? Well, I pull for him."[2] Substituting for his countryman, Rojas collected two hits with an RBI and a run scored, accounting for both of the Phillies' runs in their 2–0 victory over the Pirates. Art Mahaffey, whom the Phillies had signed right out of high school in 1956, tossed a four-hit shutout.

In the series finale, Rojas, back in center field, banged out three hits in four at-bats. Shortstop Dick Schofield singled in the winning run in the bottom of the ninth for a 6–5 Pirates win.

It was around this still early juncture that the Phillies' manager decided to make public his strategic designs for some of his players. Mauch had been using Bobby Wine at shortstop with exceptional infield utility man Rubén Amaro as his alternate. "In late May, Mauch cited the need to give both Wine and Tony Taylor some rest," briefed one of many accounts printed about the team. "He said, 'There's more mental pressure on the second baseman and shortstop than on any other regular except catcher. Taylor and Wine have played almost every inning since spring training.'"[3]

The Phillies came back home to open their longest homestand of the season (16 games in 17 days) on May 29. In the first game of a weekend series against the Houston Colt .45s, Rojas stayed in the lineup at second base and boomed out four more hits, giving him 13 in 23 at-bats and a .565 average in the six-week-old campaign. The fourth hit was a triple in the eighth inning which knocked home the deciding run for Philadelphia in their 7–6 triumph. Jim Bunning took a perfect game into the seventh frame, retiring the first 20 Colts. He was not involved in the decision, however. After going hitless in two official at-bats the next day (a 5–1 win), Rojas slashed two singles in the Sunday series concluder. A 4–1 triumph completed a three-game sweep of the Texas team. Rojas leisurely scored the first run, following a safety and Dick Allen's home run. The four-bagger was Allen's tenth.

Bunning's record stood at 5–2 as the 25–15 Phillies entered June with a slim half-game advantage over the San Francisco Giants for the National League lead.

The hot hitting earned conspicuous playing time for Rojas; he saw action in all but four of the Phillies' 30 games in June, receiving 26 starting assignments at four different positions: second base, shortstop, and left and center fields. A pair of starts at second came in back-to-back games, June 2 and 3, in which Rojas scored the deciding run in each. In the seventh inning of the former contest, Rojas singled and came around to score as the Phillies edged the visiting Los Angeles Dodgers, 4–3. The next evening, the infielder was the only player to cross home plate, doing so in the bottom of the 11th inning after doubling. An old-fashioned pitching duel between distinguished hurlers Bunning and Don Drysdale extended the scoreless affair into extra innings.

On June 4, the infielder's bat went silent as did all of his teammates'. Dodgers pitcher Sandy Koufax hurled the third of his four career no-hit games. In a minor victory, Rojas was the only Phillies batter not to strike out against the splendid left-hander, who fanned 12 and walked one. Koufax faced the minimum 27 hitters after his free pass recipient Dick Allen was thrown out trying to steal. An impressive Thursday night crowd of 29,709 onlookers were treated to the historic achievement.

The Phillies concluded their long home stay by taking three out of four games from the New York Mets, including a Sunday doubleheader sweep on June 14. During the series, the team's center fielder unveiled a protective batting accoutrement that became standard wear in baseball. Rojas, in a reminiscent aside, identified his countryman's widely adopted contribution: "Tony González had a great arm, could cover a lot of ground. He was the first player to wear a batting helmet with a protective flap over the ear." As a left-handed batter and too-often sufferer of beanings, González tailored his shielding cover over his right ear.

The following weekend in New York, the teams played a similar series, this one consisting of two twin bills and five games. The concluding Sunday, June 21 doubleheader was played on a picture-perfect weather day that also fell on Father's Day. Rojas started both games at shortstop.

In the first game, James Paul David Bunning matched the meteorological setting and threw the first perfect game in the National League since 1880, becoming the first pitcher to toss no-hitters in both leagues in the modern era.[4] Retiring all 27 batters he faced in a 6–0 win, Bunning went to a three-ball count twice. In the fourth inning, the infallible pitcher struck out the Mets' Ron Hunt swinging on a 3–2 pitch that appeared out of the strike zone. The right-hander, who required only 90 pitches to hurl his historic gem, identified the pitch as a high slider that might have been called a ball. Striking out 10 batters, the Phils' ace singled out his slider, followed by his curve, as his best pitches on the afternoon. In the eighth frame, on his second 3–2 pitch, Bunning caught the home team's Hawk Taylor looking at a slider that batterymate Gus Triandos did not catch cleanly and had to throw to first base to officially record the out.

Rojas chipped in on the offensive side with a hit and a sacrifice bunt in three at-bats. On the defensive end, Rojas recorded three of Bunning's 27 outs. Unusually, he had no assists at shortstop. The third-year player retired two hitters on pop-ups and a third when he caught a liner hit right at him by Amado Samuel for the Mets' ninth out of the contest. Rojas played the last four innings of the game in left field, where he was not tested.

"There was one difficult chance in the game and second baseman Tony Taylor took care of that in sensational style," wrote Allen Lewis in the *Philadelphia Inquirer*. "Jesse Gonder rifled a liner toward right with one out in the fifth inning. Taylor raced to his left, dove headlong, and caught the ball before it hit the ground. When he came down, however, the ball fell out of his glove. He picked it up, whirled around and threw to first from his knees to retire Gonder by at least a full step"[5]

Taylor, who handled three chances faultlessly, thought the ball would get past him. "I thought it was by," he said. "Then I dive for the ball and then I catch it in the pocket of the glove. I drop it when I hit the ground. I threw him out on my knees."[6]

In a departure from the norm and completely disregarding the superstitious customs that are so ingrained in the game, the 32-year-old Bunning was anything but introspective as his masterpiece progressed. He verbally interacted with teammates on and off the bench.

Bobby Wine, who had come in to play short when Rojas shifted to the outfield, ran into foul ground to catch the first out of the ninth inning. The Phillies' starter then struck out George Altman, pinch-hitting for Samuel. The last batter standing in the way of immortality for Bunning was a second emergency hitter named John Stephenson, a rookie with all of 27 big league at-bats under his belt. Bunning threw the left-handed-swinging Stephenson five straight curve balls, the last coming on a 2–2 count that the rookie swung over and missed. The Shea Stadium crowd of 32,026 rose to their feet cheering the opposing pitcher during the final at-bat.

Bunning's wife, Mary, and 12-year-old daughter Barbara (the oldest of his seven children) were sitting behind home plate during his one-of-a-kind effort. In a story later repeated by Mets announcer Ralph Kiner, Mrs. Bunning, after the final pitch, scampered onto the field and hugged and kissed her husband. In the Mets' broadcast booth, as the TV camera panned over the couple, Kiner colleague Bob Murphy innocently inquired, "Is that Bunning's wife?" to which Kiner answered, "It better be."

The Phillies won the nightcap, 8–2, behind six innings of strong work from 18-year-old rookie pitcher Rick Wise. Rojas chipped in with a single, run scored, and RBI in two official at-bats; he also suffered two HBP. He again opened the game at shortstop, then moved to left field in the fifth inning for Wes Covington. Wine again took over the relinquished infield spot for Rojas. The doubleheader sweep put the ribbon on the series, in which the Phillies won four games. (Boosting the team's rise in the standings, the Phillies went 15–3 against the bottom-feeding Metropolitans that season.)

The "perfect man" appeared on the *Ed Sullivan Show* that evening. Incidentally, in his next start against the Mets (August 9 at Connie Mack Stadium), he tossed five more perfect frames. Having retired 12 consecutive Mets, he was reached for an infield single, leading off the sixth inning. Bunning five-hit the Metsies, 6–0.

As is often the case with no-hitters, Bunning was not sharp in his encore start on June 26. Matched up against Bob Gibson of the St. Louis Cardinals, he gave up 10 hits and four runs in seven innings. Cardinals leadoff batter Curt Flood doubled off the Phillies' pitcher in the first inning. But Gibson was not at his best either, permitting two two-run home runs in eight innings. One of them was by Cookie Rojas, into the left field seats at Busch Stadium, his second of the season and first to clear the outfield fence. Catcher Clay Dalrymple smacked the Phillies' third two-run homer of the game in the final frame, lifting the road club to a 6–5 victory. The other circuit clout was struck by Dick Allen, his 15th. The Phils' most valuable utility man made the defensive play of the night. Playing shortstop, Rojas made a diving stop on a hard-hit ball by the Cards' Bill White with two outs and runners at first and third in the bottom of the eighth inning. Rojas threw to second for the force out, maintaining the 5–4 Cardinals lead. After that opener of a four-game set, Rojas started the next three games in center field. St. Louis won two of the three to split the series.

Rojas was the Phillies' center fielder five days later on July 1, when he tripled and scored a run against Sandy Koufax. The Dodgers' ace prevailed, 3–2, in his home ballpark. Mauch's men gained a split the next evening in the brief two-game set in Los Angeles, carrying the day by the same score. All the scoring came in the first four innings. After pinch-hitting for center fielder John Briggs in the fourth frame and taking over his position, Rojas provided a defensive gem in the seventh inning that would have made repeated highlight reels had there been any in the day. The written testimony: "Rojas' legs were pumping when he reached up and hauled down the ball at the 385-mark—and then slammed into the fence. He hit hard and bounced back in a heap on the red-clay warning track. He was knocked out for a minute or two. He still had the ball in the pocket of his glove."[7]

The potentially damaging salvo came off the bat of John Roseboro, leading off the inning. "It was a career play," said an admiring Gene Mauch. "It was the kind of play Cookie can be proud of for the rest of his life. Not too many center fielders would have been that daring."[8]

"I didn't see the wall," said Rojas, whose glasses survived the confrontation. "I was looking at the ball."[9]

The Phillies traveled to San Francisco for a Fourth of July weekend series, sweeping three games from the Giants to move into first place and stoking legitimate pennant talk around the league. The Pennsylvania club hit the All-Star break on July 5 with a first-place record of 47–28, one-and-a-half games better than the second-place Giants. The Cincinnati Reds and Pittsburgh Pirates trailed both clubs, six and seven games out, respectively. St. Louis, the least of the five first-division teams, was 10 games behind Philadelphia.

Three players from the league-leading squad were selected for the All-Star Game. Standout right fielder Johnny Callison was the sole position player, while Jim Bunning and Chris Short, the Phils' number two starter with seven victories and a dazzling 1.59 ERA, were named as the Phillies' pitching representatives. Beginning the season in the bullpen,

Short had become a starter when regular rotation man Ray Culp injured his arm. A left-handed amateur discovery inked by the Phils in 1957, Short, 26, was finally coming into his own this season.

Third baseman Dick Allen, who was making a name for himself with his hitting and slugging as the Phillies' top run-producer, was edged out of an All-Star selection by the Cardinals' Ken Boyer and the Chicago Cubs' Ron Santo. (Speaking of names, Allen, whose given name was Richard, had expressed his preference to be called "Dick," as he was known to family members and friends back home. The request went unheeded by the Philadelphia, and thus, national press, who insisted on calling him "Richie." Allen perceived "Richie" as more connoting a pre-teen's name, in his mind, and chafed against it.)

In the Mid–Summer Classic, Callison brought clamoring attention to his league and indirectly to his team when he delivered a thrilling, three-run, bottom-of-the-ninth-inning home run to cap a four-run senior circuit rally to upend the American League, 7–4. The game was played at Shea Stadium, inaugural-year home of the New York Mets. Bunning hurled two scoreless innings; Short was touched for two runs in one stanza of work.

Soon after the second half resumption of play, Rojas displayed his exceptional gifts with the glove and bat within a few days of each other. On July 19 at Crosley Field, in the back end of a doubleheader, the all-purpose fielder opened the game in center field, took over at shortstop in the eighth inning, and moved behind the plate in the bottom of the ninth. The Reds, trailing 4–2 entering their last at-bat, scored once on a double and single, but fell short as Chris Short, in relief, secured the final out for a 4–3 Phillies win. Rojas flawlessly caught the deliveries of relievers Short and Rick Wise and notched a putout when the young Wise struck out the Reds' Johnny Edwards for the second out. The Reds won the opener, 7–4.

The remarkable utility man had his best offensive day of the year on July 23 at Milwaukee, a game in which the lead changed hands four times in the final three innings. With two outs and the game tied, Rojas doubled home the decisive runs in the top of the tenth inning as Philadelphia, banging out 18 hits, defeated the Braves, 13–10. Rojas crossed the plate after two passed balls by Braves catcher Ed Bailey. It was the third hit of the game for Rojas, who also scored three times and drove in as many runs. Opening the high-scoring affair in left field, Rojas finished it at second base, as Mauch used 21 players, including seven pitchers, to nail down the win. Callison clubbed two homers and pushed home five runs.

A second consecutive game with three hits followed for Rojas, in the road opener of a four-game face-off with the St. Louis Cardinals. Adding offensive support to a six-hitter pitched by Short, Rojas tripled and singled twice; he scored a pair of runs and drove home two others in the Phillies' 9–1 pasting of the Cardinals July 24. Short secured his ninth victory.

The Phillies' handy-man player began receiving more attention as local writers started digging into the success of the team. "Rojas is the delight of Mauch, the ingenious manager of the National League–leading Philadelphia Phillies," wrote one such inquisitive reporter. "So far this season Mauch has played the 160-pounder at six different positions and calls him 'one of the most dedicated players in the game.' The reason Mauch moves Rojas around so much isn't just because of his defensive prowess, but in recognition of his .318 batting average."[10]

With their two most potent bats in Allen and Callison and their two most effective pitchers in Bunning and Short at the fore, the top-of-the-heap Phillies went 19–10 in August to build a 5½ game advantage over Cincinnati in the NL standings.

Allen himself had built an impressive first-year resumé, to the point of gaining print recognition for consideration for baseball's two biggest offensive awards. One such press notice tied together the flash he displayed with his wardrobe to his work with the bat, following a particularly good day at the plate on August 23: "Richie Allen wears orange shoes, four-button suits and sports jackets with buckles on the back. Now he's trying to stick a couple of feathers in his cap. A leading contender for not only Rookie of the Year but Most Valuable Player honors, the standout dresser and outstanding third baseman belted two homers and a single, driving in four runs Sunday as the National League leading Phillies walloped Pittsburgh, 9–3."[11]

An ungracious Allen all but dismissed the significance of the awards. "There's no money in it," he said. "Let them put up $1,000 for the Rookie of the Year and it would be worthwhile. I have a family to support. As it is, Rookie of the Year doesn't mean a thing."[12]

Meanwhile, Rojas continued to receive praise for his varied repertoire. "Cookie is a rare man in a craft where the specialist is lionized," another writer pointed out. "The plaudits go to the Mayses in center field and the Koufaxes on the mound. Utility men usually get their moments as pinch-hitters or when a regular is hurt. Few have had as much to do with the everyday success of their team as Cookie."[13]

Though willingly adapting to his manager's penchant for moving around some of his players like chess pieces, Rojas said that the effort was not without difficulties, in particular at one exacting diamond spot. "Shortstop has been the toughest to learn," he admitted. "It's not the ball coming off the bat—it's making the plays around the bag. Like the double play. The second baseman makes his pivot, steps out of the way and then throws. He never sees the runner. The shortstop has the runner coming right for him when he crosses the bag."[14]

It was around this time that Rojas expressed his positional preference without sounding selfish. "I'd rather play second base," he stated. "It's my position and it's better to play at one place every day than to be moving around. If you stay in one place, you can get adjusted and you'll play better. But I'll play anywhere, as long as I play."[15]

Rojas was not the only multifaceted player on the Phillies. "Ruben Amaro, who can play any infield position expertly, has done everything Mauch has asked of him and done it well,"[16] reminded one team writer.

Yet, in another team retrospective, Rojas could not help but receive the most ink:

> The Philadelphia story is one of skillful manipulation. Take the shortstops, Bobby Wine and Ruben Amaro. The one with the hottest bat at the moment starts. Amaro frequently switches to first base in late innings for defensive purposes. Wine more recently has closed games at third base because Allen has been handicapped by a pulled groin.
>
> Cookie Rojas, until this season a non-descript utility man, has been a lifesaver at bat and in the field. The bespectacled Cuban has played three infield and outfield positions and even caught a ninth inning of a winning game in Cincinnati. "We were protecting a one-run lead, and Cookie didn't drop a ball," recalled Mauch.[17]

Considered the emergency catcher, as the Phillies carried two backstops, Rojas had caught in a spring training game on March 20. During the regular season, Amaro participated in 58 games at first base, accruing 154 innings without an error. The mention of Allen as "handicapped" must have been exaggerated, as the rookie slugger played in all 162 games on the Phillies' schedule. So did the top-notch Callison in right field. Wes Covington (left) and Tony González (center) received the majority of outfield playing time with Callison. Tony Taylor anchored 154 games at second base. Bobby Wine was the primary shortstop, with Rojas and Amaro as the principal understudies. Clay Dalrymple was the starter behind the plate. The Phillies were weakest at an expected infield power spot. John Herrnstein produced a wincingly poor slash line (.234/.288/.360) in 125 games at first base.

Behind Bunning and Short on the pitching depth chart were Dennis Bennett and Art Mahaffey, both 12-game winners. These were the coterie of players most responsible for propelling the pace-setting Phillies to their 19–10 record in August and 12 more wins in 21 games through September 20, for a 90–60 mark. The 90th win was tossed by

Bunning, 3–2 over the Los Angeles Dodgers at Dodger Stadium, in the final game of a four-game split. It was the right-hander's 18th victory against five defeats, and both runs were unearned in the nine-inning effort. Rojas scored the game's initial run after singling in the opening frame. With the win, Mauch's marauders upped their lead in the circuit to 6½ games with 12 games to play. Coming on the heels of a tough, 16-inning loss (4–3) the previous night, Bunning's 3–2 victory not only earned the Phillies a split in the series but also a winning 6–4, three-city, western road-swing record.

Curiously, Bunning was coming off an ineffective start, on short rest, four days earlier on September 16, against the Houston Colt .45s. The staff ace allowed eight hits, three walks, and six earned runs in 4⅓ innings of work, absorbing a 6–5 road defeat. Making the outing more inconvenient for Bunning was an hour and 15-minute rain delay that impeded the normal starting time of the game. The choice of starting pitcher was naturally questioned in the expected arenas. "Manager Gene Mauch tried to outsmart the baseball world by bringing Bunning with only two nights of rest, but in the end he only outsmarted himself," asserted a Texas writer, while making a further reference to Mauch and the weather. "The infield, having been covered all day, was as dry as Mauch's throat when the final out was made and the Phils had failed."[18]

Mauch was apparently intent on wresting one final victory over a weak foe in the final meeting of the season between the two clubs. "I don't expect these people to score off Bunning," Mauch said after the game, not bothering to mention the Houston club by name. "If you want to criticize it, go ahead. I'm not going to explain anything I do. I'm going to kick them just like I've been doing all year." Mauch was referencing the 13–4 record the Phillies had compiled against the Colts heading into their final clash. "I felt okay," commented the scrutinized hurler, who had tossed a 10-inning, complete-game win (4–1) against the Giants three days earlier. "I just didn't have good control. When you have your control, you don't need real good stuff, because you can get the ball where you want it."[19]

Fall Into Oblivion

Following the 10-day western excursion, Mauch's team flew across country to play the next evening at home, their 22nd game in 21 days without an off-day. Awaiting them were the second-place Cincinnati Reds, as well as a robust Monday night crowd of over 20,000 well-wishers. Not surprisingly, the Phillies owned the best record in the

National League at home, 46–28, where they were lined up to play the next seven (in a row) of their final 12 games on the schedule.

At Connie Mack Stadium on September 21, the Reds' John Tsitouris shut out the Phillies on six hits. The home team left eight runners on base and went hitless in eight tries with runners in scoring position. The only run of the game was scored on a sixth-inning steal of home by Chico Ruíz with two outs and Frank Robinson at the plate. The audacious play by the Reds' third baseman, who was a five-time minor league base stealing champ, was viewed for a long time as not a smart baseball play. The closest actors on the Phillies to the mouth-gaping try, from third baseman Allen to catcher Dalrymple, all derided the move. But now, 21st-century analytic study has revealed that the attempt was *not* "probably the most stupid play in baseball history, so stupid that it worked," as Phillies pitcher Art Mahaffey, off whom Ruíz pilfered the plate that evening, still contended more than four decades after the fact.[20] Far from it actually, according to Win Expectancy calculations involving the base stealer's and Robinson's success or failure probabilities.[21] Mahaffey pitched from the full windup, seemingly ignoring this contribution to the rookie Ruiz's success, which came on an 0–1 pitch. Mauch labeled the daring dash as "boneheaded." Reds manager Dick Sisler stated that Ruíz could have "kept on running," if he hadn't made it, indicating severe repercussions for the player. From the beginning, talent bias certainly played a part in the historic criticism. "Had Jackie Robinson, Ty Cobb, Pete Rose or Rod Carew pulled off that steal, the move could well have been portrayed as brilliant in light of their stature," proposed a more contemporary researcher.[22]

"It just came to my mind," said the swift Cuban humbly after the game. "In this game, you either do or you don't."[23]

Ironically, in the Phils' prior defeat—the 16-inning loss to the Dodgers—Willie Davis had stolen home, with two outs and Ron Fairly at the plate, for the winning run. On the mound, in his first game of 1964 since being recalled from the Arkansas Travelers, the big club's Triple A minor league affiliate, was rookie Morrie Steevens. A southpaw, Steevens had been summoned from the bullpen to neutralize the left-handed-hitting Fairly. On his third pitch, Davis raced home successfully.

In game two of the series with the Reds, Cincinnati's best pitcher, Jim O'Toole, held the Phils to two runs and eight hits in a breezy, 9–2, complete-game victory. Chris Short (17–8) took the loss, giving up six earned runs in less than five innings. Breaking a scoreless tie in the third, a two-run homer by Robinson set the tone for the rest of the game. Ruíz walked twice, scored a run, and stole a base after being plunked by the losing pitcher. Over 21,000 disenchanted ticket buyers filed out of Connie Mack Stadium following the final pitch.

On September 23, the Reds raked in the third game by a 6–4 score. Ruíz homered, and Vada Pinson provided the big offensive blow—a seventh-inning, three-run home run—off reliever Ed Roebuck (his second long ball of the game). Timely hitting again escaped the home club, which managed only a pair of hits in 10 tries with runners in scoring position. Reflective of his team's performance, Rojas (playing center field) went hitless in seven at-bats in the second and third games, after sitting out the controversial opener. Suddenly, with the three defeats, the Phillies' lead quickly dropped to 3½ games over the sweeping Reds, who were three back in the loss column. The Cardinals and Giants were five games behind.

Undaunted, the Phillies organization began accepting World Series ticket orders. The team had not appeared in a Fall Classic since 1950, and 63,000 ticket requests were received on the first day of availability.

The Phillies' field leader remained confident after the consecutive setbacks. "We're on top, and that's where we're going to stay," Gene Mauch said. The Phillies' top brass sounded equally positive. "We're still 3½ games ahead, and that's what counts," stated John Quinn. "I'd rather be 3½ games ahead than 3½ behind."[24]

Nine games remained on the Phillies' schedule, the next four at home. On Thursday, September 24, the Milwaukee Braves opened a four-game encampment at Connie Mack Stadium. With Bunning's turn on the hill on tap, Mauch's team was primed to stop the mini-slide against the 78–73, fifth-place club, 11 games off the pace and mathematically eliminated from contention. But Mauch again found himself on the defensive, in front of the press, following a Bunning defeat, this time 5–3. The ace pitcher was touched for three runs in six innings. Reliever Jack Baldschun surrendered the deciding runs. Braves catcher Joe Torre tripled twice and drove home three runners. The Phillies scored all of their runs in the bottom of the eighth inning. Rojas tallied one of them following a pinch-hit appearance.

Mauch was questioned for starting two rookies in the important game, Alex Johnson and Adolfo Phillips, who along with Allen amounted to a third of the lineup with little or no major league experience prior to this year. (Johnson debuted in July; for Phillips, it was his first big league start. Allen saw action in 10 late-season games for the Phils in September 1963.) Johnson and Phillips combined to go 0-for-6, with a run scored for Phillips. The stellar Allen went 3-for-4 with an RBI. Mauch explained that he had reports informing him that both Johnson and Phillips had hit Milwaukee starting pitcher Wade

Blasingame well in the Pacific Coast League. Blasingame was quoted as saying that he had never faced Phillips in the lower leagues.

Rojas worked his way into the lineup the next evening as over 30,000 Friday night fans showed up expecting to root their wobbly team to a much-needed victory. Again, as a pinch-hitter in the eighth inning and staying in on defense, Rojas earned three total at-bats as the game went 12 innings before the Braves yanked out a 7–5 win. Chris Short took the ball for the Phillies, only three days since his loss to O'Toole and the Reds. Short pitched admirably, nicked for two earned runs (three total) in 7⅓ innings. He left trailing, 3–1, but Johnny Callison got him off the hook with a game-tying, two-run circuit clout in the Phils' half of the eighth. In the top of the 10th, with the score tied at 3–3, Joe Torre socked a two-run home run. (Torre went 11-for-19 in the four games with seven RBI.) The Phillies excitingly tied the score in their half-inning, thanks to a Dick Allen inside-the-park homer with Rojas, who had singled, on base. The visitors broke the deadlock two innings later on an RBI single and a throwing error by catcher Clay Dalrymple. The home team, which went an impotent 0-for-8 with runners in scoring position, was unable to respond. Pinch-hitter John Herrnstein grounded out with two runners on base to end the game. Not one to second-guess himself, Mauch openly wondered whether he should have walked Joe Torre in the first extra frame. "My choice on who to pitch to wasn't very good," he admitted, while qualifying it with the notion of a costly pitcher's mistake. "But then, managers in these situations don't think in terms of hanging curves."[25]

Remarkably, with the five consecutive losses and a like number of Reds' wins, the Phillies lead had now shrunk to 1½ games over an inspired Cincinnati club and 2½ over an also suddenly hot St. Louis squad. In fourth place, the San Francisco Giants were 3½ behind the tottering circuit leaders. It was clear to those closest to the Phillies that the team was now feeling the strain from their worst losing skid of the year (five games). "Mauch for the first time looked downhearted," wrote one insider. "His voice was low as he sat behind his desk. His answers were polite. In the locker room just across a tiny hallway, the players dressed silently and left."[26]

In the third game of the series, the Phillies could not hold a 4–3, ninth-inning lead and endured another stinging loss, with Rojas ejected for the first time in his career. In front of a paid Saturday crowd of 14,380 and another 12,000 young "knothole fans" in attendance, Art Mahaffey made his follow-up start to the 1–0 defeat by the Reds, which had begun the Phillies' fateful slide five days earlier. He went 7⅓ innings with three runs allowed. Working in his fourth straight game and on his 39th birthday, Bobby Shantz, who had pitched out of a jam not of his doing in the eighth inning, was tagged with the loss. Braves rookie Rico Carty tripled in three runs off Shantz (two earned) in the final inning to propel the visitors to a come-from-behind, 6–4 win.

Following Carty's crippling blow, which came with no one out, Ed Roebuck relieved and the side was retired, helped by controversial umpiring calls, leading to several expulsions. With one out and Carty on third, the Braves' Mike de la Hoz hit a sinking liner to left which Rojas appeared to catch at his shins on the dead run. But third base umpire Ed Vargo ruled the ball "trapped," allowing Carty to score after Rojas' throw home was too late. Rojas was "wild-eyed" over the trap call and had to be restrained by his manager and teammate Rubén Amaro—but not before he was ejected by Vargo. Second base umpire Shag Crawford was consulted by Vargo, and Vargo reversed his call. That sent Braves manager Bobby Bragan and de la Hoz into a tizzy and, as a result, both were given the heave-ho by Vargo. The same arbiter thumbed out Joe Torre after the Braves' catcher added some unkindly comments and gestures. When order was restored, Roebuck tossed to third base on an appeal play, and Carty was called out by home plate umpire Al Forman for leaving too soon, following Rojas' catch. Carty stormed out of the dugout to confront Forman, but managed to avoid what could have been the fifth ejection of the half-inning.

Saving his second game of the season, the great Warren Spahn, the eighth Braves pitcher of the contest, retired the side in order in the bottom of the ninth. Continuing to falter in the clutch, Mauch's gang went 1-for-7 with yardstick opportunities to plate additional runs. The loss, the Phillies' sixth in a row and ninth in 11 games, coupled with the Reds' seventh straight win the same day, left the Philadelphians clinging to a half-game lead with six to play.

On Sunday, September 27, 20,569 fans arrived at Connie Mack Stadium for the final home game of the schedule and for what one week earlier had shaped up to be an appreciative celebration day for a city and its pennant-clinching team, with an anticipatory look ahead to the opening of the World Series slated that year for the park of the National League champions. But instead, the fans present, mirroring all of the Phillies' faithful, must have been overwhelmed with feelings of anxiety, perplexity, and disbelief over the most inopportune nosedive of their stumbling club.

As the game commenced, from the upper deck of the left field stands hung two signs. One read "Scalp Those Braves." The other, twice as big, "HELP!" Both clubs brought their hitting shoes to the ballpark, but the Braves brought more of them and did more damage, cranking out 22 hits and handily defeating the home favorites, 14–8. Facing the same team for the second time in four days, Jim Bunning started and recorded only nine outs before he was pulled. He was charged with seven earned runs on 10 hits. As early as Friday, presumably after the Phillies' defeat that night, Bunning revealed to the press that he had approached his manager to volunteer for his short-rest starting assignment. (Bunning had pitched Thursday night, and Sunday's game was an afternoon affair, lessening the rest period further.) "I thought it was a game we had to win," Bunning said, "and I wanted to try and do it. I knew he [Mauch] was hurting for starters." Bunning, who had the only Phillies victory in the last 10 games, said he "felt fine" after the game and insisted that only one of the 10 hits against him was hit hard. "Plays we made before, we're not making," was all he could offer as to the reason for his team's plummet.[27]

"The world is crashing down on the Phillies like an avalanche cascading down Mt. Everest," wrote one local columnist, providing a view into the current temperament of the disintegrating team's leader and criticism over recent moves.

> It's terrible, but all Gene Mauch does is sit there like Mahatma Ghandi or someone, calmly. It's enough to make Billy Penn cry, and all Gene Mauch does is play the role of the calm, though beleaguered captain going down with his ship. The thing is, of course, that this calm bit is unlike Gene Mauch. It could be said that Gene Mauch precipitated the fall when he pitched Jim Bunning with two days of rest in Houston. It could be said that he played one hunch too many when he put Adolfo Phillips in center field for his big league debut instead of Cookie Rojas the other night.[28]

It was Phillips' first game as a starter. Mauch had been ejected six times in 1963; this season, he was booted off the bench once, for arguing balls and strikes on May 17.

Failing Mauch again was his bullpen. He brought in Dallas Green to relieve Bunning, trailing 5–3, after the starter gave up five straight hits to open the fourth inning. Green had not pitched for the Phillies since July 25, following his demotion to the minors, and had been recalled with the September roster expansions. The right-hander (and future successful manager of the Phils) permitted three runs to cross the plate (two inherited). He was tagged for four more runs in the following frame when Milwaukee broke the game open.

Lost among the 12 hits accumulated by the Phillies were three consecutive home runs hit by Johnny Callison, all over Connie Mack's imposing right field wall. Callison topped the 30-home run and 100-RBI marks with this game's slugging. Dick Allen, 12-for-24 in his last five games, collected three hits. Incidentally, it had been revealed that some Phillies' players had made pricey purchases against their anticipated World Series shares, while Callison, at the same time, adhering to the old adage of not counting chickens before they are hatched, had warned about the premature excess. Now the press could not avoid reminding everyone of Callison's caution with practically every daily mention of him. Rojas made an unsuccessful pinch-hitting appearance in the ninth inning.

Mauch remained optimistic, insisting that four victories in their remaining five games would assure them of the pennant.

The Phillies, who had briefly surrendered the top spot after the All-Star break, had been in first place every day since July 16. Now, on the morning of Monday, September 28, after a Sunday doubleheader sweep of the Mets by the blazing hot Reds (their eighth and ninth wins in a row), Mauch's reeling club (90–67) had dropped one full game below the summit. The team traveled to play a three-game series against the Cardinals in St. Louis, beginning that evening. Bob Gibson, a 17-game winner and a pitcher on the cusp of stardom, was their opponent on the mound. On the hill for the Phillies was Chris Short, making his fourth start in 11 days. The left-hander, in three prior starts against the Cardinals that season, was 3–0, all complete games with one shutout.

Performing in his second consecutive start on two days' rest, Short pitched less effectively than his previous outing against Milwaukee, going 5⅓ innings, allowing seven hits and three earned runs. The Cardinals tacked on two insurance runs against reliever Jack Baldschun, as Gibson, pitching into the ninth, permitted only one run in a victorious 5–1 outing. Outfielder Mike Shannon drove in three runs, and first baseman Bill White stroked three hits for the winners. The Phillies managed just five hits (0-for-7 with runners in scoring position). Johnny Callison knocked in the Phillies' lone run on a force out. Rojas was given the night off.

Following the win, the Cardinals nosed past the Phils into second place, one game behind the idle Reds. Mauch chased away reporters from the post-game clubhouse with a mild oath. After about 20 minutes (a waiting period that he had set and which had not been honored by the early arrivals), he opened the door to the press. He made clear he was having none of the "blame game." "No, I haven't chewed out the club," he said. "You can't. There's no way you can get on this club. They've given me so much of themselves all season. They—all of them—can look anybody in the eye when it's all over … win, lose or whatever."[29]

Many in the press corps were still waiting for Gene Mauch to explode, to get tossed out of a game, to do something to kickstart his inert squad. But during the bad interval, the manager unusually transformed into the polar opposite of his fiery self. One newsprint observation revealed an afflicted manager who had decided to keep things, for better or worse, bottled up: "In the heat of competition, especially after a tough loss, Mauch has been known to lose control of his tongue and temper. But this is a restrained Mauch, outwardly a model of tranquility and affability as he discusses his team's fading pennant chances. His tone is a positive tone despite the mental anguish and deep hurt inside."[30]

Others were more direct in disapproving of the manner in which the 38-year-old pilot went about things. This criticism of the embattled manager was reprinted from the *Los Angeles Herald-Examiner* of September 29:

> Gene Mauch drove the Philadelphia Phillies into the National League lead with tough, fiery leadership. He taunted his players when their skills failed. One time he sprayed a buffet of spare ribs and fried chicken to the four walls of the clubhouse. He stung his players as a jockey does a thoroughbred and eventually it led him to the front of the pack. Strangely, Mauch changed his tactics last week in the great Philadelphia disaster. He began to defend his players. He minimized their misdeeds during the blowing of leads in four of seven losses at home. If the championship is lost, it will be clear that the Phillies needed the buffet bombardment last week.[31]

Mauch deflected the criticism of which he was certainly aware and continued to project a stoic attitude: "We've won four in a row before. We can do it again. Sure we've lost eight in a row, but we haven't quit. You can't blame this defeat on pressure. We didn't beat ourselves. Gibson was simply too much for us. He pitched a strong game."[32]

The four remaining games on the schedule which Mauch had forecast to win became an impossibility when the snakebit team lost again—for the ninth time in a row—the next evening, 4–2. Dennis Bennett, the team's number three starter, got only four outs before being yanked by his desperate manager. Bennett allowed five hits and three runs. For a change, the Phillies received strong relief pitching from five bullpen men. In concert, their offense was lacking, however, as the beguiled team managed only one extra-base hit, a double by Rojas, among seven total safeties. Displaying the persistent futility that had marred the losing streak, the team failed miserably with chances to score (1-for-9 with runners in scoring position, Triandos' two-run single). The run-producer, Callison, was under the weather and did not start, though he pinch-hit with success in the seventh inning and stayed in the game.

Becoming a 20-game winner for the first time, the Cardinals' Ray Sadeki hurled into the seventh inning before tiring. Appearing in his fifth straight game, knuckleballing reliever Barney Schultz got Dick Allen to pop up with two runners on base to end the seventh inning and finished the game from there with no further trouble. The Cardinals benefited from timely hits from four players, who each drove in a run, among their 10 hits.

The Reds, meanwhile, had their nine-game winning streak stopped by Pittsburgh. The Cardinals' win, their seventh in a row and eighth in nine games, placed them in a dead heat with Cincinnati at the top of the league, both clubs with 91–67 records. The 90–69 Phillies were 1½ games behind with three to play. Mauch utilized 22 players in the game in an apparent all-out effort to stop the fall into oblivion. St. Louis manager Johnny Keane used 10.

The visitors' locker room at Busch Stadium was directly below the home club's. Mauch's dejected crew had to endure hearing exuberant goings on above them as the Cardinals celebrated their rise to first place. The Redbirds had been practically in lock step in wins with Cincinnati in making up the daunting ground to catch and pass the Phillies over the past nine days. In the silent clubhouse, a defiant Mauch said, "Don't bury us yet. We're not dead yet."[33]

Following the second crushing loss to the Cardinals on September 29, Phillies management announced that they would delay mailing out more World Series tickets sold which they had been authorized to print by the National League the prior week.

The next evening, the last day of September, Phillies management also received a painful reminder of a talent misevaluation from four years ago. The team had released veteran pitcher Curt Simmons, a franchise-grown product, in May of 1960. Three days after he was cut, Simmons was signed by St. Louis. A left-hander, he had several productive seasons with the Cardinals and was now enjoying his winningest campaign at age 35.

Simmons received the start in the series finale and beat the Phillies, 8–5, to complete the sweep and drive another nail in the Phillies' coffin. It was the pitcher's 18th win of the season, and it raised his record to 16–2 against his former team since his release (4–0 this season). The southpaw did not permit a hit for the first six innings. Ahead 8–0, he was touched for a two-run homer by Alex Johnson in the seventh and an RBI triple by Rojas in the eighth, with two more runs (one earned) charged to his ledger after his removal in the ninth.

The losing pitcher for the Phillies was starter Jim Bunning, starting another game on short rest—his fifth start in 15 days. As with his other outings on two days' rest, he was ineffective. Removed with one out in the fourth inning, the Kentuckian was knocked around for eight hits and six runs, all but one earned. He yielded a two-run homer to Cardinals catcher Tim McCarver. Three Phillies errors behind him did not help matters. Bunning refused to acknowledge the obvious—that he was not the same pitcher without an extra day away from the mound. "I don't care what people think about the two days," he said. "I had good stuff. I made one mistake to McCarver. Other than that, I don't feel I have to apologize to anyone. We ought to kick ourselves for being lousy. It's all our own fault. All of our own fault."[34]

The losing streak had now matched or surpassed historic National League collapses and entered into comparisons of nightmarish, cinematic fantasy. "Think of it," explained one columnist. "Future generations will be told this incredible horror story September after September, that the Phillies of Philadelphia led the league by six and a half games with two weeks to play and couldn't win another game. Children will shriek, adults will shiver, managers will faint. The legend will take its place alongside such classics as the Dodgers of '51 and Frankenstein and the Wolfman."[35]

As if to keep out the demons, Mauch kept the clubhouse closed for 30 minutes after the last pitch.

Cincinnati, meanwhile, suffered their second straight shutout defeat to the Pirates, this one a 16-inning, 1–0 marathon, allowing the 92–67 Cardinals, now winners of eight straight, to take possession of first place by a full game. Both squads had three games remaining, while the Phils, 2½ back and on the brink of elimination, had only two to play.

"You keep pinching yourself hoping you will wake up," confided Rubén Amaro, at the nadir of the Phillies' September woes. "You hope you will wake up and it will be like it was. The last week at home was terrible. I was so much on edge that even my little boy called me Ruben, like my wife does when she is mad at me."[36]

The Gene Mauch–led Phillies had lost 23 straight games over a three-week-plus period in the summer of 1961. They were a bad baseball team, losing 107 games in a 154-game season. For its manager, franchise, civic leaders, and faithful fans, that terrible losing streak had to pale in comparison to the excruciatingly ill-timed, calamity that had now occurred before everyone's disbelieving eyes despite a vastly improved club.

The Phillies had played 31 games (12–19) in the 30 days of September without respite. They had lost a staggering eight games in the standings in 10 days. On Thursday, October 1, the downtrodden team had their first day off since the last day of August. With their remaining two games scheduled against the Reds, the Phillies had flown into the Queen City and were in town as the Reds salvaged the final game of their series versus the Pirates with a 5–4 victory. The Cardinals, at home preparing for a weekend-closing series versus the lowly New York Mets, were also idle.

The National League announced the coin-toss winners for where a best-of-three series would open in the event of a tie between two or more clubs. General managers of the three teams in contention were present in NL President Warren Giles' office for the doings. The only path to the post-season for the Phillies would be a three-way tie, if the Cardinals lost all three of their games to the Mets, or a four-way tie if the Mets swept and the Giants (-3) took their three remaining games against the Cubs in San Francisco. Lots were drawn to establish the possible matchups between the four clubs in a round-robin playoff structure. For the Phillies, everything was contingent on winning their two final games versus Cincinnati.

On Friday, October 2, at Crosley Field, it appeared that the Phillies' longshot-scenario would be closed out. The woe-begotten team trailed 3–0 after seven innings. Their infield defense had betrayed Chris Short, pitching on normal rest for the first time in two weeks. Three errors in the sixth frame (one each by Taylor, Allen, and Wine) allowed the Reds to score two unearned runs. Short was removed in the seventh after plunking Reds shortstop Leo Cárdenas, which caused both benches to empty. Cárdenas menaced Short with his bat before being detoured by catcher Clay Dalrymple.

Perhaps the incident helped resurrect the Phillies, as the seemingly left-for-dead team tallied four runs in the eighth inning and carried through to a 4–3 win. Dick Allen's two-run triple tied the score, and Alex Johnson's single put the Phillies up for good. Johnson, patrolling left field, had made the defensive play of the game earlier. In the fourth, with two men on base, Johnson raced back, angling to his left, to spectacularly flag down a long drive by the home team's Deron Johnson. The runners, on first and second, had been off with the pitch, and both were doubled off their respective bases on relay throws for a triple play! Johnson threw to cutoff man Bobby Wine to Tony Taylor at second to double off Vada Pinson, and the throw to first baseman Vic Power nabbed a frantic Frank Robinson. It was the third triple play pulled off by the Phillies that year, all on the road (May 17 versus Houston and August 15 against New York). In spite of the terrific catch, Mauch removed Johnson (and his bat) in the bottom of the eighth. The manager shifted Rojas, who was playing center field and had scored one of the rallying runs, to left and placed Tony González in Rojas' vacated spot. Jack Baldschun pitched a perfect eighth and ninth for his 21st save. Ed Roebuck was the winner in relief of Short.

In St. Louis, the same evening, the Mets' Al Jackson outdueled Bob Gibson with a stunning 1–0 victory, maintaining the Phillies' faint heartbeat of hope for the flag. Mauch remained realistic: "About the only satisfaction we have tonight is getting this losing thing over with, this losing business. If the pencil doesn't get us, we got a chance."[37] San Francisco also won, thrashing the Chicago Cubs, 9–0. In fourth place, they moved two games in back of St. Louis with two games remaining.

In a new town with new reporters, Mauch was asked whether he had any regrets about pitching Bunning and Short on short rest during the stretch drive. His answer addressed only one of the men and completely diverted the question from what Bunning did on two days' rest to how he responded on normal rest afterward. "The first time I pitched Bunning with two days' rest was at Houston," Mauch replied. "He came back three days later and shut out Los Angeles for eight innings and won the game. It didn't seem to hurt him then."[38] (It was actually four days later, on normal rest.)

While Mauch justifiably engendered a long line of critics, not everyone was willing to pile on. "It's ridiculous to criticize manager Mauch for the smash-up even if he pulled a rock or two, and we aren't saying he did," wrote one defender. "On the contrary, we feel that it is a tribute to his managing genius that he kept the Phillies up there as long as he did, in view of the fact that his pitchers and his makeshift lineup did not mature before the show came down."[39]

Another Mauch advocate blamed the length of the season: "For manager Gene Mauch, who did a tremendous job of managing, the season simply lasted too long. Over the old 154-game schedule they would have been champs."[40]

A quirk in the schedule had the Phillies and Reds not playing on Saturday, October 3. Proving momentum is only as good as your next day's starting pitcher, the St. Louis Cardinals again lost to the last-place Mets, 15–5, that day. After winning eight in a row, the Cardinals, who could have clinched the pennant with a win yesterday or today, were battered out of their own ballpark. The Mets jumped on 20-game winner Ray Sadeki and five other pitchers for 17 hits, including five home runs. Gaining half a game in the standings, the 92–69 Reds moved into a first-place tie with St. Louis, and the Phillies, 91–70, inched to within one game of both. The Cubs defeated the Giants, eliminating the northern California club from pennant contention.

In the junior circuit, the New York Yankees, in their own battle for league supremacy, clinched their 29th circuit flag with an 8–3 victory over the Cleveland Indians at Yankee Stadium. It was their record-tying fifth consecutive pennant and first under rookie manager Yogi Berra.

October 4 dawned with two teams in position to win the National League pennant, and a third (the Phillies) whose best hope was for a tie with the other two (setting up the first three-way playoff for the pennant in history). Expectedly, one of the largest crowds of the season, 28,535, crammed Crosley Field for the Sunday afternoon finale. The Phillies had Jim Bunning, who had lost his last three decisions, hurling on normal rest.

Reds manager Dick Sisler selected John Tsitouris to oppose Bunning. Sisler, who had taken over for Fred Hutchinson following the sobering cancer diagnosis that led to the longtime skipper stepping down from the Cincinnati club in mid–August, may have been influenced by his pitcher's previous outing versus the Phils in reaching his decision. Mostly a starter with an ERA in the mid-threes, Tsitouris had shut out the Phillies, 1–0, on six hits on September 21—the game that cast Mauch's troupe off on their shocking 10-game losing skid. The Reds' field leader opted to use the right-handed Tsitouris (9–12) over 15-game winner Jim Maloney. Four days earlier, Maloney had hurled 11 innings of shutout baseball against the Pittsburgh Pirates, striking out 13, in the Reds' 16-inning, devastating home loss.

As it turned out, it would not have mattered, unless Maloney had been able to duplicate his last outing, as Bunning blanked Sisler's club, allowing only six singles. Resoundingly backing Bunning, who fanned five and walked one in picking up his 19th win, were 12 Phillies' hits and 10 runs. Tsitouris, who was 2–1 against Philadelphia on the year, both complete game victories, did not last the third inning. Dick Allen socked two homers (#28, 29) and drove in four runs. Tony González scored twice and knocked in as many. Rojas entered the game as a defensive substitute for left fielder Wes Covington in the seventh inning. He batted once but was not involved in the one-sided, run-scoring activities.

The worst team in baseball had beaten the hottest team in baseball for two consecutive days in St. Louis. That unrealistic trend came to a screeching halt not long after the completion of the Phillies-Reds game. Although the scrappy Mets held a 3–2 lead after 4½ innings, the Cardinals erupted for nine runs in their next four turns at the plate and coasted to an 11–5, pennant-clinching victory. Bob Gibson, who suffered the 1–0 defeat two days earlier in the series opener, was called on to relieve starter Curt Simmons in the fifth inning. Gibson, who would gain prominence in the upcoming World Series against the New York Yankees, guided the Redbirds through to victory with four innings of bulwark hurling, permitting two runs while walking five. Barney Schultz recorded the last two outs.

"No manager ever took a 10–0 victory harder," sportswriter Frank Dolson summed up perfectly. "I wish I had done as well as the players," said Mauch. "They did a great job. That's all I have to say." Dolson also wrote, "Asked later if he meant to imply he had done some things wrong, Mauch snapped, 'I'm not implying nothing.'"[41]

What could be categorized as collateral losses from the Phillies' collapse were made public as part of another report: "Extra box seats were being built. World Series tickets were ready to mail, the press box was enlarged, programs were printed at a cost of at least $25,000 and hotels were sold out. Restaurant, night spots, novelty concerns were set for a booming business. Estimates range as high as $3.5 million loss for the city's business people."[42] As a small consolation, the Phillies' turnstile count of 1,425,891 (fourth-highest in the league) established a record-breaking home attendance mark.

Mauch additionally lamented, "If we had just done as well against the Cardinals as the Mets, we'd be in high cotton today."[43] Though another apparent misdirected point on his part, it does provide a valid view of how the schedule conspired against Mauch's team. The Phillies had to play every day of September (31 games), including playing in Philadelphia the night after completing a West Coast swing, flying cross-country from Los Angeles. Six decades ago, that kind of trip had to be much more trying—and tiring—than a similar one today. With modern-day scheduling, all big league East Coast teams reserve an off-day following such trips. In what would have been a perfect day to "recharge their batteries," the Phillies were forced to take the field. They were shut out, 1–0, in what has now become known as the "Chico Ruíz game."

The sole scheduled off day in September for the Phillies was used as a makeup date from an earlier rainout. "On an August night on which Sandy Koufax was supposed to pitch for the Dodgers in Philadelphia," wrote Steve Wulf a quarter-century later, "the Phils' front office called the game on the merest hint of rain. The game was rescheduled for Sept. 8, and on that night [Frank] Thomas broke his thumb. 'I don't get hurt, we win it all,' Thomas would say 25 years after the injury."[44] (The night was August 3 and Philadelphia newspapers do not make mention of a needlessly rained out encounter. One would think that a draw like Koufax is not easily dismissed by any opposition administrative hierarchy.)

But travel burdens aside, the strength of comparative schedules down the stretch did no favors for the Phillies, while undeniably assisting their chief competitors. One later analysis bore this out: "The Reds and Cardinals were playing teams (including the Phillies) with a combined winning percentage of .483 [starting] on the morning of September 21 [Chico Ruíz game], while the Phillies were going against teams (Reds, Braves, Cardinals) with a combined winning percentage of .544—a significant difference."[45]

The Cardinals did win 28 out their last 39 games ... but it would not have made a difference had the Phillies not disintegrated.

Tony Taylor had been with the Phillies through tough times, through the 23-game losing skid in 1961. He reaffirmed in a 2004 anniversary interview that the 1964 implosion had been impossible to shake. "It's still here," he conceded. "We worked so hard, and to see it break so easy and the way it happened, it still hurts and I still cannot believe it.... Wherever you go, people remind you." Yet in spite of the outcome, he would not have traded the experience. "I'm proud to be part of that team. It was a great team, a team that played to win. I can say now that in baseball, anything can happen."[46]

Ten years later, as part of a series of Philadelphia newspaper articles on that season's 50th anniversary, Cookie Rojas clung to a broader perspective on his team and their misfortune.

> Of course, I remember 1964, but it comes to a point where you have to forget about the bad times and start talking about the good times. It seems like it goes only in one direction. It was very disappointing, no question about it, 1964, for all of us that were involved. There's nothing you can do about it. You have to live with it, and we lived with it and have gone our different directions now.... You can't keep thinking about '64; otherwise, you'll be a miserable guy. It's gone. It's something that happened. It happened. It was very unfortunate, especially disappointing to the fans in Philadelphia, who are the best, I think, in the country, because they know the game well and they demand 100 percent effort. I think we gave them that, and they realized that, and that's why at the end when we came over to Philadelphia after the last game of the season, there was about 2,000 people in the airport. I think that was in appreciation of what kind of year we had.[47] [Newspaper articles of the day put the number even higher.]

Inevitably, it all fell on Gene Mauch. Sixty years of generational scrutiny has not lightened the load, even though he received the unequivocal backing of his general manager from the outset. "A manager must end it as fast as he can and that's the way Mauch handled it when he started Jim Bunning at Houston on September 16 with only two days' rest," stated John Quinn after the final game. "Gene went with his best. He had to. I can't fault him."[48]

Mauch was never able to satisfactorily justify the move. He publicly stated that Bunning on two days' rest against Houston was better than on full rest versus Drysdale and the Dodgers, which was the matchup the Phillies faced the following day (September 17). Mauch sold his best pitcher short with his inability to face facts.

Preparing for the stretch run, a proactive Quinn tried to keep his team stocked. He traded for Frank Thomas during the first week of August to address the Phillies' inherent weakness at first base. Thomas welcomely produced 33 RBI in 36 starts and a .294 average in 39 games. Another August pickup by Quinn was Bobby Shantz, to address a left-handed need in the pen. When Thomas broke his thumb [in the makeup game versus the Dodgers] a little more than a month after being acquired from the Mets, Quinn obtained Vic Power to help fill the void.

A writer from the time said that he had witnessed Mauch manage approximately 800 major league games, had never seen a better manipulator of personnel during a contest, and never saw a better job of managing than Mauch did for 145 games that season. But, he qualified, "I never saw him manage as badly as he did the next 15.... It is difficult to believe the Phillies could have fallen so far so fast had Mauch employed his pitchers differently, especially in the last three weeks of the season. In fairness, it must be said that without Mauch and his managerial talent, the Phillies might never have been a contender."[49]

With respect to his singular, in-game deployment of personnel, this contemplative view of Mauch's alternating use of key infielders, at times, required a stretch of one's imagination: "When it was over, manager Gene Mauch had wrung eight homers and 68 RBI out of his shortstop(s), shuffling Amaro and Wine out of the lineup based on biorhythms only he detected, based on the opposing pitcher, the day of the week, the phases of the moon."[50]

Simply put, there was no rhyme or reason to some of the arbitrariness of Mauch's moves, and he was reluctant to give explanations. Yet, as put by another supporter, "all season long the Phillies were a team short on solid depth responding spiritedly to the artful gerrymandering of lineups by Gene Mauch."[51]

According to Wine, Mauch was one of the first managers to employ double switches: "I was playing shortstop," he recalled years later, "and Gene came out to take out the pitcher. He told me I was out of the game, too. I said, 'Why me? I didn't give up the home run.' It was the first time I was involved in a double switch."[52]

The Phillies were 28–18 in one-run ballgames, an achievement the manager can usually hang his hat on. The 92 wins Mauch guided the team to set a club record. The club posted identical 46–35 records home and away.

Tempering the harsh scrutiny on the manager, Mauch had to deal with injuries to rotation men. Dennis Bennett, who was the Phillies' Opening Day pitcher and won eight of his first 12 decisions, developed a sore shoulder as the season progressed. He went 1–8 after the promising beginning. Bennett posted three resurgent starts in September, winning all of them, including a 1–0 victory over Juan Marichal and the Giants on September 11 in San Francisco. Following the third win, his 12th, his arm weakened, and he was beaten twice during the infamous losing streak.

With the fourth man in the rotation, Art Mahaffey, Mauch unwarrantedly appeared to have lost confidence in him during a crucial period. Mahaffey's regular turn was skipped over to place a not fully rested Bunning on the starter's hill on September 16 versus Houston. With Bunning making another start four days later, Mahaffey, with 12 wins on his pitching ledger, stood idle for eight days before taking the mound again in the Chico Ruíz game. Although healthy, Mahaffey made only one more start, September 26, when the Phillies' bullpen lost a one-run, ninth-inning lead to Milwaukee, a game he was in line to win.

Mauch, through no fault of his own, lost an alternate option in starter Ray Culp. A sophomore pitcher and winner of 14 games as a rookie, including an impressive five shutouts, Culp had been part of Mauch's starting rotation to commence the season. Unable to reproduce his excellent rookie campaign due to elbow problems, his last victory came on July 22. An eight-game winner, Culp threw fewer than 10 innings following his final start on August 15, and none after September 12. Bunning and Short started 19 of the Phillies' final 33 games.

No writer then speculated that Mauch, in pitching Bunning out of turn on September 16, was trying to set up the pitcher to open the first game of the World Series without an extended "down time." As the rotation was playing out with Bunning going every fourth day, from his regular start on September 13, Bunning's last start of the season would have come September 29, eight days before Game One of the Fall Classic. The Phillies had three games to play after the 29th with scheduled off-days in between the final two, so Bunning could not have been worked in without upsetting his normal rest schedule of three days. Though the tight-lipped Mauch probably never let on, this conclusion was drawn by historian Bryan Soderholm-Difatte, in a Society for American Baseball Research Journal article in 2010. Pitching Bunning every fourth day, following his September 16 short-rest, poor outing, would have put Bunning's last start on October 2, in Cincinnati in game 161, leaving four days of rest for his ace before the World Series opening on October 7. Mauch did not have the luxury of exploring a five-man rotation over the final two and a half weeks. "With Culp out, Bennett hurting, and no depth in his rotation" wrote Soderholm-Difatte, "[Mauch] appears to have decided that keeping to the rhythm of three days' rest between starts was preferable and took the gamble of starting Bunning—presumably just this once—on short rest against the woeful Houston Colts, in order to set him up to have proper rest before his final regular-season start on October 2."[53]

No manager ever had to go through what Gene Mauch did over those final 14 tortuous days of the 1964 season. Everything that could have gone wrong did. Nothing broke his or his ill-fated team's way during the 10-game death spiral. And he remained defiant to the end. Sitting in the front row on the Phillies' flight home from Cincinnati, Mauch told Sandy Grady of the *Philadelphia Bulletin*: "To hell with 'em. I'm not going to defend myself to anybody. Inside I know I did everything I could do to win."[54] He refused to accept the misuse of Bunning, deviating from the issue as he had constantly done as the season wound down. "All I know is that between the 275th and 284th innings Bunning pitched for us he threw shutouts. Is that an overworked pitcher?" he posed.[55] The reference was to Bunning's marvelous last start of the campaign. But it avoided distinguishing between "misused" and "overworked." Bunning obviously had quite a bit left in his tank, but clearly only when his engine was permitted to cool sufficiently in between revving up. Bunning also would not admit to a weakness on his part, or in Mauch's strategic (mis)use of his abilities.

John Quinn and Gene Mauch were the first to disembark the plane on the team's return home from Cincinnati. On a Sunday night, several thousand people welcomed the Phillies home at International Airport in Philadelphia. Some of the placards held high read: "Welcome Home Phillies. We love You Anyway—Always Our Champs. Skin 'Em Alive in '65. Wait Till '65."[56]

A photo in the *Philadelphia Inquirer* showed Mauch twisting his fingers through chain-link fencing in a handshake gesture with greeters. A raised poster visible in the photo's background proclaimed "Welcome Phillies You Played Like the Champs You'll Be." Though reaching the post-season was still a dozen years away for the franchise, the next day (October 5), it was announced that Mauch was given a new two-year contract, in effect extending the contract Mauch had in place that was set to expire at the end of 1965. After a meeting with Phillies owner Bob Carpenter and GM Quinn, Mauch was awarded a new two-year deal running through the end of 1966. Terms were not divulged, but a raise from his $40,000 salary was understood.

While the ultimate prize agonizingly escaped Mauch, for the Phillies and their fans, individual plaudits should not remain unrecognized.

Leading off with our protagonist, Cookie Rojas was penciled into the starting lineup by his manager 80 times during the year. Rojas appeared in 29 other contests as a pinch-hitter, pinch-runner, or defensive substitute. He finished with a .291 average in 340 at-bats. He roamed every outfield position over 509 innings, accumulating 110 putouts; he made only four errors, all as a center fielder.

Because of his versatility, Rojas continued to receive positive press, including from one writer at the end of August who could not have imagined how prescient his opening words would be: "A great many things will be remembered about the 1964 Phillies after they have taken their place in Philadelphian lore—and what Cookie Rojas, the wonder second baseman did this year will certainly not be the faintest memory."[57]

With a .971 fielding percentage (10 errors), Rubén Amaro won the NL's Gold Glove Award at shortstop, though he only played 79 games at the position, and Bobby Wine played more games (108) than he at the spot. (Wine won the GG at short in 1963.) Players voted for the award.

Dick Allen, who wore horn-rimmed glasses like Rojas, received 18 out of 20 first-place votes in Rookie of the Year Award balloting, as he led the league in runs with 125 and posted a fearsome .939 OPS. On the last day of the season, the third baseman became the 17th rookie to rack up 200 hits in a season. (Earlier, Tony Oliva, in the AL, had reached the total as the 16th first-year-man to do so.) Allen led the Phillies with an imposing 8.8 WAR accumulation. Ken Boyer of the pennant-winning Cardinals was named NL MVP. Boyer and Johnny Callison (second in the voting) each accrued a WAR of 6.1. Willie Mays, with a monstrous 11.0 WAR and .990 OPS, finished sixth. Allen placed seventh in the writers' tabulations. (OPS, on-base plus slugging, is a 21st-century performance-measuring tool that combines on-base plus slugging percentages. Front office executives and other baseball talent evaluators have come to view OPS as a truer reflection of a player's offensive prowess. An on-base of .350 and a slugging mark of .450 are considered good; therefore, an OPS of .800 describes a productive hitter.)

Undeniably, it was an unforgettable season. But not all of it should be encapsulated under the heading of "Phillies Phold," one the disparaging labels the collapse has received. "The Phillies held first place for 150 days," reminded one later review. "The most integrated and likeable team in many years had created 'Phillies mania.' There was a newly awakened sense of interest in baseball in the old Quaker City caused by this team that resulted in more blacks, whites, and Hispanics in the stands, despite summer racial rioting just around the corner from the stadium in North Philadelphia."[58] The Phillies fielded at least four minority first stringers: Covington, LF, González, CF, Allen, 3B, Taylor, 2B. Plus Rojas and Amaro were first off the bench, and African American rookie John Briggs, and two September additions, Vic Power from Puerto Rico and Panamanian Adolfo Phillips, were part of the team.

In that diversity aspect, it should be mentioned that Candida Rojas deserved a great deal of credit for her unheralded approach to spousal support.

> What I remember most about Philadelphia is that when we got there the players' wives sat in different groups at the stadium—Black and Hispanic and White wives. I went to the ticket manager, or the one who handled the players' wives' tickets, and told him to mix up the seating with the tickets. He did and we stopped being a segregated group amongst ourselves. Mary Bunning, Jim's wife, supported me. Everyone except for one wife, who shall remain nameless, was behind the idea. I said to myself if we [wives] don't get along the players might not either. If we get along, the players will too. I was raised with Blacks and Whites sharing communal settings.
>
> It was the same thing when we got to Kansas City. I brought change in that respect with the wives. I really believe it's the reason Cookie had such good relationships on the team, that last to this day.

A season-ending editorial headline in the *Philadelphia Inquirer* attempted to mitigate its sports fans' anguish by glibly asking, "How about those Eagles?"

Four

Major League All-Star

Cookie Rojas luckily did not have all winter to idly contemplate "what might have been?" He returned to Puerto Rico and the Arecibo Wolves to begin a new winter campaign on October 22—exactly one week after the final World Series pitch was hurled by Phillies adversary Bob Gibson. Rojas took with him or was forwarded a full team member share of $1,165.63 as part of the Fall Classic's revenue pool distributed to the first division clubs of both leagues. (Full World Series shares of $8,622.19 and $5,309.29 were given to the winning and losing participants, the St. Louis Cardinals and New York Yankees, respectively.) The return marked Rojas' fourth straight winter playing for Arecibo.

Also joining the Wolves that off-season was fellow Cuban Mike Cuéllar, a left-hander who had completed his full rookie season with the St. Louis Cardinals. Former Cuban Sugar Kings manager Tony Castaño was hired to help lift the young franchise out of the cellar the team had landed in the previous winter. At the end of the 70-game schedule, the Wolves exceptionally improved from last year and finished in second place with a record of 38–32 in the six-club league.

Cuéllar and Detroit Tigers rookie Denny McLain shared top laurels on the mound. Each posted a 12–4 record. McLain, hurling for the Mayagüez Indians, led the league in strikeouts with 126. The 20-year-old right-hander missed a chance for a league-leading 13th victory in his final start, January 17, dropping a tough, 2–1 decision to Castaño's team. Two solo home runs, one by Rojas and the other by Félix Torres, negated an otherwise fine effort by the future 30-game winner. George Culver, a Cleveland Indians prospect, pitched a two-hitter.

With 7⅓ fewer innings pitched than McLain (127 to 134⅓) and a negligibly superior ERA, 2.06 to McLain's 2.08, Cuéllar was bestowed dual prestigious honors with the Most Valuable Player and Outstanding Pitcher Awards of the Puerto Rican Winter League. Pennant-capturing manager Preston Gómez of the Santurce Crabbers edged out Tony Castaño in the Manager of the Year voting.

In the first round of the playoffs, Mayagüez—which had concluded the campaign in third place, two games behind Arecibo and 5½ games in the rear of Santurce—defeated the upstart Wolves, four games to three, with McLain winning the decisive game in the Wolves' home park. The score was 5–3, with all of the visitors' runs unearned, the end result of a dropped fly ball with the bases loaded by Wolves flychaser Román Mejías. McLain, who had won game five, in relief, two days earlier, notched his second victory of the playoff round.

Wolves losing pitcher George Culver would not soon forget the fateful encounter, in which Mayagüez culminated a three-games-to-one deficit comeback and aggravated the Arecibo faithful to no end. "After the game, our fans were throwing rocks and bricks at their bus," said Culver, who had fared well against the Tigers' right-hander in a previous clash, tossing a one-hit, 4–0 victory. "After beating McLain earlier in the series, I remember fans coming to the plaza in Arecibo—they were celebrating, and it was a great feeling."[1]

Another worthy anecdote, by extension, also reflected winter league *fanáticos'* displays of negative and positive "passion." According to Bob Swift, Mayagüez manager, delirious Indians followers met the damaged team bus outside of the city limits and initiated a welcoming parade of cars two miles in length. As the winner of the deciding game, McLain was hoisted on people's shoulders and carried to the town square, where he abruptly had his pocket picked in the excitement. The next day, McLain's wallet was found but without the $30 he had in it. When the town folk found out about the incident, they began a collection and raised $110 (no small amount) to give to McLain.

The Indians could not keep their momentum going as they were defeated by Santurce in the championship series that followed, four games to two. Crabbers ace and MLB veteran Juan Pizarro hurled victories in games two and six to lead the way. A nine-game winner for Santurce, Pizarro won four games in the two playoff rounds.

Rojas and family left Puerto Rico to return to their home in Miami, where he soon departed for the Phillies' spring training facilities in Clearwater. There, he joined his Phillies' teammates, the majority holdovers from last season.

We can imagine Gene Mauch imperiously buckling his belt strap and hitching up his stirrups as he faced the familiar sights and sounds of spring training on the first day, less than five months after the Phillies' debacle for the ages. He arrived February 23, one day ahead of the reporting date for pitchers and catchers. Mauch would not discuss the most recent season. He warned reporters that his response would be "next question" to any inquiries on the ruinous end of last fall.

"We're going to get ourselves in the best shape possible and go after 'em again," Mauch said he told his players in the private orientation meeting when the full squad arrived. "With Stuart and young Alex Johnson in there maybe we'll even things up against lefties," he added, referring to off-season addition Dick Stuart and the Phillies' under-.500 showing (32–34) against southpaw pitchers the prior year.[2] Stuart, who was acquired from the Boston Red Sox in a straight-up trade for pitcher Dennis Bennett, was a notoriously bad fielder who Mauch predicted would club 40 home runs. The first baseman fell short of Mauch's projection by 12, but his long ball totals and 95 RBI were a definite upgrade to a stark lineup weakness. The manager also forecast that his team would win more games than last year. Apart from Stuart, pitcher Bo Belinsky was the only other notable addition to the team.

Mauch retained most of his coaching staff. The exception was Al Widmar, the Phillies' pitching coach since 1962. The recently retired Cal McLish was named his replacement in December 1964, with Widmar reassigned to groom minor league pitching prospects within the organization. Peanuts Lowrey returned as first base coach, George Myatt reassumed third base box duties, and Bob Oldis continued as bullpen coach.

To get the club ready for the exhibition schedule, the Phillies held an intrasquad game on Sunday, March 7. The Tony Taylors defeated the Cookie Rojases, 5–4, in 10 innings. It is presumed that both men managed their respective clubs. Rookie John Briggs socked a three-run home run against Rick Wise and doubled home a fourth run to power Taylor's club over the Rojas nine. Rojas was singled out for making two exceptional plays at second base. It was an interesting pairing of opposing managers as through much of the off-season, there was speculation that Rojas would displace Taylor at second base.

Mauch confirmed that the keystone position was up for grabs early in camp. He said, "Cookie Rojas will vie with Tony Taylor at second and if he beats out Taylor, everybody will know he is a good player—if they don't already."[3]

But in the days leading to Opening Day, Bobby Wine was hospitalized with a bad back, and Rubén Amaro developed a pinched nerve in his back. Rojas was viewed as the infield savior, although sounding more and more like a reluctant one. "Shortstop is the hardest job in the infield," he said. "You are in almost every play. It needs a real good arm. I have a good arm, but I am used to throwing three-quarter sidearm from second base, and my throws sink. So I have to cheat on hitters. I can't play back on hitters like Wine and Amaro." Rojas also mentioned the burdening mental aspect associated with his versatility. "Sometimes I would start a game in center field and finish it at shortstop or second base, a completely new situation. You have a lot more on your mind when you have to play more than one position."[4]

Following a three-hit game by Rojas in Miami versus the Baltimore Orioles on April 4, Mauch proclaimed, "If the season opened tomorrow or the day after tomorrow, Cookie would be the shortstop. He's playing as if he wants to be the shortstop. I think he can handle it."[5]

However, a week later on the eve of Opening Day, Mauch threw cold water on the notion, announcing that a recovered Rubén Amaro would be the shortstop and that Tony Taylor would not be pushed aside at second.

Expecting to be a starter somewhere, Rojas was stung by the news. "Sure, I'm unhappy, and it goes deeper than that," he told the press. "I'm bitter about it, very much so. After the spring I had, I think I deserve to be in the lineup some place. I don't care where."[6]

Mauch explained that he felt Rojas' ability to play multiple positions was more valuable to the team than as a regular, designated position player. Mauch added that his plans were for Amaro and Wine to play short and to platoon Rojas and the left-handed-swinging Tony González in center field.

Those intentions further soured some of the press box pun fanciers, as one, in a near lament, wrote: "It was observed the other day that we were set to root for Bobby Wine and Cookie Rojas to start at shortstop and second base for the Phillies, respectively, just so we could write about 'The Plays of Wine and Rojas' without music."[7] The play on words was spun from the 1962 movie *The Days of Wine and Roses*, which won the Oscar for its title song.

In the first big program of the season, Mauch's team clashed with the renamed Houston Astros in their new "space-age" stadium. On Monday, April 12, three days after Houston and the New York Yankees had inaugurated the enclosed, air-conditioned stadium in an exhibition game, the Phillies and Astros took the grass field of the often-dubbed "Eighth Wonder of the World."

Even though it was a new season, it was apparent that it would be some time before out-of-town writers let the Phillies forget what had happened six months earlier. "It seemed only right that the Phils should open the league season in the spectacular Harris County Domed Stadium," penned one needling journalist. "The Philadelphia Phillies, remember, are essentially the same baseball team which took off like Gemini II last summer only to lose nine of its final 10 games and crash in despair."⁸ (The Phillies lost 10 in a row before winning their final two games.)

Twenty-two of the 24 NASA astronauts were present and threw out first balls to a like number of Astros. Barely settled in, the astronauts witnessed the game's leadoff batter, Tony Taylor, single to left field for the stadium's first hit for posterity. Taylor was left stranded, to the delight of the 42,652 mostly Astros fans.

In the exhibition inaugural, Mickey Mantle had belted the first home run in the indoor baseball stadium's history. But it wasn't enough as the Astros came out on top, 2–1. The first official home run came two innings after Taylor's single, rocketed over the center field wall, more than 400 feet from home plate, off the oversized bat of Dick Allen. The brawny Allen was known for regularly swinging weighty Louisville Sluggers of up to 42 ounces. (By comparison, Bryce Harper now uses a 31-ounce bat.) Shortstop Rubén Amaro, who had singled, crossed the plate ahead of Allen. It was all the scoring in the game. Chris Short dominated Astros batters, permitting only three singles and a double (to second sacker Joe Morgan) in tossing a shutout. The southpaw walked three and struck out 11. Allen, Taylor and Tony González each collected two hits among the Phillies' 10 for the game. Stuart went 1-for-3. Rojas watched the activities from the bench.

After a travel day, the Phillies opened their home campaign versus the San Francisco Giants on April 14 and lost, 5–2. Willie Mays homered off Jim Bunning, and Gaylord Perry and Bob Shaw combined to hold the Phils to just five hits. Wes Covington accounted for the home scoring with a two-run circuit blast. It was Bunning's first loss to the Giants after beating them four times in 1964.

The next day's game was rained out, and with a scheduled off-day on Good Friday, the team did not take the field again until Saturday, the 17th. The Los Angeles Dodgers came to town. Short outdueled Don Drysdale, 3–2, with Jack Baldschun picking up a two-out save. The Phils only managed four hits, but two of them were home runs which produced the needed scoring. Covington hit his second, and Johnny Callison smacked his first with a man on base.

On Easter Sunday, the Phillies faced their first left-handed starter, and Rojas was presented with his first opportunity to make an official mark on the young season. That left-hander was Sandy Koufax. In his first at-bat, Rojas singled off the future Hall of Famer, who was making his initial 1965 appearance on the mound due to a swollen pitching elbow. Opposing Koufax was recent addition Bo Belinsky. Obtained from the California Angels for two prospects, Belinsky was tagged for three runs in five innings—and the eventual 6–2 loss. Playing center field, Rojas got two hits off the Dodgers' feared southpaw. Rojas made a backhand, running-at-full-tilt-catch, robbing John Roseboro of an extra-base hit in the sixth frame, leaving an imprint on the wall he hit with his bracing feet in left-center. (It was the second time in less than a year that Rojas had denied the Dodgers' catcher an extra base hit with an outstanding outfield grab; the first occurrence was also a wall-banger, in Los Angeles on July 2, which Gene Mauch praised.) Koufax's bothersome elbow had been diagnosed as traumatic arthritis, and he had hurled only three innings since March 30. He was wild, walking five, while striking out seven in the game. Yet Dodgers manager Walter Alston allowed him to throw nine innings. Dick Stuart's two-run home run scored the only runs for the home team.

Two starts later, on April 26, Koufax was back on the bump against the Phillies in the final game of a four-game set at Dodger Stadium. Chris Short and Jack Baldschun combined to defeat Koufax, 4–3; Rojas doubled and tripled against the Dodgers' ace, who had previously beaten the Phillies nine straight times, dating to 1961. In the ninth inning, Rojas walked, stole second, and scored the fourth and decisive run on a Clay Dalrymple single. Charged with three runs earlier, Koufax was pinned with the loss.

The "man of all positions," as he was sometimes called by the press, Rojas continued his platoon role for Mauch in center field for the first two months of the season, holding up his end of the deal with a .303 batting average and 1.000 fielding average. Meanwhile, carrying a 20–24 record, the eighth-place Phillies were seemingly not intent on backing up their manager's pledge of winning more games than last year. Starting on June 1, Mauch penciled in Rojas' name as a starter (mostly second base) in the Phillies' next 40 games, leading into the All-Star break on July 10. The previous day, Tony Taylor had been hit on the forearm *twice* by pitched balls by Pittsburgh Pirates hurler Don Cardwell. Coincidentally or not, the Phils started playing better, going 25–15 in those games and moving up to fourth place in the standings behind league-leading Los Angeles.

In those early games, Rojas crunched his first pair of round-trippers, coming in back-to-back games, June 6 and 7. On the former day, in the second game of a twin bill, a Rojas three-run homer and four RBI were upstaged by three fence-clearing wallops by Johnny Callison. Dick Stuart also went deep as the Phillies completed a sweep of the Chicago Cubs with a 10–9 victory at Wrigley Field. The first game had gone in the Phillies' favor, 2–1.

The next day, making a return trip to Connie Mack Stadium were the Los Angeles Dodgers. On the hill for the Dodgers was Sandy Koufax, whose teammates had their way with three Phillies pitchers, including starter Lew Burdette. Koufax coasted to a 14–3 win, his tenth in his last 11 decisions versus the Keystone State team. Though reached for nine hits, he fanned 13, becoming the first pitcher to top the 100-whiff mark in either league. The home club's scoring came on long balls. The winning pitcher identified the culprits in his post-game comments: "Stuart hit a fast ball—a real good one. And the ball Rojas hit in the sixth [a solo blast] was also a good fast ball."[9] In three games versus Koufax, Rojas had gone 5-for-11 with a double, triple, and home run.

Rojas hit his third home run on June 12 in an exciting Connie Mack Stadium Saturday matinee in which the home club scored three times in their last at-bat to pull out a 5–4 win versus the Houston Astros. Rojas' third-inning four bagger accounted for the second Phillies run.

The Phillies finished June with a 38–34 record, 5½ games in back of the top-perched Los Angeles Dodgers, with three other clubs also ahead of them.

Based on seniority, Mauch was chosen to guide the NL All-Stars in the 1965 Mid–Summer Classic. Pennant-winning and World Series champion manager Johnny Keane had changed leagues to manage the New York Yankees. The players around the league chose the starters, and afterward it fell upon Mauch and opposing manager Al López to select the substitutes. (Yogi Berra had been fired by New York after losing the World Series to the Cardinals.) Dick Allen was chosen by his peers to open the game at third base for the senior circuit. Mauch chose Octavio Rojas as one of four back-up infielders, one catcher and four substitute outfielders to represent the elder loop. Rojas went into the break with a slash line of .302/.378/.399.

The game was held at Metropolitan Stadium in Minnesota on July 13. Milt Pappas of the Baltimore Orioles opened the game for the AL and was promptly greeted with a home run by leadoff batter Willie Mays. The NL jumped out to a five-run lead after two innings. The Giants' Juan Marichal, who had flung a two-hit shutout three days earlier against the Phils, threw three scoreless frames and became the first Hispanic player to be named MVP in an All-Star Game. Rojas pinch-hit for Marichal in the fourth inning and flied out. It was Rojas' only action in the star-studded game, which featured eight Latin American players (four from each league) for the first time. The NL, after ceding their early lead, won, 6–5, with Mauch as the winning manager.

Of incidental note in Marichal's July 10, 7–0 whitewash of the Phillies, the second hit came off the bat of Rojas, a harmless ninth inning safety. In the first stanza of the contest, Willie Mays and Phils catcher Pat Corrales were both removed from the game after a violent collision at home plate, wherein Mays scored the Giants' second run with two outs. Having taken over backup duties following Gus Triandos' mid–June sale to the Astros, the rookie Corrales was sent to the hospital for observation as he obviously got the worst of the crash. Mays scored all the way from first base on an infield hit and error, following Dick Allen's high throw that sailed over the head of first baseman Dick Stuart. Mays never stopped running and would have been out on right fielder Johnny Callison's relayed throw home. But the dynamic player not only knocked the ball free from Corrales' grasp but also knocked Corrales unconscious. On top of it all, the catcher was charged with an error. Apparently intent on giving Clay Dalrymple the day off, Mauch signaled for Rojas to move from second base to behind the dish. Rojas unexpectedly ended up receiving the tosses of three pitchers over the remaining 25 outs, recorded four putouts, and assisted on two others. He and reliever Jack Baldschun permitted one stolen base in the game. Rojas even had enough left to bear down in the ninth for his base hit against the resplendent Marichal. A near-sellout Saturday afternoon crowd of 32,031 was on hand.

Ten days prior to the All-Star Game, the Phillies encountered some crisis management issues involving two of their players, Dick Allen and Frank Thomas. The pair engaged in fisticuffs during batting practice following a racially insensitive comment Thomas made to Allen. Thomas, 36, Stuart's back-up at the initial base, pinch-hit a homer in the game that followed. He was then placed on irrevocable waivers and was picked up by the Houston Astros a week later, July 10, for the $20,000 waiver price. The incident, however, hung over Allen unfavorably and began the love-hate relationship that developed between Allen and the city's fans until his ultimate departure from Philadelphia several years later.

Since reaching the majors, Allen had exposed the racial hostility he experienced while in the minor leagues in Little Rock. He was the first Black player to suit up for the Arkansas capital team. Upon his airport arrival in Little Rock, "there was a picket carrying a sign that said, 'Don't Negro-ize Our Baseball.'"[10] Unable or unwilling to grasp the paradox of Allen the athlete and Allen the African American communing in a Jim Crow state, the Northern press often offered subtle pushback when reporting his grievances, mentioning that Allen had been voted the minor league team's most popular player and been gifted a new suit.

The reliable player appeared in 161 games for Mauch during the season, but his offensive numbers fell below his glowing rookie year statistics. His WAR of 6.1 easily remained at All-Star level, but his slugging numbers diminished, and his already-high strikeout rate increased. He was still a good player but not yet elite—much like his team. The

Phillies were still considered good, and the club finished the season nine games above .500, but would not contend for the pennant all year. They regressed to a second-division standing in the league, behind five other clubs, including the pennant-winning Dodgers. By the way, in Rojas' final meeting with Sandy Koufax (August 18), the infielder went 2-for-3, raising his offensive numbers to 7-for-14, including a double, triple and homer, against the majors' winningest pitcher (26–8).

Due to the two-month head start he received, Taylor was able to edge out his Cuban teammate in games at second base, 86 to 84. Rojas still played in 142 games, accumulating 578 plate appearances, one of the highest totals on the team. In 55 outfield games (42 starts), he made only one error and recorded six assists, a proportionally high number. In all, Rojas defended *seven* different positions, including two games behind the plate and one at first base.

The other catching assignment came on July 18. But the indispensable player barely had a chance to don the tools of ignorance for a second time, as he was ejected from the game for arguing a ball-four call after only a few pitches caught. In the seventh inning, Rojas had been switched from second base in a road matchup against the St. Louis Cardinals. On a 3–2 pitch to the Cards' Phil Gagliano, the first batter of the inning, Rojas stated too vehemently his case for a strikeout instead of a fourth ball with umpire Lee Weyer and was tossed.

The game at the initial sack occurred on September 16. Prior to the first pitch, the Phillies had designated the evening as "Cookie Rojas Night." Occasions usually reserved for special events or popular members within a franchise's history, the tribute was a testament to Rojas' performances and popularity in the three short years he had suited up for the Philadelphia team. The Rojas family gifts included a TV set, stereo equipment, and a wristwatch for wife Candida, who accompanied her husband on the field, along with their toddlers, Octavio Jr. and Michael. Mr. Dominic Forte, the father of south Philly born-and-bred pop singer and actor Fabian, presented Rojas with a pair of handmade cufflinks. "The Italian community of Philadelphia was behind that night, as I remember," said Rojas.

When the game commenced, Rojas was not in the starting lineup, but Gene Mauch substituted for both of his first basemen, and Rojas was pressed into duty at the new position in the final inning. He was not tested as Phillies rookie Ferguson Jenkins secured the final three outs of the Phillies' 8–6 win over Milwaukee without involving his freshly minted first baseman. Rojas admitted later it was the first time in his life that he had played first base in a game. All during his "tribute night" week, sports fans checking daily league batting averages in their local newspapers would have seen Rojas' name in the top 10, hovering around .300.

Two weeks later, eliminated from the race, the Phillies' pitching staff exhibited highly exceptional hurling in four straight games over the final weekend of the season. Seven Phillies pitchers permitted only *one* earned run in 49 innings against the New York Mets.

In the first game of a twi-night twin bill, Jim Bunning two-hit the wretched club from Queens, New York, on Saturday, October 2. (A rain-out the previous evening precipitated the dual encounters.) The 6–0 Shea Stadium blanking was Bunning's 19th win. Rojas went 4-for-5 with a run scored and one pushed home. The second game resulted in a sensational pitching duel between Chris Short and Rob Gardner. Both hurlers went 15 innings without permitting a run. Two relievers from both sides stretched the game another three unblemished innings before the contest was called a 0–0 tie due to curfew at the end of the 18th inning. The opener began at 5:30 p.m., and the final pitch was thrown at 12:50 a.m. Gardner, a rookie left-hander making only his fourth major league start, yielded only five hits (one of them to Rojas, who also stole a base); the Mets' pitcher walked two and fanned seven in the magnificent undertaking. The only extra-base hit the 20-year-old September call-up allowed came in the top of the 15th frame to Tony González. In the Phillies' third at-bat, with Rojas on third base, Gardner reached back and struck out Dick Allen for the final out of the inning. "I thought, I'm not going to walk this guy," said Gardner after the experience. "I just threw the ball as hard as I could and he swung through it. As I walked off the mound, he looked at me and just shook his head."[11] The equally spectacular Short struck out *18* Mets while being reached for nine hits. He permitted three free passes in the speculatively sky-high-pitch-count game. One double play was turned behind him.

Meanwhile, much earlier in the day, the Los Angeles Dodgers, with Sandy Koufax on the mound, defeated the Milwaukee Braves, 3–1, to clinch their second pennant in three years. The complete game victory by Koufax was his 26th, tying Carl Hubbell's record for most wins in one season by a National League southpaw since 1900.

In a story released the next day, one of the Phillies' outfielders, Wes Covington, publicly criticized his manager. "This club should have won the pennant the last couple of years," said Covington, part of an alternating brigade of flychasers on the Phillies. "We had the horses. I've been on pennant winners. I would never say it unless I had been in a position to see what it takes to win a pennant. Is it easier to find ballplayers or is it easier to find a manager?"[12]

The Phils and Mets, forced to replay the 18-inning tie, played another doubleheader on Sunday. In the lidlifter, Ray Culp, who had regained his rookie-year form of 1963, emerged victorious with a four-hit, 3–1 suppressive exploit of the hapless Mets squad. In his 14th win, the run against Culp was unearned. Rojas, roaming both corner outfield positions at different times, collected two hits to raise his average to .303. The second engagement went 13 innings, ending in the same score with the Phillies again on top. Another September-summoned minor leaguer, Grant Jackson, hurled the first nine innings in his second big league start; he was nicked for one run. Two other first-year tossers split the whitewash chores over the final four frames, with Ferguson Jenkins picking up his second major league win. The manager did not play Rojas in the nightcap, probably intent on preserving the infielder's .300 average. Jack Fisher pitched all 13 innings for New York to fall excruciatingly to a record of eight wins and 24 losses for the year. Mauch used Covington as a pinch-hitter in both games, apparently brushing off his comments. (Covington would be traded over the winter.)

With the four season-closing victories, Mauch's club ended the campaign a disappointing 85–76, in sixth place, 11½ games in arrears of the Dodgers. With four season-closing losses, Casey Stengel's Mets finished 50–112, three games poorer than last year.

The .303 batting average for Rojas was eighth-highest in the circuit and one point better than Dick Allen for best on the Phillies, and only Allen registered a higher on-base percentage on the club (.375 to .356). Rojas slugged at .380, and his 2.3 WAR rated sixth on the Phillies and third-highest among position players. The top two, Allen (voted in) and Callison (Mauch selection) were NL All-Star colleagues. Rojas led the NL in at-bats per strikeout (1 in 15.8AB) and even received enough down-ballot votes to appear in the MVP voting results list.

A Franchise-Crippling Trade

At the time, MLB rules prohibited players with more than three years' experience from playing winter ball, unless you were a native of the operating league's country. Therefore, Rojas, now a four-year veteran, had to explore other options over the winter of 1965–1966. He was enticed back to Puerto Rico, and Arecibo, for a fifth winter campaign, in a new capacity—as manager of the team. San Francisco Giants rookie Rigoberto "Tito" Fuentes replaced Rojas as the club's second baseman.

"When I managed in Puerto Rico there was always a big to-do with Rubén Gómez and Orlando Cepeda," recalled Rojas. "Juan Pizarro had a tremendous fastball. He was the best pitcher, such a hard-throwing left-hander."

Arecibo made the playoffs but had to scramble at the end to do so. Winners of their last five games, the Rojas-guided club qualified as the fourth seed with a 34–36 record. The Wolves took the league champion Mayagüez Indians to a first-round limit of playoff games but succumbed in the seventh-game decider, 7–1.

While Rojas was writing out lineup cards in his first month as manager of Arecibo, John Quinn pulled off a striking trade with the St. Louis Cardinals on October 27. In a six-player swap, the Phillies' GM obtained first baseman Bill White, shortstop Dick Groat, and catcher Bob Uecker in exchange for pitcher Art Mahaffey, promising outfielder Alex Johnson, and backstop Pat Corrales. The deal upgraded two key infield spots for Gene Mauch, with the five-time All-Star Groat and White, a four-time Mid–Summer Classic selectee. Both players' most recent All-Star appearances were in 1964. A month afterward, 30-year-old Rubén Amaro was sent packing to the New York Yankees for three-years-younger Phil Linz. And prior to spring training, Dick Stuart was shipped off to the New York Mets to clear the way for White.

John Herrnstein, White's potential backup at first, tied White and Johnny Callison for most spring training home runs with four. In the final week of spring camp, Rojas took the mound for the final inning of a "B" squad game and retired the side in order. Since pitching was the only position Rojas had not played since becoming a major leaguer, the exercise would portent a rare achievement in baseball history to which Rojas would tie his name.

Bill White needed little backup as he failed to see action in only three of the Phillies' 162 games. Even though the future president of the National League got off to a horrendous start with the bat in April (one HR and a .143 average), the Phillies were clearly committed to their acquisition. Eight days into the season, on April 21, the Phillies included Herrnstein, along with rookies Adolfo Phillips and Ferguson Jenkins, to the Chicago Cubs, in a deal to obtain veteran pitching help. The Cubs surrendered hurlers Larry Jackson and Bob Buhl in the 3-for-2 transaction.

On the surface, the trade appears not only explainable but favorable to the Phillies, even though Jackson and Buhl would turn 35 and 38, respectively, over the summer. Both men were reliable starters, with Jackson a former 24-game-winner and a legitimate innings-eater. The two pitchers appeared to be solid, complementary additions to the workhorse duo of Bunning and Short. Bunning, 34, was coming off a

19–9 campaign, including seven shutouts (2.60 ERA), while Short had started 40 games and relieved in *seven* others, accumulating just shy of 300 innings pitched and an 18–11 record (2.82 ERA). Topping 200 innings, Ray Culp, with his 14 wins, had seemingly overcome his previous arm issues. But no other pitcher won more than seven games for Gene Mauch's 1965 club. Belinsky and the aged Burdette had been busts. Of course, no one could have predicted Jenkins' enormous success. But the need to win now, with a current, competitive team on the field, might have made the turning over of prospects, like Jenkins and Phillips, easier. The trading of Jenkins undoubtedly crippled the Phillies franchise, as the right-hander set the league afire with six consecutive 20-win campaigns, starting in 1967. The Cubs improved as a team over that period, while the Phillies regressed.

That upgrade for one club and decline for the other was still a year away as the Phillies began the 1966 season on April 13 at Busch Stadium. Rojas made the first Opening Day start of his career. The four-year veteran was assigned the left field pasture by the ever-tinkering Gene Mauch. The manager had announced that Rojas would be the Phillies' second baseman against right-handed pitchers and would patrol left field versus portsiders. Rojas went 1-for-5, a bunt hit, in the game started by Curt Simmons. Chris Short pitched into the 10th inning, allowing two runs, and the soon-to-be-traded John Herrnstein delivered a pinch-hit single to plate the decisive run in the top of the 12th inning, for a 3–2 season-commencing victory. Ray Culp saved the win, striking out the side in the lower half of the frame. The Cardinals sent another left-hander, Larry Jaster, to the mound the next day, to conclude the two-game series. The Phillies rode a three-run circuit blast from Dick Allen in a four-run first inning to a 5–4 victory. Rojas went hitless in three at-bats.

Jim Bunning opened the Phillies' home schedule the following day, April 15, against Sammy Ellis and the Cincinnati Reds. Both right-handers pitched well, allowing two runs each, but were not involved in the decision. Second baseman Rojas collected two hits, including a single to start a two-run, ninth-inning rally to carry the Phils to a 4–3 win. With one out, Rojas scored the tying run on a hit by Clay Dalrymple, and two batters later, John Briggs singled home the game-winner, to the acclaim of the 29,007 hometown faithful.

Facing seven left-handers in their first 11 games, Rojas found himself roaming the outfield the majority of the time. Without sounding as if he were complaining, he astutely conveyed his defensive preference, again implying that his range was better on dirt surfaces. "Going from the infield to the outfield caused me some trouble," he said. "In the outfield I stand with my hands on my knees. In the infield I keep my hands away from my body. That enables you to break for the ball better."[13]

After those first 11 games of the Phillies' schedule, Rojas was hitting .341 (14-for-41). Then he was temporarily felled for six days with an acute case of bronchitis. Because of scheduling and rainouts, Rojas missed only two games. When he returned, Mauch kept him at second base more and more. The overcalculating manager decided to realign the left side of his infield, moving Allen to left field, while playing Tony Taylor and even Dick Groat at the third base. This gave Bobby Wine more playing time at shortstop.

Rojas' average suffered following his illness, but he regained his stroke toward the end of May, as the Phillies concluded the month with a 22–20 record. Six teams in the National League were within eight games of first place, occupied by the San Francisco Giants. The Phillies were six behind. From May 27 to June 11, Rojas hit in 16 out of 18 games, including 11 in a row, to boost his batting average up near .300 again.

On June 16 at Crosley Field, Rojas enjoyed his first and only five-hit game in the major leagues. It came during a 19-hit onslaught by the

A record eight Latin American players (four from each league) participated in the 1965 All-Star Game at Metropolitan Stadium in Minneapolis. From left: Félix Mantilla, Roberto Clemente, Tony Oliva, Cookie Rojas, Juan Marichal, Zoilo Versalles, Vic Davilillo, Leo Cárdenas (author's collection).

Phillies in a 12–5 drubbing of the home favorites. With five singles in his pocket, Rojas batted again in the ninth and sliced a ball down the right field line that was foul by inches, before grounding out. "I'm not complaining," said the man with a 5-for-6 in the box score. "A handful of hits isn't too bad for one night's work. I wasn't thinking of any records. I was swinging the bat ... waiting for my pitch and hitting it where it is pitched."[14]

Over the past two seasons and the first two months of the current campaign, Rojas displayed a hitting prowess that he had never shown at any lower level of competition. "In the minors you're swinging against eager, wild kids," he explained. "I was never relaxed up there [at the plate]. It's true that in the majors, the pitchers go for your weakness, but the ball is always around the plate somewhere."[15] Rojas also mentioned placement in the batting order as affecting his hitting. Batting lower in the order, Rojas said, he felt more pressure to drive in runs, and he was more comfortable slotted higher in the lineup.

A few games prior to the All-Star Game, the never-satisfied manager of the Phillies decided to play Rojas in center field, shifting Tony González to left. The left-handed-swinging González had started the year in left, playing against right-handers, and then switched to center when Mauch moved Allen to the outfield and stayed with Rojas at second base. After a two-week trial in center, Rojas came back to second base.

At the end of July, three teams were tied for first place, with the Dodgers, Giants and Pirates separated by percentage points. The Phillies (55–49) and Cardinals (54–48) were next in line, both 5½ games from the top spot.

During summer's hottest month, Mauch's club lost ground to the front-runners.

In September, the pennant picture developed between three teams, and Mauch was not managing any of them. Heading into the final week of the season, the fourth-place Phillies had been eliminated from contention. But the Phillies were in a position, thanks to scheduling, to influence the final standings. Their final two series were at home against the top contenders, Pittsburgh and Los Angeles.

First up were the Pirates. On Monday, September 26, Mauch's men defeated the second-place team, 5–4, in 11 innings. John Briggs stroked a game-winning single; Rojas, playing left field and second base, went 2-for-5 with an RBI squeeze bunt. With an inning of help out of the bullpen, Jim Bunning won his 19th game. The loss, coupled with a Dodgers victory over St. Louis, dropped Pittsburgh 2½ games behind Los Angeles. The Pirates lost another half-game in the standings the following evening when their game against the Phillies was rained out and Los Angeles beat the Cardinals for a second straight day.

Making up the postponement with a doubleheader on September 28, Bunning made his regularly scheduled start in the first game and fell, 2–1. Four Pirates pitchers held the Phillies to five hits, Rojas not among the successful batters. In the nightcap, Rojas, who played left field in both games, was more productive with two singles in five at-bats. But the Pirates' Bob Veale outclassed Larry Jackson, 4–2, to complete the sweep. Together with a Dodgers loss the same evening, the Pirates regained the ground they had lost over the prior two days, as they left town.

An off-day on Thursday was followed by a season-ending, three-game set versus the first-place Los Angeles Dodgers, who had upped their lead to two games over idle Pittsburgh, with a 2–1 win hurled by Sandy Koufax in St. Louis the same day.

In the Friday opener, Chris Short provided an assist to the Pirates with a 5–3 victory over the visitors, his 19th. Bill White cleared the fences with two men on base in the seventh to cap the Phillies' scoring. Hurling his 19th complete game, Short permitted seven hits, issued six walks, and fanned eight in the strenuous effort. Rain prevented the Pirates and third-place Giants from playing the initial contest of their campaign-concluding series in Pittsburgh. Their previous one-game card for Saturday was upgraded to a twin bill.

On Saturday, October 1, weather intruded on the Phillies-Dodgers matchup, forcing a doubleheader on Sunday. Meanwhile, the Giants won both of their games versus Pittsburgh to slide into second place, two games behind Los Angeles (eliminating Pittsburgh). In a last-gasp push, winners of five in a row, the San Francisco team had placed themselves in a position to tie for the pennant. It would not be easy. On the final day of the campaign, they would have to beat Pittsburgh again and hope for the Phillies to sweep the Dodgers. That would force the Giants to play a make-up game against the Cincinnati Reds on Monday, which if they won, would tie them with their archrivals and force a playoff for the pennant.

The intrigue was enough for over 23,000 fans to populate Connie Mack Stadium for the season-closing doubleheader on October 2. In game one, Jackson pitched effectively into the seventh inning with three runs allowed, and the Phillies scored twice in the eighth for a 4–3 comeback win. Short pitched the final two frames and scored his 20th win, entering the charmed circle for the initial time, the first Phillies hurler in 11 years (Robin Roberts). With the Giants-Pirates outcome in doubt, Dodgers manager Walt Alston called upon Sandy Koufax to take the mound in the nightcap. Koufax had thrown a complete game three days earlier versus the Cardinals. Jim Bunning opposed Koufax. The Dodgers' left-hander was warming up as news came that the Giants had pulled out an extra-inning win in Pittsburgh. If Bunning and the Phillies could beat Koufax, the Giants would inch to within one-half game of the lead and head to Cincinnati to play their 162nd game.

With an opportunity to win 20 games for the second time in his career and his first in the National League, Bunning faltered. He gave up a two-run circuit clout to the Dodgers' Willie Davis, an RBI single to Dick Schofield, and a sacrifice fly by John Roseboro, before he was pulled after five innings. The two-day-rested Koufax took a 6–0 lead into the bottom of the ninth. The Phillies tagged the tiring hurler for three runs, two earned, before he buckled down and secured the final three outs for a 6–3, pennant-clinching win. It was his 27th victory (most by a left-handed senior circuit pitcher in one season since 1901), with an *equal* number of complete games. Phillies outfielder Jackie Brandt struck out to end the game. Perhaps no one pondered it then, but Brandt would be the 2,396th and final strikeout of Koufax's wondrous National League career. The game and its fans would see him only once more from the mound, in four days, in the second game of the World Series. Koufax's afflicted left elbow would force an early retirement at age 30. Rojas went 0-for-3 with a sacrifice bunt.

In the happy Dodgers clubhouse, Koufax was all smiles. The likeable left-hander's personality could not be masked, even in a *San Francisco Examiner* report: "Sandy is known with affection among his teammates as 'Super Jew.'" The nickname tickles him. He roared in the locker room when, asked to explain the Dodgers' victory, Lou Johnson announced proudly, "It was Black Power, White Power, and 'Super Jew.'"[16]

The Phillies won two more games (to reach 87) and finished higher in the standings (fourth, eight games behind) than they had in 1965. Bunning, with his third straight 19-win season, may have produced his best year, tossing over 300 innings for the first time. An outstanding WAR of 9.0 was a career best and surpassed everyone on the team, including Dick Allen (7.5). In his third full season, Allen opened league eyes wider to his potential for greatness with a .317 average, 40 home runs, and 110 RBI. This despite not starting a month of games early in the season due to a shoulder injury sustained while attempting to steal a base. No one had analytics in their sight yet, but the slugger topped every peer in both leagues with a 1.027 OPS and an OPS+ of 181, which is a whopping 81 percent better than what is considered to be an average player.

Analytically, as well, 15–13 Larry Jackson significantly outpointed 20-game victor Chris Short in Wins Above Replacement, 4.7 to 2.5. Six-game winner Bob Buhl, the other pitcher obtained in the Ferguson Jenkins departure, was a well-below-average hurler, with a 76 ERA+ compared to the league average rating of 100.

Playing every outfield position and two games at shortstop, Rojas could not maintain his early hot hitting, his average settling at .268. He set career highs in games (156), the majority at second base, at-bats (626), and hits (168). He sent six souvenirs into the bleachers.

Defending All Nine Positions

Due to an earlier directive, veteran big leaguers were not permitted to play winter ball except in their native countries' leagues. In early October, the new commissioner, "William Eckert, with the help of his coordinator for Latin affairs, Cuban Bobby Maduro, overturned [Ford] Frick's edict," reversing a decision that disadvantaged one group of foreign-born major league players.[17] Eckert realized the flaw that existed in that only Cuban major leaguers, who had no professional league to which to turn, were adversely affected. The commissioner announced that experienced Cuban players could play in the winter of 1966–1967 in the international circuits of their choosing—with their MLB club's permission.

Rojas was free to go back to take the field as a player in the land that continued to welcome so many of his countrymen. Rojas returned to Arecibo for the sixth consecutive winter, his fifth as a player. In an uneventful campaign for Rojas and the Wolves, the club repeated their 34–36 record from last winter and were again bounced in the opening playoff round, this time in four straight by the Santurce Crabbers. (Suiting up for Santurce, Tony Pérez geared up for what would be the first of his seven 100-RBI campaigns in the major leagues by leading the PRWL in batting [.333], hits [87], doubles [18], triples [4], and, naturally, runs batted in with 63.)

It turned out to be Rojas' last winter season as a player in Puerto Rico. According to historian Thomas E. Van Hyning, Rojas compiled a .272 average with seven home runs and 94 RBI in his five winter league campaigns.

Spring training mandatory reporting date for the entire Phillies' squad was March 1. The Phillies tried to cut Rojas' pay because his batting average had dropped from .303 in 1965 to .268 last season. Rojas countered that his RBI total had increased from 42 to 55, and his home runs had doubled to six. As a result, Rojas did not return the first contract the Phillies mailed to him. But apparently after making his point, he soon signed on the dotted line a slightly revised contract and arrived in camp a few days after the deadline.

Although Rojas was not technically a holdout, one Phillies player was certainly conspicuous by his absence. With the leverage of his huge 1966 campaign, Dick Allen held out for a higher compensation level than originally offered. He eventually signed, to the relief of everyone associated with the Phillies, for a reported $75,000. Allen's first day in uniform at Jack Russell Stadium was March 19. He was a particularly welcomed sight because Bill White was recovering from a torn Achilles tendon that he had suffered playing paddleball in a St. Louis gymnasium in December and was doubtful of being ready for the season opener.

A few days later, March 22, the Phillies announced that Gene Mauch's current contract would be extended for one year, through 1968, at a speculated $50,000-a-year range. In a press conference held at Clearwater's Jack Tar Hotel, Phillies owner Bob Carpenter said he didn't want Mauch to manage the season with the uncertainty of a one-year contract (something Carpenter and his fellow owners never had trouble subjecting upon their players).

Entering his seventh season as manager, Gene Mauch had guided the Phillies from the bench longer than anyone in the modern era. The now-41-year-old had taken over in 1960 after predecessor Eddie Sawyer resigned his duties after the first game of the season. After five Opening Day wins, Mauch lost his first season christener on April 11; the Phillies' opponents were the Chicago Cubs. From Wrigley Field, the 1967 inaugural also marked the first televised game in "living color" on Philadelphia Phillies fans' television sets. What failed to come "alive" for most of the game were the Phillies' bats, as former Phillie Ferguson Jenkins outpitched Jim Bunning, 4–2. Since his trade, Jenkins had progressed in one year to the point where Cubs manager Leo Durocher had enough confidence to name him the team's Opening Day pitcher. Manning second base, Rojas "squeezed" home one of the runs allowed by the hurler, who was nicked for six hits and two walks, while striking out five.

Jenkins' parents received the chance to attend a big-league game pitched by their son for the first time. Though Delores Jenkins was visually impaired and could not see any of the 129 pitches thrown by her only child over nine innings, it did not impede the emotions of the day from surfacing. "Mother has about four percent vision in one eye and six percent in the other," explained the winning pitcher afterward. "I know she couldn't see beyond the third base coach, but just the atmosphere of the crowd thrilled her."[18] Jenkins' mother carried a transistor radio, and tears welled in her eyes with every inning-ending cheer from the more than 16,000 devotees who braved the 41-degree game-time temperature.

Fewer than 2,700 followers showed up the next day, as the Phillies erased a three-run deficit to win, 5–4, in 11 innings. Rojas homered into the "last row of the left field bleachers" for his team's first two runs, and Dick Allen knotted the score at 4–4 with a two-run bleacher blast of his own in the seventh. Playing first base for the injured White, Tony Taylor scored the winning run on a wild pitch. Center fielder Tony González hauled in a deep drive with two men on base for the final out, which came in the waning light of the cold and cloudy day. The contest may not have been permitted to continue past the half-inning in the non-lighted venue. Rick Wise got the win with five frames of scoreless relief. The scheduled third game of the opening set was postponed due to inclement weather.

The 1967 Connie Mack christener began and ended as expected on April 14 against the New York Mets. The Phillies jumped on Mets starter Jack Fisher early, lashing out eight hits and plating four runs in less than three innings. Rojas and Tony González collected two hits apiece and scored twice. Chris Short held the National League patsies in check the entire way, cruising to a seven-hit, 5–1 victory. A nice Thursday evening turnout of 26,649 enjoyed the proceedings.

Rojas was struck with the scourge of all ballplayers—an early-season slump. Following his second hit on April 14, he went 0-for-15 and 1-for-27, before singling twice in a contest on April 27 at Forbes Field. In between, Mauch used the injured Bill White in what could only be described as a Mauchian maneuver.

On April 21, the manager inserted White, who had not played yet because of his Achilles injury, into the leadoff spot in a road game against the New York Mets. Knowing White could not play defense and that he would have to pinch-run for him if he reached base, Mauch let White bat, ostensibly to have him face "live pitching." White grounded out. Bobby Wine replaced White; Rojas, penciled in at shortstop, moved to second base and lineup card-listed second baseman Tony Taylor shifted to White's position at first base. Subsequently in the game, Rojas slid back to short on defense and Taylor back to second base, the result of other Mauch substitutions. Jack Fisher defeated Jim Bunning and the Phils, 6–3. Saving White for a pinch-hit appearance would seem to have accomplished the same thing and made for a more stable defense and neater scorecard.

That same month, Bobby Wine replaced Dick Groat at shortstop on a full-time basis. Suffering from severe ankle inflammation which required hospitalization, Groat had no choice but to step aside. Upon his recovery, the former National League batting champion was sold to the San Francisco Giants in June and retired after the season, as he approached his 37th birthday.

Also on the mend, White wasn't ready to return to the lineup in full capacity for another five weeks, until near the end of May. By that time, the Phillies were a struggling ballclub, better only than the perennial doormats, the New York Mets and Houston Astros. During this period, voters in Philadelphia narrowly approved a second bond issue that assured the building of a new sports stadium, one to accommodate not only the Phillies but also the Eagles. Construction on the multi-purpose structure was expected to begin in the fall of next year.

Dick Allen broke a power draught of 31 games without a circuit blast on June 1 versus L.A. It came off Claude Osteen, with two men aboard, at Dodger Stadium. His fifth home run of the season backed Larry Jackson's 6–1, complete-game win. With the low power output and the Phillies' under-.500 record, it was reported that Gene Mauch and Allen were the two Phillies most regularly booed by Philadelphia baseball enthusiasts. Much more exposed than Mauch, Allen received the brunt of the paying patrons' audio ire. The third baseman had taken the unusual course of wearing his batting helmet on defense, one of the more shameful indictments that could be made against Philadelphia sports followers.

Catcher Bob Uecker, in comments defending his teammate Allen, discerned the negative reputation Connie Mack Stadium attendees had attained. "The fans here are the toughest anywhere," Uecker said, while revealing a side of off-beat humor that would flourish in his long, post-playing career. "You know, I think the fans go down to the Schuylkill River to boo the scuijers. They'd probably boo an Easter egg hunt, too."[19] Uecker would be spared hearing any more vocal displeasure from the locals soon thereafter. He was traded on June 6 to the Atlanta Braves for catcher/outfielder Gene Oliver.

Rojas viewed fans' expressions of annoyance as something that should not be carried around as a big distraction. In later years, as a veteran, he was often asked what advice he offered to younger players in this respect. One of his replies: "I tell them to concentrate on baseball, not worry about the fans. You're going to make errors, and they're going to boo. They boo because they care. And when you get a hit, they're going to cheer."[20]

On the day he was traded, Uecker saw action in both games of a twi-night doubleheader, as did Clay Dalrymple. In the nightcap, Rojas was called in from the infield to catch the final inning. Having been victorious, 8–6, in the opener, the Phillies completed the sweep, 9–8, with Rojas receiving the three-up, three-down heaving of reliever Turk Farrell. Dick Allen crushed a ball that flew over the 70-foot billboard atop the left field upper deck, completely out of Connie Mack Stadium, for a two-run home run. Turk Farrell had rejoined the Phillies that season to strengthen the bullpen. Originally signed as an 18-year-old amateur pitcher back in 1953, he debuted for Philadelphia in late 1956. After four full seasons under his belt with the team that drafted him, Farrell was traded to the Los Angeles Dodgers and then claimed by the Houston Colt .45s in the expansion draft in the fall of 1961. General manager Quinn purchased Farrell from the Astros for $35,000 in early May.

In the second game of another twi-night doubleheader on June 30, Rojas completed the adroit defensive endeavor of playing every diamond position. The 28-year-old took the mound in the final inning of a lopsided affair between the Giants and Phillies and wrote his name into the record books where very few others have landed. Having used five pitchers over eight innings, Mauch summoned his specialty player to the Connie Mack Stadium mound to obtain the last three outs owed to the San Francisco Giants, who led, 12–3. Rojas surrendered a single to the Giants' Tom Haller, the first batter he faced. Third baseman Allen got the first-time hurler into further trouble when he overshot first base on a routine throw after fielding a ball hit by Hal Lanier. With runners on first and second, Rojas buckled down after the error and got compatriot Tito Fuentes to hit into a force play, shortstop to third base, erasing Haller. Pitcher Juan Marichal flied to shallow left field for the second out. Rojas now faced Willie Mays with two men on. One of the Philadelphia writers compared the matchup to local heavyweight boxer Joe Frazier versus jockey Willie Shoemaker. Rojas threw the "Say Hey Kid" two balls, then Mays fouled a pitch to left. On the fourth offering, the peerless center fielder lofted the ball to short right for the third out. Those left of the 26,618 paying supporters on the evening cheered loudly for Rojas as he walked stoically off the mound—very much unlike the grinning position players of recent years who have made a mockery of pitching in one-sided games with managers attempting to spare bullpen arms. (A new rule limiting the use of such wayward arms went into effect in 2023.)

Securing his 11th win, Marichal retired the Phillies in order in their final turn, gaining a split for his club, losers in the opener, 10–3. "He's too good a player to be doing that," the great right-hander said, meaning Rojas and alluding to the fact that it was considered almost demeaning for a non-pitcher to take a major league mound. "You mean to tell me in a doubleheader that's all they can find for him to do?"[21] Still struggling at the plate, Rojas had not played in the lidlifter, nor in the second contest up to that point. "I wanted to throw strikes," Rojas said of his performance. "I threw all fastballs and two changeups. Nothing fancy. It was a thrill getting Willie Mays out, but my heart was in my throat when he came up."[22]

Rojas' lack of hitting cost him playing time in July. The club, meanwhile, through 100 games, was one win below the break-even mark. A four-hit game by Rojas on July 25 started him on the road to recovery at the plate, which included hitting safely in 22 of 25 games and a much-needed, nearly fifty-point boost to his average to a respectable .260.

Also playing more respectably were the 68–62 Phillies, who climbed into fourth place by the end of August. However, the 83–51 St. Louis Cardinals had established themselves as the class of the league, holding a 10-game advantage over their closest competitors, the Cincinnati Reds. The Phillies were 13 games behind.

On September 10, Rojas hit the first grand slam of his career. He clubbed it into Connie Mack Stadium's left-center field upper deck seating, off Cecil Upshaw of the Atlanta Braves. Jim Bunning picked up his 16th win in the 10–5 final.

Without any of last year's drama, the Cardinals clinched the pennant on the Phillies' home turf on September 18. Not that there was much chance of catching the eventual 101-win Cardinals, but Mauch's team received a crushing blow on August 24, when they lost Dick Allen for the remainder of the season. The All-Star third baseman damaged tendons in his right hand during a home repair accident involving the headlight of his automobile.

After three straight 19-win seasons, Jim Bunning posted another stellar year, perhaps his best since entering the National League. He led the league in starts (40), innings (302⅓), and strikeouts (253), and tied for most shutouts (6). Bunning lost *five* 1–0 decisions and another, 2–0. In the last of those slimmest-of-margin defeats, on September 27, the Phils' ace dueled Mike Cuéllar of the Houston Astros into extra innings of a scoreless stalemate in the Astrodome, before Chuck Harrison's single drove in Rusty Staub with two outs in the 11th frame. It was the last of Bunning's 16 complete games that season, tying a career high. The 17–15 right-hander posted a career-best 2.29 ERA while accumulating a team-pacing WAR of 8.0.

With Allen missing the last five and a half weeks, outfielder Tony González edged Allen for the highest WAR total among position players, 5.4 to 5.3. The 30-year-old Cuban outfielder, with a .339 average (second in the league to Roberto Clemente), an .869 OPS and 147

OPS+ in 149 games, racked up his best all-around season. With 10 stolen bases, he matched Tony Taylor for the second-most on the club. The underappreciated Allen robbed 20 bags (a career high), as the Phillies pilfered 79 bases as a team, equaling their 1962 level.

Rojas, who blamed his poor start on trying to pull the ball too much and feeling a need to drive in runs, salvaged his batting average with a final .259 showing. Displaying a distinct mastery with the bat, Rojas led the league in sacrifices with 16.

Perhaps over-punishing the team's 82–80 record, Phillies attendance was 828,888, last in the league, a drop of nearly 280,000 from last season's more than 1.1 million turnstile count.

Five

All-Time Phillie

A new winter baseball-playing country beckoned Cookie Rojas soon after Connie Mack Stadium was shuttered for business until the spring. After six winters in Puerto Rico, the Rojases traveled to South America to continue the head of the family's year-round ballplaying. The Caracas Lions team Rojas joined had a distinctive Cuban flavor. Pitchers Luis Tiant, Diego Seguí, and Aurelio Monteagudo, along with outfielder José Tartabull, were on the 20-man roster. The manager was Reggie Otero.

"It was Otero that got me to go to Venezuela," said Rojas. "He had been managing there for many years. We had strong teams down there."

"We lived at residencia Taormina in Caracas," recalled Candida Rojas.

The 1967–1968 Venezuelan league consisted of six teams, four residing outside of the country's capital city. University Stadium in Caracas opened in 1955 and could accommodate up to 35,000 *aficionados*. A capacity crowd was on hand to inaugurate the season on October 12, as the intercity rivals Caracas and the Navigators of Magallanes met. In his Venezuelan debut, Rojas had two hits and two RBI to support Diego Seguí's 5–2, complete-game victory.

Led by Seguí's 12–1 record and outfielder Vic Davalillo's .395 league-topping hitting mark, Otero's team won the pennant. Rojas finished fifth in batting with a .320 average. Seguí tied Eddie Watt (Orioles) for most wins in the regular season. Watt hurled for the third-place La Guaira Sharks, who were managed by native major league standout Luis Aparicio. Tiant produced the league's best ERA at 1.53 while posting an unpretentious 6–5 record.

The top four teams (Caracas, Aragua Tigers, La Guaira, Valencia Industrialists) engaged in a round-robin playoff with each team playing the other three times. The two clubs with the best records advanced to a final best-of-seven championship. Seguí led the way with four additional victories in as many starts for Caracas, which gained a home-field series advantage against the runner-up Aragua team. Based in Maracay, the Aragua club and Caracas finished with identical 6–3 playoff records. Seguí broke the tie with a 5–3 victory on February 5, his fourth of the post-season. (The Lara Cardinals and Magallanes were the circuit's also-rans.)

Defending their 1966–1967 championship, the Otero-led Lions repeated as undisputed league champions in the final, head-to-head series.

Rojas may have received a dispensation from the club around its championship run. In Miami, on February 3, his third child, Victor Manuel, was born. The third Rojas son went on to have success in baseball broadcasting with the MLB Network and Anaheim Angels, and more recently he was the president and general manager of the Frisco Roughriders, a minor league affiliate of the Texas Rangers.

> Our life always revolved around baseball. We did travel to Puerto Rico and Venezuela and the Dominican, mostly during school winter and holiday breaks. We had a house in Kendall Lakes [Miami]. I remember when we were in Little League. There were four different fields. My mom would take a chair and bounce around from field to field to watch each one of us play, if were playing at the same time. All of us had that bond, that connection to baseball growing up.
>
> I would hear my mom whistling and that meant to come home. Not to say that my Dad could not discipline us. He was more the sleeping dog you did not want to wake. To a certain degree that's how I am now. Dad was a disciplinarian in a way that he wanted things done in a certain way and we were supposed to be a certain way—yet he was never hard on us, even from a baseball perspective, from a failure perspective. I never once remember my Dad talking negatively about baseball to me, about a game or a performance—never. Conversely, he was never one of those "too high guys." He was even keel, keep things in check, don't get too high, too low. Lessons I share with my son Tyler today.
>
> Not one thing stood out with my dad. He got across to us the standard life lessons of: be smart, be wise, be alert at all times. I tell people all the time to try and imagine what it had to be like culturally, to be able to come over from Cuba with no money, and dealing with what's going on back home and oh, trying try carve out a major league career. To have that perseverance, sticking to what you do best. To be good at what you do, to be who you are and not try and live outside your means, that's what most stands out to me.[1]

"He did what he was asked to do," added Victor. "He was the ultimate team player. The ultimate utility guy. People talk about utility players like Mark DeRosa and Ben Zobrist, people who could bounce around from position to position—that's what my dad did in the 1960s and 70s. He was giving himself up for the good of the team."²

"Cookie played like he practiced," Gene Mauch said of his most functional player. "He was always very well prepared. He had average speed, marginal power and marvelous hands. He worked at becoming adept at situational baseball. If the ball had to be bunted, if it had to be directed with the bat, he could do it against any and all people. Cookie practiced better than any player I ever had. He made himself into a winning player and a successful player."³

As the VWL played out, hot stove rumors circulated that the San Francisco Giants were interested in obtaining Cookie Rojas. The talk was all but dismissed by the time Rojas (with another mouth to feed) joined his teammates in Clearwater to prepare for the 1968 season. Making ready for his ninth season at the helm and eighth spring training, Gene Mauch told reporters, early in camp, that he thought the Cincinnati Reds were the team to beat in the National League. Mauch would have to open the campaign without his best pitcher over the last few years.

Almost two months after his 36th birthday, Jim Bunning had been traded on December 15. John Quinn moved his best pitching asset to the Pittsburgh Pirates for left-handed pitcher Woodie Fryman and three untested players: infielder Don Money and pitchers Bill Laxton and Harold Clem. "In our opinion, we have acquired three of the best prospects in the minor leagues,"⁴ said Quinn. Fryman and Money (who was the key piece in the deal) would have extended major league careers, though not so much with the Phillies. Laxton would be a bust, and Clem never made it to the Big Time. It was another proactive move by the Phillies' general manager, and judged by the overall results, not one to fault. Bunning would never again be the excellent moundsman he had been.

With perhaps a youth movement in mind, Quinn also dealt— announced on the same day—pitcher Dick Ellsworth and backup catcher Gene Oliver to the Boston Red Sox for catcher Mike Ryan. Oliver would turn 33 by Opening Day; Ryan was 26. Ellsworth, 6–7 in 21 starts for the Phils, had been obtained a year earlier from the Chicago Cubs for Ray Culp. A 28-year-old left-hander, Ellsworth, would put things together for the Red Sox in 1968, hurling just under 200 innings and notching 16 wins.

Quinn and Mauch were counting on the return of Dick Allen and Bill White from injuries. The former All-Star first baseman had been limited to 95 starts at first. Allen had played in 122 games before his season-ending hand injury. Mauch decided to move Allen to left field as a measure of protecting the wear on Allen's recuperating right hand.

Both White and Allen were in the Phillies' Opening Day lineup on Wednesday evening, April 10, at Dodger Stadium. So were prospects Don Money (SS) and Larry Hisle (CF), both debuting in the major leagues. Both hit toward the lower end of the batting order. Hisle collected two hits and a run scored, and Money had one hit with two RBI. Chris Short, the heir to Bunning as staff ace, blanked the Dodgers on four hits. Tossing his second Opening Day shutout in four years, Short struck out 10 and walked no one in the 2–0, 1:53-minute stifling. The whitewash was a harbinger of the season which became known as "The Year of the Pitcher." On the whole, big league hurlers dominated hitters to the extent that had not been seen since Dead Ball Era times. Rojas went 1-for-4.

An anticipated, low-attendance crowd of 28,138 showed up. The majors were customarily scheduled to christen the new campaign on Monday in Washington. But the assassination of civil rights leader Dr. Martin Luther King and the subsequent funeral postponed the major league schedule for two days and eliminated one of the two games the Dodgers and Phillies had scheduled. The Academy Awards ceremony, taking place in Los Angeles, was held the same night as the Dodgers' opener, after being delayed two days from its usual Monday annual telecast day.

The Phillies hit the early skids, dropping their next six games, the longest such string of reverses for a Phillies team since the crucifying setbacks at the finish of 1964. In the second loss, Rojas gleaned four hits on April 12 at the Astrodome. It was Woodie Fryman's initial venture in a Phils uniform. Fryman couldn't get through the fifth inning; he was tagged with a 5–2 loss to Houston. The sixth loss came back at Chavez Ravine on April 16, following a doubleheader defeat by the Giants at Candlestick Park two days earlier. A previous off-day for the Phillies and travel day for the Dodgers was used to make up the bereavement-postponed game from a week ago.

Although the season was barely a week old, Mauch and his club were already subject to harsh criticism in the press. On the day of the Phillies' home opener, April 17, one prominent scribe railed that "the Phillies are 1–6 and snugly in last place. Blame that on a worried, restive, confused group of athletes and their leadership from front office to field. The Phillies died somewhere on a road trip that took them from Clearwater to Los Angeles, to Houston, to San Francisco, back to Los Angeles and finally home to the nation's capital of bad baseball."[5]

After flying through the night, the Phillies righted the ship in their first contest on home turf. Also making the all-night flight were the Los Angeles Dodgers, as they were programmed to be the Phillies' opponents. At the evening home opener, what was described as "Philadelphia's world famous Cardinal Dougherty High School Band" provided the headline pre-game entertainment, while a city managing director tossed out the first ball. In a well-pitched game, Fryman, requiring a four-out assist from Turk Farrell, beat Don Drysdale, 3–2, for his initial win in a Phillies uniform. Ahead 2–1 in the fifth inning, Drysdale was ultimately beaten on a two-run home run by Cookie Rojas in the lower half of the inning. "I was trying to punch the ball for a hit," said a modest Rojas. "With a runner on first and Johnny Callison coming up, I just wanted to keep things going. He gave me a high fastball and I punched at it. It got up in the air and the wind did the rest."[6]

It was reported that after arriving at his Beverly, New Jersey, apartment at noon, Rojas was operating on one hour of sleep for the game, after being awakened by one of his sons (unidentified) at 1:00 p.m. Perhaps it was Mike, celebrating his fifth birthday, wanting to know what his father had gotten him for the occasion. With his game-winning blow, Rojas ended up providing a present the whole family could celebrate.

A small gathering of discontented fans paraded a banner in the stands throughout most of the game, reading "Bunning's Gone. Who's Next? How about Mauch?" The manager was asked if he had seen the sign. He answered in the affirmative and declined further comment. In the game, Mauch used his seventh different lineup in eight games. Don Money had been shipped to the minor league San Diego Padres, and Larry Hisle, the other rookie Opening Day starter, would soon be joining him on the same Pacific Coast League team.

On the last day of April, instead of traveling with the team, Dick Allen, without permission, drove to a scheduled game in New York. Mauch benched him. The Phillies could have used his bat as Don Cardwell outdueled Chris Short, 1–0. Allen pinch-hit for Short in the eighth inning and flied out. Rojas took the collar. Allen returned to the lineup the next evening.

Turk Farrell and Dick Hall had been salient cogs for Mauch's bullpen last season. This year, only Farrell turned in a repeat performance with 12 saves and four wins in 54 relief appearances. The second of those victories was picked up when the Phillies rallied for two bottom-of-the-ninth-inning runs, on May 19, to squeak out a 4–3 victory over the St Louis Cardinals. As a side note, it seemed as if Rojas was trying to avoid arousing sibling jealousy by duplicating the home run present he had given Mike the previous month with another clubbed for birthday boy Octavio Jr., who turned seven on this day. A solo shot, accounting for the second Phillies' run, Rojas targeted one of the eight future Hall of Fame hurlers he would take deep in his career. Coming off two shutouts in a row, 23-year-old Steve Carlton surrendered the Rojas dinger, but ultimately he was not the pitcher of record in the happy decision for Phils fans. The one-run win completed a three-game sweep of the top-of-the-heap Cardinals and moved the 17–16 Phillies into fourth place, only 2½ games in arrears.

In the Phillies' next game, Rojas experienced the highs and lows of the sport within the span of a half-inning. At Wrigley Field on May 21, in top of the ninth inning, the second baseman cleared the ivy with two outs and two men aboard. The clutch blow capped a four-run ninth and knotted the contest at 5-all. Mauch had pinch-hit for Clay Dalrymple in the comeback inning, after having done the same for starting backstop Mike Ryan two innings earlier. The manager called for his jack of all trades player and inserted him behind the dish for the Cubs' last swings. Top reliever Farrell tried to send the game into extras but got into trouble straight off. A leadoff double was followed by an intentional walk and successful sacrifice bunt (by Ernie Banks), moving the runners to second and third with one out. Before the next batter came up, Mauch moved left fielder Allen to center and center fielder Don Lock to left. That next batter, Lou Johnson, fouled off the first offering and missed Farrell's second pitch—but so did Rojas behind the dish. The winning run scored from third; Rojas was charged with a passed ball.

Though he made no excuses, in Rojas' defense, he was nursing a bad back, enough to make him miss a week of games immediately following the catching duties. During the time away from the bench, it was written that Rojas' wife had to help him slowly up the stairs leading to their apartment. The 15-step climb could take as long as 10 minutes to scale during the aggravated flare-ups.

Overcoming the capricious nature of back issues, Rojas returned to action on May 29. He played regularly the rest of the way, including both ends of 14 doubleheaders. Following his return, he hit in 11 games in a row, after hitting safely in his previous three contests. The 14-game hitting streak, from May 18 to June 9, was the longest of Rojas' career.

Just as Rojas was returning, another high-profile team player became absent from the team lineup for much different reasons. Dick Allen arrived late, again, for a home game on June 1 (20 minutes before game time). This displeased Mauch enough to fine Allen and send him home. Hitting .288 with only seven home runs, Allen did not play for an entire week, until June 8. That day, with the Phillies trailing 5–3, in the eighth inning at Dodger Stadium, he appeared as a pinch-hitter and grounded into a force out. The Phillies mustered no more offense and lost by the same score; Rojas went 2-for-5 with a run knocked in.

In the fifth frame, the Phillies scored a run against winning pitcher Don Drysdale, ending a record scoreless-innings streak of 58⅔ the big right-hander had strung together over his last seven starts. Drysdale had broken the old mark of 55⅔ held by Walter Johnson, after keeping the Phillies off the board for the first two innings. At the end of the visitors' third, home plate umpire Augie Donatelli (stemming from a complaint by Mauch) intercepted Drysdale coming off the mound, grabbed him by the wrist, and ran his fingers through the pitcher's hair to examine him for a foreign substance. None was found. Drysdale was unfazed but was eventually removed from the game in the seventh inning after surrendering three runs (two earned). Afterwards, his post-game comments captured the plaintive sentiments of many in the country, only two days after the assassination of U.S. Senator and presidential aspirant Robert F. Kennedy: "This was one of those nights, the kind when you just run out of steam."[7]

The evening prior, Mauch had reason to be steamed at his second baseman. Rojas was thrown out to end the game in an attempted steal of third base with the tying runs on base. Trailing 2-zip in the top of the ninth inning, with two outs and Johnny Callison on first and Rojas on second, Rojas took off for third. He was thrown out by Dodgers catcher Jeff Torborg for the 27th out of Claude Osteen's shutout. Mauch said of the bad play: "I don't criticize ballplayers who play as hard as Rojas."[8]

After sitting on the Phillies' bench for 10 days—the duration of the team's western road swing—Allen returned to the Phillies' lineup, June 11. Prior to the game—in which Allen homered, the only scoring in a 5–1 home loss to the Houston Astros—he got together with owner Bob Carpenter for an hour-long meeting. A backstory report provided more clarity on the situation: "Allen has refused to conform with rules laid down by Mauch and has been fined repeatedly. On a recent trip to the west coast, Mauch suspended Allen and told him he was not returning to the lineup until he came and said he was ready to live by the rules."[9]

Four days later ... the Phillies fired Gene Mauch. Quinn and Carpenter broke the news to Mauch in a phone call to Los Angeles, where the former manager had flown the prior day to be with his ill wife. "I'm not of a mind to talk to anybody about it," Mauch said. "I bear no grudge against the Phillies. They have been good to me."[10]

Allen, who was clearly not happy, said, "I suppose they'll blame it on me."[11] The "they" presumably meant the fans, the press, and any other potential critic in the greater Philadelphia area. Despite four stellar years with Carpenter's team, Allen had not been able to gain an ingratiating foothold with anyone who seemed to matter in the City of Brotherly Love. It is clear, though, that Allen did have at least one sympathetic and important ally in Carpenter.

Had Allen been slugging better, had Mauch given Allen more leeway with his idiosyncrasies that perhaps a non-minority player would have received, had the Phillies been winning more, then things might have been different. But Mauch had avoided the hammer long enough. The feud with Allen and the team's losing record (26–27) notwithstanding, accountability had finally arrived for 1964 for Gene William Mauch.

Bob Skinner was elevated from his managerial post as the Phillies' minor league skipper in San Diego to pilot the club for the remainder of the season. The Phillies played worse under him than Mauch, who left the team as the winningest manager in franchise history. (Mauch's 646 wins, with 684 losses, in 8¼ seasons was surpassed decades later by Charlie Manuel's 780–636 mark in 10¾ campaigns.) The 1968 club settled in eighth place (76–86), a handful of games ahead of the league inferiors, the Mets and Astros.

At Dodger Stadium on August 11, Rojas recorded 10 assists at second base, two shy of the major league record for a nine-inning game (held by multiple players). Don Drysdale blanked the Phils, 1–0. Rojas reached the big right-hander for two of the Phillies' four hits on the afternoon. On August 16 at Connie Mack Stadium, Rojas collected his second four-hit game of the season. He knocked in three of the Phillies' five runs, but the visiting San Francisco Giants rallied for three scores in the top of the ninth to pull out a 7–5 decision.

Rojas made an excellent case for the Gold Glove Award. Playing in 150 games, he led all NL second baseman in fielding percentage (.987) and putouts (365). The decision-makers, who were the managers and coaches of the circuit, voted the award to Glenn Beckert, the Chicago Cubs' smooth-fielding second sacker. Playing in five more games than Rojas, Beckert had a poorer fielding percentage of .977, committing *nine* more errors than Rojas' 10. Digging deeper, Beckert raked in 356 putouts and 461 assists to the 365 putouts (first in the circuit) and 424 assists of Rojas, who was involved in turning 110 double plays (tops in the league) compared to his counterpart's 107. A dip into analytics revealed that both infielders exhibited exceptional range, with Beckert's range factor/per game at 5.27 to Rojas' 5.26.[12] Bill Mazeroski of the Pirates bested all second basemen with a per-game range factor of 5.54.

In the "Year of the Pitcher," Rojas enjoyed a career-high in dingers with nine.

Edwardian Suit and Ruffled White Shirt

Likely still bothered or worried by the recent back troubles, Rojas skipped winter ball. For a time, he took a job as a public relations rep for a local automotive agency.

The Phillies' selfless utility man was in camp in Clearwater when Dick Allen arrived to his usual press-driven fanfare, March 8. It was an anniversary of sorts. Exactly one year earlier, the mercurial player had left camp and was AWOL for three days before returning. A photo in various newspapers preceded his arrival, showing Allen, a family man with a wife and three children, in Miami with Joe Namath at the opening of Namath's new restaurant in late February. The celebrated New York Jets quarterback had recently pulled off the NFL's most impactful upset in the Super Bowl, held two months earlier in the same city. According to press clippings, the mustachioed Allen showed up that first day to Phillies camp dressed in an Edwardian suit and ruffled white shirt; he went to the clubhouse and shaved his mustache.

Certainly with Allen in mind, the Phillies announced that an eight-foot fence was being installed at Connie Mack Stadium, traversing the left-center field bleacher wall to the right-center field scoreboard, with the aim of reducing the distance to center field from 447 to 410 feet. The 60-year-old facility, the oldest in the major leagues, sported the second-most expansive center field dimensions, behind Forbes Field, in the league. All hitters at CMS not only had the long, straightaway outfield distance with which to contend, but also the 64-foot-high, right-center field scoreboard which peaked over the 34-foot high corrugated wall extending across the outfield from the right field foul line.

The Phillies kicked off the 1969 season in a recognized homer-friendly venue on April 8. An unusually warm, early spring day enticed a standing room crowd of over 40,000 to Wrigley Field, the best-attended opener in modern team history. Phillies manager Bob Skinner presided over his first season christener, while Phillies starter Chris Short prepared for his fourth and Cubs mound designate Ferguson Jenkins for his second, both against his old club.

Outpacing everyone, by far, Ernie Banks made his 16th—and best—Opening Day appearance for the Cubs. Banks hit two home runs, numbers 475 and 476 lifetime, both against Short, and drove in five runs. But the home team required a two-run, walk-off, stadium-shaking blast by pinch-hitter Willie Smith in the bottom of the 11th inning to upend the Phils, 7–6. Rojas went 2-for-4 with a run scored, as neither starter was around at the finish. Banks received the largest pre-game introduction ovation. No doubt the proudest of the applause was provided by Banks' father Eddie, in for the occasion from his Dallas residence.

Before the game, from a spot near the dugout, the sunny-disposed Banks was spied attracting pre-game attention. "It was an assembly line deal, an usher serving as a middle man between the youngsters and their idol," noted a Chicago writer. Banks exclaimed between signing autographs, "I'm happy. Is everybody happy?"[13]

Last year's disappearing rookie prospects, Don Money and Larry Hisle, both 22, were in the season's initial lineup again, but this year both were on the club to stay. Coming off a top-grade season in San Diego and with no real challengers, Money had won the shortstop role in spring camp. Hisle, signed by the Phillies out of high school, had also shined during his playing time in the same minor league city. The young shortstop issued an early statement to the club and its followers that the job was his to keep by cracking two Wrigley bleacher bombs and driving in five runs in the one-run, extra-inning loss.

Rojas did not have much of an early chance to get acquainted with his new keystone mate as the 30-year-old infielder suffered back spasms while taking infield practice in the team's next scheduled stop in Pittsburgh. Rojas was sidelined for all but six April games, missing his club's home opener.

The same first month, Skinner's squad suffered a serious blow to the pitching staff. After only two starts, Chris Short was disabled on April 21. He would endure season-ending back surgery in June, with just the two appearances to show for his season.

On May 1, an off-day, Dick Allen missed the team plane to St. Louis for a three-game weekend set scheduled against the Cardinals. He arrived the next day *during* the first game at Busch Stadium. He was fined $1,000 by Skinner and was forced to sit out the following day's game as well. Allen returned to the lineup for the Sunday series finale and had two hits and two RBI. Behind Grant Jackson's seven-hit shutout, the Phillies won, 5–0, and completed a road sweep over the defending National League champs.

Baseball was celebrating its centennial in 1969 and, in the spirit, the Phillies asked their followers to select an all-time Phillies team. Voting took place in April and May. When the results were tallied, three infielders of the Phillies' famed "Whiz Kids" 1950 pennant-winning team were acknowledged by the fans, as well as one Octavio Victor Rojas. Around the horn, Willie Jones, Granny Hamner, Rojas and Eddie Waitkus were ballot-honored. At catcher, Andy Seminick was selected as the Quaker City team's best receiver. Robin Roberts and Rojas' contemporary, Chris Short, tabulated as opposite-throwing pitching preeminents. Playing his third position in as many years, Dick Allen had been shifted to first base at the start of the season. After only two months at the initial base, Allen was barely edged out by Waitkus, a full-time Phillies first baseman for only three seasons. The Allen vote was splintered as he also received consideration at third base and the outfield.

In the outfield, Chuck Klein, Richie Ashburn and Del Ennis rounded out the 1950s-centric team. Roberts was voted the greatest Phillie ever by the voting group of slightly more than 26,200. The team balloting was part of an inclusionary process that resulted in the Baseball Writers' Association of America announcing the greatest team and players of the designated 100-year history of the sport.

"I never thought anything like this would happen to me," said Rojas, who referred to the recognition as one of the greatest honors he had ever received. "As a boy I heard of Robin Roberts and Richie Ashburn, but I never thought I'd be picked on a team like this with such great players."[14]

In early August, the Phillies invited their all-time team to Connie Mack Stadium. All but Chuck Klein, who died in 1958, and Willie Jones (prior commitment) returned to be celebrated. Baseball Commissioner Bowie Kuhn presented the honorees with engraved wrist watches and framed photos.

By this point in the campaign, the Philadelphia Phillies were far back of the Chicago Cubs in the National League's newly formed Eastern Division. Major League Baseball had expanded in 1969 with four new teams, two in each circuit, and the leagues were split into two, mostly geographically-based, six-team divisions. The division winners would face each other to determine a league champion.

On August 7, the Phillies were scheduled to play an exhibition game against their Reading, Pennsylvania, farm club. Dick Allen announced to his manager that he would not participate in the game. Allen had recently come off a suspension of 26 days by Skinner, for missing the start of a doubleheader in New York on June 24. (The distracted player was visiting a local racetrack where one of the horses Allen had an interest in was soon to compete.) Owner Bob Carpenter had intervened on Allen's behalf to get him reinstated on July 20.

That same day, the Apollo 11 lunar module landed on the surface of the earth's satellite. Rojas recalled a sneering quote of his acknowledging the return of Allen to the team that made the Philadelphia newspapers: "I said, 'This must be the greatest day in history. The astronauts reach the moon and Richie Allen comes down to earth.'"

But when Carpenter would not back Skinner in another disciplinary move over Allen's intentions to skip the exhibition game, Skinner resigned.

The temperamental Allen had taken to scrawling cryptic words in the dirt area of the first base bag he defended. On August 5, Allen spelled out "OCT 2" and "PETE" at the same time, before ground crews erased it in between half-innings. Although October 2 was the season-ending

Although Rojas (right) only spent a short time with the St. Louis Cardinals, he had an opportunity to meet then–home run king Roger Maris in 1970 (courtesy Cookie Rojas).

date for the 1969 campaign, the meanings were unknown to everyone, apparently, except the writer. Allen also traced out "BOO" on another occasion, an obvious defiant response to fans.

"Richie Allen is a great player," said Skinner, in parting. "I wish him the best of luck. His next manager, too."[15]

Phillies coach George Myatt, who had skippered two games last season in between Mauch's firing and Skinner's arrival, took over the club's helm the rest of the way. The Phillies were 44–64 under Skinner. With only one pitcher on the team with more wins than losses (Rick Wise, 15–13), the Phillies fell further under Myatt, winning only 19 of their remaining 54 games. Landing in fifth place, inflicted with 99 losses, they were pitifully only 11 games better than the expansion 110-loss Montreal Expos—who were managed by Gene Mauch.

Spiked on the right heel on a force play at second base September 20, Rojas missed the last 12 days of the campaign. Plagued by a bothersome back and the season-snipping injury, Rojas played in 110 games, his fewest as a starter with the Phillies, and his offensive production correspondingly dropped to his rookie and sophomore-year lows.

The Trade That Would Change the Economics of Baseball

Four days before the start of the World Series, in which the New York Mets amazingly culminated an unpredictably rapid rise from perennial cellar dwellers to champions of the baseball world with a four-games-to-one Series victory over the powerhouse Baltimore Orioles, the Philadelphia Phillies and St Louis Cardinals initiated a blockbuster trade. Phillies fans would no longer have Dick Allen to boo—at least not as a hometown performer. The team's most productive and talented and disenchanted player was sent packing in a seven-player swap.

Also, Cookie Rojas' tenure in Philadelphia came to an end. Highly touted prospects, Larry Bowa and Denny Doyle, in the Phillies' minor league infield pipeline made Rojas expendable. He was attached with right-handed hurler Jerry Johnson to the big exchange, which originally netted the Quakers four Cardinals in return: catcher Tim McCarver, southpaw pitcher Joe Hoerner, and outfielders Byron Browne and Curt Flood.

Although the nearly 32-year-old Flood was a star, the three-years-younger McCarver was said to be the player most coveted by the Phillies, who were bereft of backstop talent for years. Allen, who obviously needed a change of scenery, said he was glad to be out of

Philadelphia. "Six years in this town is enough for anybody," he commented, with a swipe at his general manager. "I'm glad to be away from Quinn and all of them. They treat you like cattle."[16]

A day later, Curt Flood threw a potential monkey wrench into the consummated deal with a stance of non-cooperation. A seven-time Gold Glove winner with six seasons with a .300 or better batting average, Flood announced: "Under the circumstances, I have decided to retire from organized baseball and remain in St. Louis where I can devote full time to my business interests."[17] Flood, who expressed "surprise and disappointment" at the news, had a photography and painting business. Cardinals GM Bing Devine would eventually compensate his Phillies counterpart John Quinn with two substitutes for Flood, one of them rookie Willie Montañez. (Over the years, it's most often written that Flood refused to report to the Phillies in much the same manner Jackie Robinson decided to retire rather than suit up for the rival New York Giants, following his stunning trade to that team in the late 1950s.)

Flood could not shake the disillusionment the trade brought and bravely challenged—through litigation—major league baseball's contractual clauses that indentured all players to their teams—all the way to the highest court in the land. After defeats in lower court rulings, the United States Supreme Court, on appeal, upheld (5–3 vote) major league baseball's anti-trust exemption, established decades earlier in the same high court. Although Flood was defeated at all turns, the high-profile legal battles shone light on how the game was allowed, in effect, to set its own rules when it came to arbitrary treatment of its most prized commodities. Two and a half years following Flood's reverse, in December of 1975, arbiter Peter Seitz sustained the legal grievances filed by the Major League Baseball Player's Union on behalf of pitchers Dave McNally and Andy Messersmith, who argued that they were free to sign with any team after refusing to sign contracts with their current clubs. Seitz ruled in favor of both players on the grounds that the owner's standard contract did not specifically stipulate for how long the signing player was bound to his team. After exhausting all legal appeals that upheld the Seitz decision, in response, MLB relented and reworked the "reserve clause" wording of the standard baseball contract that previously had practically perpetually bound the signer to his team. Eventually, this paved the way to negotiate the now–long established free market system of player movement after six years of major league service with one or more teams.

The business side of baseball leaves not only affected players in a forced readjustment course but, in most cases, their families as well.

The Rojases were one example. "We were able to buy our first house near Philadelphia in 1969," remembered Candida Rojas. "We lived in Willingboro. And then Cookie gets traded to St. Louis!"

Complicating matters further was the welcomed arrival of the Rojases' fourth and last child, Roberto Arturo, born November 11, 1969. Rojas forsook winter ball, no doubt, to help out at home.

"I remember when Bobby was born," said elder brother Tab. "They wouldn't let us all in Mom's hospital room. So from the outside, we all waved up at Mom's window, where she was holding up Bobby."[18]

Today, Bobby Rojas is a human resources executive living in Naples, Florida, and is a married father of three children. He was following an athletic baseball career in college when an injury permanently sidelined any such ambitions.

> I was the only brother not born in Miami. I was born in Willingboro, New Jersey. To me, I didn't see anything special in my Dad being a ballplayer. It was like one of the many jobs that a grown-up might have. I guess I didn't know any better, at the time. The older I got, of course, the more I began to appreciate it.
>
> I got to be a bat boy in Kansas City, which was very cool. What most stands out is to be able to see and have an on-field interaction with somebody like Rod Carew. He and George Brett became my favorite all-time players.
>
> Later, when I was at the University of Alabama—I was a first baseman/relief pitcher—I got a chance to spend a full week with Carew in California. This would be in the '90s when he had a baseball academy. I ended up suffering a third-degree a/c joint separation of my clavicle after taking a fall on the bases and that put an end to any baseball hopes I had. But Carew was such a professional. He broke down hitting, the art of hitting, in such simplistic terms. He was a humble man, too. Being at that facility with him during that time was an experience I will never forget.
>
> I remember for years and years there was a baseball glove in a framed, glass case in our house. I always asked my Dad about it, and he would just say the Hall of Fame keeps asking for it. That glove reflected my Dad's versatility, the selfless player he was, always about the team, versus chasing numbers. How do I help my team? How do I help others? That's what I learned most from him and that's how I try to live my life today.

Rojas Sr. caught the chicken pox from one of the older boys, which delayed his reporting to his new team's spring camp in St. Petersburg, Florida. But not long after his March 9 arrival, one of the Gateway City's longest tenured sportswriters profiled Rojas as a way to introduce him to his new followers. "Rojas worked as one of the most versatile utility regulars in baseball history," informed Bob Broeg. "Except for that brief fling on the mound, the moves hadn't been gimmicks, either. He played everywhere else as an aid to a club that almost won the pennant in 1964."[19]

While his immediate family had grown by one recently, it was revealed that Rojas' extended family had been reunited through his selfless efforts. "From 1961 to '68 he arranged for 23 of his relatives to come to the U.S.," wrote Broeg. "The last two were grandparents who have since died."[20]

"Every chance we got we'd bring out family members through third countries," said Rojas. "My father, uncle emigrated to the United States from Spain. It took time and money, but it was all worth it."

Wearing uniform number 11, Rojas seemed destined for a return to a utility role with the Cardinals in 1970, as Julian Javier had been manning second base for St. Louis since 1960. The transition back to a non-starter was difficult for the nine-year veteran, reflected in no greater part than by his poor batting average. In late April, however, Rojas substituted for Javier for a week's worth of games, when the latter came down with a sore back.

On May 21, Rojas returned to Philadelphia for the first time since his trade, but the spotlight, understandably, was on another individual. A writer from a suburban Philadelphia newspaper described part of the Cardinals' initial visit to the City of Brotherly Love: "They sang Richie Allen's song at Connie Mack Stadium Thursday night—BOO! Allen, whose stormy career with the Phillies included a fist fight with a teammate, missed planes, missed games, suspensions, and a running feud with booing fans, took his return to town in stride."[21] Allen hit a two-run home run; Rojas, subbing for an indisposed Lou Brock in left field, went 1-for-3. Phillies stalwart Tony Taylor's run-scoring single in the bottom of the ninth inning lifted his team to a 4–3 walk-off win.

With Brock and Javier back in place, Rojas' playing time grew more limited. It did not help that he was hitting barely .100. A couple of days before the June 15 trading deadline, Rojas was traded once again—in what turned into a beneficial move that reenergized his career and brought his embraceable style of play to a new baseball audience.

Candida Rojas recalled the particulars: "I had arrived in St Louis with my four kids. I don't remember the name of the hotel we were staying at, but one day after shopping in the supermarket across the street, I came back to the hotel. The concierge asked if I heard the news. I said no. *Cookie was traded to Kansas City.* I grabbed my kids and drove to Kansas City. I took my sons everywhere with me."

Six

Happy to Be a Royal

The trade to Kansas City occurred June 13, two days before the trading deadline. Rojas had to clear waivers from every other National League team before he could be moved. The one-for-one exchange sent obscure outfielder Fred Rico to St Louis. The team Rojas and family joined was one of two second-year expansion franchises added to the American League's Western Division in 1969. Currently, both the Kansas City Royals and newly relocated (from Seattle) Milwaukee Brewers were, as expected, bringing up the rear in their division.

Rojas had his doubts about joining a new team that was not expected to be competitive. "When they traded me to an expansion team, I figured this was the end of the line," he disclosed a year later. "I flew to San Diego and stayed with Preston Gómez for two days. He explained that Kansas City was a young team, and I could help the inexperienced players."[1]

As a result of the trip, Rojas joined the Royals with a changed outlook. "This is the best for me. I want to be with a team that needs me," he said following the transaction. "The only way I can produce is to play regularly. I don't think I can hit .300 but I can hit .260 and I can do things to help win games, like hit behind the runner. I'm happy to be with a good, young club. We're going to win some ball games."[2]

The newest Royal made a successful debut on June 16 against the Boston Red Sox. At Municipal Stadium—the former domicile of the American League Athletics and current Royals home ballpark—Rojas, playing at his preferred position and batting second, collected two hits and an RBI. He was on third base, with new teammate Amos Otis on second, when Boston's Reggie Smith hauled in Lou Piniella's long, potentially game-tying drive to end the game in the Red Sox's favor, 7–5. Smith banged off the wall, holding on for the game's final out.

Ten days later, Rojas collected his first four-hit game in almost two years. One of the four singles knocked in a run, but the visiting

California Angels edged the Royals, 5–4. The Royals had a group of rotating players holding down second base, but after Rojas arrived, he joined shortstop Jackie Hernández as the club's new keystone combination, until Hernández lost his starting placement in late July.

A few days after Royals manager Bob Lemon benched the light-hitting Hernández, Rojas went on a hitting spree, collecting 10 hits over four games from July 30 to August 3. The newcomer continued his good swinging with his second four-hit effort in less than two months, on August 7. The safeties were timely in nature as each one produced an RBI, coming in the back end of a home doubleheader, handily won by the Royals, 10–2, over their expansion counterparts, the Milwaukee Brewers. It was the second four-RBI game for Rojas in less than two weeks. On July 25, the 31-year-old infielder homered and singled, providing half of the Royals' runs in their 8–4 doubling up of the Cleveland Indians at Cleveland's Municipal Stadium.

Later in August, the player few thought would reach the major leagues appeared in his 1,000th game. On Monday, August 17, at Robert F. Kennedy Stadium in Washington, Rojas played in his four-digit-milestone game. He did not celebrate the occasion, going 0-for-3 and being removed before his fourth at-bat. The Royals were one-hit by Washington hurler Jim Hannan, 7–0.

After being made aware of his accomplishment, Rojas commented, "This is my life. And I hope to keep it my life for a long time." He also gave a hint of his desire to remain part of the game once his playing days were over. "I want to play as long as I can—as long as I don't embarrass the club or myself. And I hope to stay in the game after that time."[3]

A disastrous, 106-loss season by the Chicago White Sox prevented the two expansion teams in the Western Division from vying for last place. As it was, the sophomore squad of Bob Lemon finished in a dead heat with the Milwaukee Brewers, both with records of 65–97.

Perhaps Rojas' greatest contribution those last few months was the air of professionalism, in manner and action, he brought to the young Kansas City club. Though not yet fully known, going forward, the budding Royals fan base would become very pleased that Cookie Rojas had become part of their team.

All-Star in Both Leagues

Rojas returned to Venezuela for a second time in the winter of 1970–1971. His objective that off-season had a more defined purpose. The trade out of Philadelphia had disenchanted him. "I didn't say anything because it looked like the Cardinals were going to be a contender," Rojas revealed later in the upcoming MLB season. "But I didn't get to play. All I did was sit on the bench and get fat. I went from 170 to 181. I hadn't played winter ball for two years. So, I went to Caracas. I got myself in real good shape—down to my 170 pounds."[4]

Showing he was getting the job done, a rounding-into-shape Rojas was one of four unanimous All-Star selections in the Andean League. Again suiting up for the Caracas Lions, the Cuban infielder was one of three proven or about-to-be-proven major leaguers picked, including St. Louis Cardinal Vic Davalillo (Caracas) and Houston Astro Bob Watson (Lara Cardinals). The fourth selection on all the ballots was Atlanta Braves' organization catcher Faustino Zabala (Lara). Watson headed the circuit in home runs and RBI. Thirty broadcasters and writers chose the non-pitching participants, pitting a team of imported players versus a club composed solely of native Venezuelans in the extravagant exhibition game.

The All-Star game traditionally halted the VWL during Christmas week. Played on December 23, the Venezuelan nationals pounded out 17 hits to the 14 cranked out by their foreign opponents, in squeaking out a 7–6, walk-off victory. A bottom of the ninth inning, run-scoring single by Minnesota Twins outfielder César Tovar (Caracas) decided the contest. A crowd of 20,000 paid their way into University Stadium. No other statistics on the game are available. Pompeyo Davalillo, manager of first-place Caracas, guided the Natives; Lara's Tony Pacheco piloted the Imports.

Caracas won the pennant and faced the third-place La Guaira Sharks in the playoffs. Magallanes, fourth-best in the circuit, took on the second-place Lara Cardinals. Caracas and Lara were both ousted in the first round by the lower-tiered clubs. La Guaira defeated Magallanes and went on to represent Venezuela in the recently resurrected Caribbean Series.

As the latter events played out, Rojas prepared to report for the first time to the spring camp of his American League team, in Fort Myers, Florida. For the first time, Rojas had a say in what uniform number he would wear. "I chose number one," he said, "because it gave the impression of being first, and I liked that connotation as both a player and veteran."

The man who had snatched Rojas out of St. Louis orchestrated two other important trades that significantly improved his team. On December 3, 1969, Royals general manger Cedric Tallis had obtained center fielder Amos Otis, along with right-handed pitcher Bob Johnson, from the New York Mets for third baseman Joe Foy. Almost a year to the day later, and less than six months following the Rojas–Fred Rico exchange, Tallis sent Johnson, catcher Jim Campanis, and Jackie Hernández to the Pittsburgh Pirates in exchange for catcher Jerry May, pitcher Bruce Dal Canton, and shortstop Freddie Patek.

In Pittsburgh, Hernández would make history as part of the majors' first all-minority lineup fielded by the Pirates, September 1, 1971, against the Philadelphia Phillies.[5] He also reached the height of professional glory and a personal revalidation, of sorts, as the Pirates' shortstop in their pennant drive through the playoffs and World Series championship that same year. Starting all four of his club's division playoff games and six of the seven Fall Classic contests, Hernández recorded the final assist of the final out of the seventh game, won by Steve Blass and the Pirates, 2–1, over the Baltimore Orioles.

Rojas and the 27-year-old Patek, who was 5'4" in height, meshed right away as the Royals' middle infield defenders in 1971. "That Patek has all the tools," touted Rojas a couple of months into the season. "He's made a big difference in our club; he's a hellava ballplayer."[6]

"Even though I was the oldest, I barely remember his Philadelphia years," admitted Tab Rojas. "I most recall Kansas City, how that ballclub came together. It was a fantastic time once everything started clicking. I loved watching my dad and Freddie Patek turn the double play. It was a thing of beauty."[7]

The partnership was made even more pleasing for Royals fans by the offensive contributions of both players as well. From the start of his first full season in Kansas City, Rojas possessed a sharpened batting eye. He had four multi-hit games in the first six the Royals conducted on the road to open the campaign.

The team's seventh game did not prove lucky. On April 12, 1971, the Royals lifted the curtain on their home schedule at Municipal Stadium. The largest crowd for a Royals season opener, 32,728, and biggest at the park since 1955, the debut year of the former Philadelphia Athletics franchise in their new Midwest territory, came out on a warm evening to cheer their 3–3 team. While the weather was pleasant, the treatment of the Royals by the visiting team's starting pitcher was anything but. Minnesota's Bert Blyleven three-hit the home team, notching a 2–0 victory, his second whitewash in a row—and one of 60 he would spin in his Hall of Fame career. Rojas reached the just-turned 20-year-old hurler for the only extra-base hit he allowed, a double.

Though he would not have to wait quite as long as Blyleven for Cooperstown recognition, Bob Lemon was at the helm in his first full campaign as Royals manager, having taken over about a third of the way through the 1970 season for underachieving Royals skipper Charlie

Metro. About a month into the season, Lemon already had singled out his up-the-middle tandem of Patek and Rojas as giving his club a different look and, with their fielding, of taking pressure off the pitchers by not having them feel that they had to make a perfect pitch every time.

After the Royals' first 42 games, Rojas was hitting .310, highest at his position in the AL. "[I'm] finding the holes. I'm seeing the ball real well and hitting strikes," the rejuvenated batter said. "That's what happens when a guy is going well."[8]

It wasn't just Lemon singing the praises of Rojas. "Why are the Royals infielders making the defensive play this season that was getting away last time?" asked one local writer. "Why are they, the infielders in particular, performing better than anyone connected with the club could have hoped? The answer you hear most is that Cookie Rojas has taken charge, that he has grown into the player-level leader the club needed so badly, that he has become the cohesive around which a unit forms."[9]

Starting May 28, the Royals tore off 12 wins in 13 games to climb nine games over .500 and pull to within 4½ games of the division-leading Oakland A's. The ninth win came on June 11 against the Boston Red Sox. Rojas provided a first-inning, bases-loaded triple off Luis Tiant to set the stage for a 6–3 Royals win at Municipal Stadium.

On June 17, Rojas reached a hitting milestone, obtaining his 1,000th career hit. In his home ballpark, Rojas tagged California Angels reliever Mel Queen for a seventh-inning single to left field. Earlier, he had recorded hit number 999, a single against starter Rudy May, as part of a three-run first frame the team used to top the Angels, 5–0. The Royals' leading pitcher, Dick Drago (7–2), hurled the six-hit shutout.

While Drago had emerged as the team's best hurler, perhaps no other player had contributed more to the team's success than Amos Otis, who was following up on an outstanding first season in 1970 with Kansas City. At the close of the current campaign, Otis would be the club leader in WAR at 5.3, while pacing the team in homers with 15 and RBI with 79. The 23-year-old also swiped 52 bases and was caught only eight times. "That Otis is the best center fielder I've seen in many, many years. He's going to be a superstar," predicted Rojas.[10]

Otis finished fifth in the fans' voting among American League All-Star outfielders. Rojas received the second-most votes on the Royals (308,636 to Otis' 411,552) and third-highest at his position. Rod Carew was the top choice at second. Davey Johnson of the Orioles came in second. Remarkably, all of Rojas' tallies were write-ins, as he was not listed on the AL computer ballot. In 1971, voting was returned to the fans for the first time since 1957. Rojas was touched by the local support, which permeated from the highest levels of the organization. He witnessed it firsthand following a road trip. "It was the greatest thing I have ever seen," Rojas stated. "Here were Mr. and Mrs. Ewing Kauffman, owners of the Royals, standing on the street corner handing out ballots. It makes a guy feel like he's four feet off the ground. It's not one of those things you can look at and forget. It will stay with me all my life."[11]

An examination of comparative numbers makes clear the reason behind the groundswell of support for Rojas. Entering the break, Carew, had a slash line of .283/.324/.360 to the .315/.368/.446 triple threat numbers of Rojas. Carew had hit only one home run in contrast to the six times Rojas had left the yard. American League manager Earl Weaver prevented a total miscarriage of justice by selecting Rojas to the special squad as a reserve player. Throughout the early summer, the Royals' second baseman had battled teammate Otis for a top-three placement in batting average in the league. The pair typically trailed the Yankees' Bobby Murcer and were well behind circuit leader Tony Oliva, hitting in the .370s.

A report on the eve of the exhibition contest noted that Rojas had invited family members from Miami and Puerto Rico to come to the big game in Detroit to see him play. "No matter what, it's going to cost me," said Rojas. "My wife had a bottle of perfume break in her suitcase all over her clothes. She had to go out and buy all new ones this afternoon. Wow."[12]

"I remember it well," said Candida. "All my good clothes were ruined. I had to scramble to buy new outfits. Don't ask me the brand name of the perfume. I probably erased it from my mind because of what happened."

The 1971 All-Star Game was an exceptionally star-studded classic, most remembered for Reggie Jackson's moon-shot home run that hit the light tower in right field at Tiger Stadium and for the participation of 20 future Hall of Famers. Weaver let Carew bat three times before substituting Rojas, who flied out to right in his only at-bat. Rojas became the ninth player to suit up for both leagues in the Mid–Summer Classic.[13] Otis, in his second All-Star Game, went 0-for-1. Reversing a string of eight defeats in a row, the AL upended their older league rivals, 6–4, on the strength of three circuit clouts by destined immortals, Jackson, Frank Robinson (ASG MVP), and Harmon Killebrew. Shortstop Luis Aparicio played the entire way for the winners, the only player to do so. Backup Leo Cárdenas of the Twins was nursing an injury.

The winning pitcher in the All-Star Game was Vida Blue. The 22-year-old Oakland A's pitcher became the youngest hurler to a win a

Mid–Summer Classic and was on course for one of the greatest pitching seasons in history. His team had pulled out to a commanding 11½-game division lead at the All-Star Game pause, as the 43–41, second-place Royals had lost their earlier winning momentum.

On July 20, a week after the clash of the baseball titans in the Motor City, Rojas kept up his forward hitting progress, accruing the ninth four-hit game of his career. Among the hits were two doubles, both off losing pitcher Mike Cuéllar, who was knocked out of the game in the third inning, allowing five of the Royals' seven runs. The Baltimore Orioles' left-hander had not lost to the Royals in six decisions since they had come into the league. "I knew he throws that screwball," Rojas said following the Royals' 7–1 victory, "and I decided to wait on him. I waited, and I got him."[14] Rojas scored twice and knocked in two runs as the principal backer of Dick Drago's 11th win.

In August, Oakland further strengthened their grip on the division, and the Royals endured a diminishing blow to their improved product on the field. Suffering a hairline fracture of his right fibula on August 21, Cookie Rojas was lost for the rest of the season. It occurred in a freakish manner, twisting out of the way of a brushback pitch by Washington Senators hurler Mike Thompson. Shifting his weight onto his right foot, Rojas said, he heard a popping sound. He suspected his spike might have caught in the dirt. Bobby Knoop took his place. The infielder, who had 11 game-winning hits to his credit, returned to Miami to recuperate.

In 112 starts, all but one at second base (one start at shortstop), Rojas hit .300 (124-for-414), sixth in the AL. He finished third on the club in RBI with 59, and fourth with 56 runs. Rounding out the stellar, albeit shortened season, Rojas recorded the best fielding percentage of any second baseman in the league at .991. He made only five errors in his curtailed campaign.

Rojas called the season his best—and most satisfying—from the standpoint of doing different things well, such as hitting in the clutch, defensive plays that helped save games, and completing the unsung tasks of moving over runners.

The Sporting News placed him on their AL All-Star team as the league's best second baseman. The peppery little infielder, as one writer referred to him, finished second in the periodical's Comeback Player of the Year Award. In the players' poll conducted by TSN, Rojas was beaten out by the Tigers' Norm Cash.

Over the winter, the Kansas City Royals held their first Baseball Awards Dinner on January 23, 1972. Among the marquee awards presented, Dick Drago (17–11) won Pitcher of the Year unanimously. Freddie

Patek and Amos Otis tied for Player of the Year honors. Rojas was voted the player who did the most to supply inspirational leadership.

A few months earlier, Rojas had joined the Royals' Florida Instructional League club, serving as instructor with an opportunity to continue rehabbing his right ankle. He missed the start of winter league play in order to complete his Florida assignment. But the Zulia Eagles, based in Maracaibo, were able to open a roster spot for Rojas, who wanted to keep testing his ankle. The infielder appeared in 25 games for Zulia, which was bumped out of championship consideration in the first round of the playoffs. The western Venezuelan team lost a seven-game series to the La Guaira Sharks. In the final series, with the winner crowned as Venezuela's representative to the Caribbean Series, Maracay's Aragua Tigers defeated the Sharks, four games to three.

Aragua's Rod Carew led the league in hitting with a .355 mark. His Twins teammate, César Tovar (Caracas), finished second at .333. The All-Star second baseman became playing manager of the team when Vern Rapp resigned mid-season. Carew, with one of his *seven* batting titles under his belt at this point, had obviously been dissatisfied with what had been, for him, a sub-par season, batting .307. He had decided on winter ball as a corrective course of action.

In the Caribbean Classic, held in Santo Domingo, the Venezuelan champion shared a second-place tie (3–3) with Dominican title holder Águilas Cibaeñas, behind the winning Ponce Lions (5–1) of Puerto Rico. Mexico's Guasave Cotton Growers placed last with a 1–5 record. The Lions and Chicago White Sox outfielder Carlos May was named MVP. Carew was selected as the tournament's top second baseman.

First Hispanic Player to Pinch-Hit a Home Run in the All-Star Game

Anticipating a mid-season move from Municipal Stadium to the Harry S. Truman Sports Complex, the Royals began working out at their new synthetic infield at Terry Park in Fort Myers, March 6. Plans for the Truman Sports Complex included completion of two AstroTurf, open-air stadiums, separately designed for baseball and football.

As previously touched on, the switch in uniforms for Rojas had also brought a change in identifying numeral to his on-field garment. A spring training report on the player brought further mention: "Rojas has had 11 seasons in the majors. He wears a distinctive uniform, No. 1, as he works in the training camp of the Kansas City Royals here. Uniform No. 1 is appropriate. If there is any Kansas City player who deserves the ranking that man is Cookie Rojas. A poll of players taken by *The Sporting News* last July named him as the best second baseman in the American League by a 2 to 1 margin."[15]

As the 1972 season commenced on Saturday, April 15, the Royals were hoping to reduce last year's wide margin of 16 games between themselves, as second-place finishers, and the 101-win Oakland A's. The first-ever work stoppage in baseball history from a players' strike had delayed the start of the campaign for 13 days. The stand-off had ended two days earlier when the owners agreed to increase health benefits by $490,000, along with a $500,000 added increment to the players' pension plan. None of the lost early games would be made up.

What no other sport can top baseball at is the special feel of renewal and hope the first game of a new season delivers to everyone involved. "I always get butterflies for the opener," stated the veteran Rojas. "Just too bad the weather wasn't good."[16]

On a 50-degree day at Municipal Stadium, the Royals edged the Chicago White Sox, 2–1, in 11 innings. Ninth-inning solo home runs by Chicago's Dick Allen (playing his first game in a White Sox uniform) and the Royals' Bob Oliver spoiled shutouts being tossed by starters Wilbur Wood and Dick Drago. In the final extra frame, with both hurlers departed, the Royals' Paul Schaal reached second with no one out. Rojas, hitless in the contest, laid down a bunt, advancing the runner to third. One out later, John Mayberry, the team's off-season acquisition, singled to bring in Schaal with the winning run. A first baseman obtained from the Houston Astros for two relief pitchers, Mayberry's first hit as a Royal made a victor out of reliever Tom Burgmeier and sent the 8,749 announced crowd home happy.

A Sunday doubleheader the next day produced about 2,600 more attendees and more happy outcomes for the home team, which swept the visiting Chicagoans, 2–1 and 4–3, in 10 innings.

The Royals lost their next six games, all on the road, then won three straight. The streaky club fell below .500 in May. On the 15th, Rojas doubled home the deciding run in a 5–4 home victory over the Texas Rangers. In the second inning, Rojas combined with his shortstop to make the defensive play of the contest. At double play depth, Rojas backhanded a grounder hit by the Rangers' Lenny Randle and flipped it with his glove hand to Freddie Patek, who forced runner Ted Ford and relayed to first for the double play. The *Kansas City Times* featured a side-by-side, three-photo sequence layout of the spectacular play. "On an Astro turf field there's hardly any dirt where you can stop your momentum to throw, so Patek and I devised the play during spring training," Rojas told the author. Municipal Stadium's dirt infield, notwithstanding, provided adequate testing ground this night. The team record stood at 10–15.

Exactly a month later, John Mayberry had his best game as a Royal to date, driving in six runs with a round tripper and two doubles, to help his team outscore the Red Sox, 13–9, at Fenway Park. Rojas' three-run four-bagger capped a six-run sixth inning that put the Royals ahead in the game for good. In spite of wins in their next two games, the 25–28 Royals had fallen 10½ games in back of first-place Oakland.

In a Sunday doubleheader on July 2 at Municipal Stadium, Rojas collected six hits and five RBI. He lashed out three doubles in the opener, which provided two scores, but the visiting Texas Rangers prevailed, 7–5, in 10 innings. In the nightcap, three singles and three RBI by the second baseman helped the Royals gain a split with an 8–3 decision.

On the same homestand three days hence on July 5, Rojas contributed to a milestone achievement by Detroit Tigers pitcher Mickey Lolich, who was coming off a fantastic 25-win season in 1971. In the fifth inning, Rojas swung through a Lolich fastball for strike three and became the left-hander's 2,000th strikeout victim. In the sixth, Kansas City knocked Lolich from the mound on their way to an 8–2 victory. Rojas had a hit and run scored.

A week later, on July 12, Rojas made his only hit of the night count—a bases-loaded home run. The 10th-inning jackpot wallop occurred at Memorial Stadium as part of seven-run frame that broke open a game between the Royals and Baltimore Orioles. The final score was 11–4.

For five games leading up to the All-Star break, Rojas filled in at third base for Royals hot cornerman Paul Schaal, even moving over to shortstop in one of the contests. Hitting .298 with a .343 on-base percentage, Rojas trailed perennial All-Star Rod Carew in the All-Star team fan voting.

Over 2,000,000 ballots were cast to decide the lineups for the 43rd All-Star Game, held in Atlanta on July 25. Carew's 832,055 votes more than doubled the 411,253 tallies Rojas received. Dick Allen of the White Sox was the AL's top vote getter with 1,092,758. Cincinnati Reds catcher Johnny Bench's name was punched out 1,229, 677 times on the computer cards, outpacing all other players. Roberto Clemente, garnering over a million fan votes, was a late scratch due to a left knee strain he suffered sliding into a bag two days earlier in Cincinnati. Willie Mays, playing in his 19th straight All-Star Game, replaced him in the NL starting lineup. (*The Sporting News* polled the players, and, at second base, Sandy Alomar of the California Angels beat out Carew, with Rojas placing third. Players were not allowed to vote for their teammates.) AL

All-Star manager Earl Weaver added four Royals to the team, including their entire outfield: Lou Piniella, Amos Otis and Richie Scheinblum, plus Rojas. Of the four, Otis was the only player who did not see action in the contest.

Rojas nearly did not participate himself. With the score, 2–1, late in the game in favor of the Nationals, Weaver later stated, he was afraid of running out of position players and had advised Rojas that he might not use him. But when second base starter Carew complained that a previous rib cage muscle pull had begun bothering him, Weaver substituted Rojas as a pinch-hitter for Rodney Cline Carew in the top of the eighth inning. With two outs and Carlton Fisk on first base, Rojas drove a ball over the outstretched glove of left fielder Billy Williams at the fence of Atlanta Stadium. The two-run home run put the American Leaguers ahead, 3–2.

"I thought it might get caught," Rojas said. "I believe it hit Billy Williams' glove. But when I rounded first I saw it was out and thought: 'I only need 630 more to catch Hank Aaron.'"[17] Rojas became the first Hispanic American Leaguer to go deep in the All-Star Game, the first Hispanic to pinch-hit a home run, and the 10th player overall to pinch-hit a four bagger in the interleague classic. Additionally, Rojas became the first Royals player to clear the fences in the starry summer extravaganza.[18]

That was the official account. But according to Rojas, there was a more involved behind-the-scenes interaction that led to the dramatic moment: "I went to get a drink of water near Weaver and started walking back to sit down when he asked if I would mind him not using me. 'Earl,' I told him, 'every player here wants to represent their team and their city.' So he said, 'okay, when Carew's turn comes up again, you bat for him.' [Bill] Stoneham was pitching. I hit a slider. It went over the fence. My wife told me that my father and father-in-law nearly fell from the second deck from the excitement." Apparently still bristling that Weaver would ask him the question, Rojas added that he refused to shake Weaver's hand after rounding the bases and had a few choice words for him. The incident, as described, did not make the papers.

"I remember that home run like it was yesterday," recalled Tab Rojas, who was 11 at the time. "I was watching the game on TV. I jumped I don't know how high off the floor in our house. I can't really tell you who else was around, there was a whole bunch of family members. But I can still see that TV set and feel that moment."[19]

AL reliever Wilbur Wood could not hold the lead, however. The Nationals tied the game with a run in the bottom of the ninth and won it in the following inning on a Joe Morgan RBI single. The largest crowd in Atlanta Stadium history—51,383—became delirious. The New York Mets' affable reliever, Tug McGraw, notched the win with two scoreless innings of work. "I thought we had them with only two innings to go," a dejected Rojas said about the 4–3 defeat. "But I guess we didn't. What do they say, the game is never over until the last out."[20]

Prior to the star-studded classic, as often happens with a player of his experience, Rojas was asked a much-recycled question: *Is there a difference between the National and American Leagues?* Obviously in good spirits over his All-Star selection, Rojas answered: "Sure, they have two different presidents."[21]

The author posed to Rojas the same question. His answer:

> The difference in the two was seen in the balls and strikes. In the National League, the home plate umpire wore his chest protection inside of his suit. In the American League the umpires behind the plate wore an inflated chest protector strapped over their shoulders. In the National League, the low strike was called more because the umpire crouched behind the catcher's shoulder. In the American, the umpire stayed directly behind the catcher, upright. They tended to call the high strike more. So one league was the "high strike league" and the other was the "low strike." The National League also tended to run more, steal more bases.

Rojas' next homer proved more fruitful. After 10 long balls in a Kansas City uniform, all on the road, Rojas smacked his first round-tripper at home. On August 9, at Municipal Stadium, the mighty mite connected in the seventh inning with a man on base against reliever Darold Knowles, providing insurance runs in the Royals' 5–2 victory over the Oakland A's. Last year's diamond phenom and this year's much-publicized holdout, Vida Blue, was the losing pitcher. The loss shrunk the A's lead to one game in the division. However, it was not the Kansas City club that was in contention. Though the win completed a three-game sweep of the defending division winners by the Royals, the 50–54 team trailed Oakland by 11 games.

The next time the teams met, in six weeks' time, Bob Lemon's club had been eliminated from contention. The Royals' final record of 76–78 (16½ games behind 93–62 Oakland) apparently did not sit well with Ewing Kauffman.

On October 3, the start of a two-game, season-closing set with the Texas Rangers, the Royals owner notified Lemon that he would not be returning to guide the team in 1973. Lemon had been the center of some controversy during the season, following his temporary benching of Freddie Patek and Amos Otis, and after being quoted as saying he was planning on retiring after the season. Lemon stressed that he had been misquoted on the latter issue. Not misquoted was virtually every layer who came out in support of Lemon following the announcement—including Patek and Otis. Rojas perhaps summed it up best: "It's baseball. You're hired to be fired. Lemon didn't do anything wrong. We didn't play good baseball for him."[22]

Kauffman introduced Lemon's replacement at the same time as he signaled his exit. In an unusual press conference, with Lemon on one side of him and his replacement—Jack McKeon—on the other, Kauffman pronounced, "I want a younger manager, and I did not want to lose McKeon from our organization." McKeon, 10 years the junior of the 52-year-old Lemon, had been piloting the Royals' Double A affiliate in Omaha. Overriding the objections of GM Cedric Tallis, who was also present and a Lemon man, the owner added, "During the next ten years, I expect to win at least five out of ten pennants."[23]

The next day, October 4, the Royals held a farewell ceremony, not to Lemon, but to Municipal Stadium. The Royals' expected midseason move to their new stadium—much like those of the Pittsburgh Pirates and Cincinnati Reds in 1970—had not been met. Now with an Opening Day eye on their new park in six months, the Royals bid Municipal Stadium adieu on a positive note, blanking the Texas Rangers, 4–0. Author of the shutout was Roger Nelson, his team-high sixth. After the final out, Nelson (11–6) ripped the rubber from the mound to keep as a souvenir from the 50-year-old ballpark.

Rojas, who was given the finale off, slipped to .261 on the season. The drop from last season is mitigated when compared to some of the league's best. With a 2-for-3 day, Lou Piniella boosted his average to .312, six points behind batting champ Rod Carew. Piniella's was one of the highest hitting marks in Kansas City baseball history, behind 1914 Kansas City Packer teammates Ted Easterly (.335) and Duke Kenworthy (.317), and the .319 performance of the Athletics' Vic Power in 1955. Piniella's outfield associates, Richie Scheinblum (.300) and Amos Otis (.293), as well as John Mayberry (.298), all finished in the top 10 in hitting. Mayberry, with 25 home runs, knocked in the second-most runs in the circuit with an even 100.

Sparkled with Lights and Shined with Newness

Over the winter months, Rojas returned to Maracaibo to play for the Eagles of Zulia, the team that took him in after his rehab stint in the Florida Instructional League the prior off-season. Rojas made a veteran's impact on one up-and-coming major leaguer while on the South

American playing fields. It would come to light in the early weeks of the ensuing spring conditioning sessions in Florida. "Two years ago there was really some doubt in my mind about my defensive play," said Toby Harrah, second-year player of the Texas Rangers. "Then I go to Venezuela, play alongside Cookie Rojas for a full season down there, set a fielding record for assists and suddenly those doubts were erased." A shortstop, Harrah gave "wholesale credit to his winter league teammate, Rojas, for his improvement. He committed only eight errors all winter for the Zulia team and led the league in defense. And the shortstops in the league include Luis Aparicio and Davey Concepción."[24]

While winter ball was in full swing in the Caribbean basin, Cedric Tallis made another impactful trade for the betterment of the Royals' franchise, December 1. Hard-pressed to top the acquisition of John Mayberry from last December, the Royals' GM, nevertheless, made an artful attempt by sending all-star outfielder Richie Scheinblum and pitcher Roger Nelson to the Cincinnati Reds, for outfielder Hal McRae and pitcher Wayne Simpson, who was trying to reignite his promising career following a devastating rotator cuff injury.

McRae was in Venezuela during this time, chasing flies for the Caracas Lions, and therefore Rojas may have been one the first new teammates to make the acquaintance of the former National Leaguer.

Rojas and McRae were part of a large holdout class Tallis had to deal with in the spring. In fact, Rojas was the last Royal to sign on the dotted line. Comments on the issue by the veteran infielder reflected the leverage ball teams still maintained over their players: "I wasn't satisfied, but what can you do? We weren't very far apart. They just wouldn't give in."[25]

Once in the fold, Rojas, like his teammates and coaches, was conscripted into new playing attire. The transformation over the years in major league baseball from baggy, wool uniforms to closer-fitting, polyester ones, continued its fashionable contraction. In the style of several National League teams, such as Cincinnati and Pittsburgh, the Royals adopted a new V-neck pullover home uniform top with form-fitting elastic waist pants. Contrasting their Royal-blue-trimmed home whites, the team also changed their road greys of last season to Columbia blue-brand visitors' vestments.

Debuting the new color road attire on opening night in Anaheim, April 6, 1973, the Kansas City Royals were bested by Nolan Ryan and the California Angels, 3–2. Left without a baseball team in the nation's capital, following the move of the Washington Senators to Texas the prior season, U.S. President and California native Richard Nixon attended the game. He ceded the traditional first ball toss to Air Force Major José

David Luna, a newly released prisoner of war, who had been chosen by the Angels for the honors. After spending nearly six years in captivity, the Vietnam veteran, who was a resident of Orange County, tossed his inaugural offering to Angels catcher John Stephenson, with the smiling president at his side.

Earlier in the day, the American League debuted something entirely new with an assigned batter to take the hitting place of the pitcher. Ron Blomberg of the New York Yankees became the first "designated hitter" against the Boston Red Sox at Fenway Park. Hitting sixth in the lineup, Ed Kirkpatrick was chosen by manager Jack McKeon as the Royals' first DH. Kirkpatrick, an outfielder by trade, went hitless in three trips, with a walk, against Ryan.

Batting second in the order, Rojas collected two hits off the Angels' fireballer, including a run-scoring single in the eighth inning when the visitors scored their runs. In his first season-opening start, Ryan allowed six safeties, struck out 12, and walked four; both runs were earned.

An offensive outburst by the Royals the next day secured Jack McKeon's first win at the helm. Two doubles and four RBI by Rojas, as part of a 13-hit attack, propelled the road team to a 12–5 victory. Off-season pick-up and a former fireballer himself, Wayne Simpson, went the distance for his first win in a Kansas City uniform. Simpson's damaged arm would not hold up, however, and his overall contribution to the team was negligible. Hal McRae registered his first hit with his new team, a double, which drove in two runs.

Rojas slashed two more doubles and a single in the series' third game as the Royals edged the Angels, 6–5. McRae, Lou Piniella, and Amos Otis all went deep for Kaycee. Rojas had come out whacking to start the season. In the three games, he went 7-for-13, with four doubles and six RBI.

After a travel day, the Royals returned home to inaugurate what one baseball writer termed "baseball's newest play-palace." Less than 24 hours after a snowstorm hit the area, the all-artificial turf Royals Stadium held its first game on April 10. (It was the only artificial surface stadium in the American League.) The largest crowd in Kansas City baseball history—39,464—came out to see it and were glad they did. Braving temperatures in the mid–30s, the big crowd watched as the Royals ran roughshod over the Texas Rangers, 12–1. Left-hander Paul Splittorff scattered five hits, becoming the park's first winning pitcher. The Royals had to borrow the rubber-bladed snowplow from the football stadium next door to clear the field in time for the first pitch. Otherwise, the stadium "sparkled with lights and shined with newness.

The fans voiced their approval of the view, the scoreboard, the hot dogs and especially the hot coffee. In addition, they also went away greatly impressed by the Royals."[26]

Rojas collected his fifth two-base hit of the campaign; he scored twice and drove in one of the dozen runs. He had this to say about his new playing turf, which provided dirt cutouts at each infield bag: "Just a little slick tonight because of the weather, and it's a little fast, but it played OK."[27] The infielder coincidently played his 1,000th game at second base and 1,296th as a major leaguer. John Mayberry, who drove in four runs and scored as many, hit the first Royals Stadium home run, a fifth-inning, wall-clearing clout.

Mayberry and the rest of Royals' swatters would have it a bit easier in their new ballpark compared to the old one, as far as dimensions were concerned. The new stadium was 330 feet down both lines, 385 in the power alleys, and 410 to straightaway center. Municipal Stadium had been 360 feet to the left field foul pole, 338 to right, 390 in left-center, 380 in right-center, and 410 to dead center. Yet the new stadium turned out to be more pitching and defense centric and, with its unconventional turf, built more for extra-base hits.

The Royals also paid tribute to a recently released U.S. captive of the Vietnam War. Lieutenant Commander Joseph C. Plumb threw out Royals Stadium's first ceremonial pitch. Union boss Marvin Miller was an invited guest of Ewing Kauffman. The only down note to the gala evening was that the $750,000 outfield fountain display was not ready for the inaugural.

Rojas hit his first Royals Stadium home run on April 18. A solo shot,

Rojas is all smiles inside the first installation of Monument Park in renovated Yankee Stadium, ca. 1976 or 1977 (courtesy Cookie Rojas).

it came against Catfish Hunter as part of a two-hit, two-runs-scored night at the dish. But Hunter's Oakland A's prevailed, 7–6, lifted by a two-run, ninth-inning home run by Gene Tenace. The next night, the Royals exploded for 16 runs and 19 hits, cakewalking past the same visiting A's squad, 16–8. Rojas scored three of the runs as the Royals notched double-digit runs for the fifth time already. Paul Splittorff won his third game without a setback for the 9–3, first-place Royals.

Nine days later, on April 27, the Royals' Steve Busby, in only his tenth major league start, no-hit the Detroit Tigers at Tiger Stadium. A 23-year-old right-hander, Busby walked six. First baseman Mayberry snatched a line drive in the ninth, off the bat of Rich Reese, to double off pinch-hitter Duke Sims, who had received Busby's final free pass. Bill Freehan grounded out to Freddie Patek for the final out. Rojas had one assist. Busby struck out four.

On May 14, Rojas was thrown out of his first game as a Royal (and first since 1969). He was thumbed out by second base umpire John Rice for arguing a safe call on a pickoff attempt at second base in the fourth inning. Rojas was so sure he tagged out the Angels' Sandy Alomar on a mound throw from pitcher Dick Drago that he took the argument too far and was sent to the early shower. Unfortunately for the Royals, one batter later with two outs, Angels DH Frank Robinson slammed one over the wall with Alomar on second. The California team scored once more in the top of the 10th inning for a 3–2 win.

The next evening, Rojas probably would not have minded an early shower against Nolan Ryan. In only its 20th game, Royals Stadium became the scene of the legendary pitcher's first of a record *seven* no-hitters. In the 3–0 win, Ryan walked three and struck out four times as many, as the Royals managed to pull only one ball all night. Only three Royals were identified as hitting the ball hard: Rojas, out on a liner to second baseman Sandy Alomar, Lou Piniella, retired on a line drive to right field, and Amos Otis, who twice hit drives to the warning track, including for the final out of the game.

Rojas capped off the Royals' most thrilling game of the young season on May 28, Royals Stadium's first walk-off win. Trailing 4–2 in the final inning versus the Boston Red Sox, the home team rallied for three runs, the first pair on a single by pinch-hitter Kurt Bevacqua. With runners on second and third and one out, Rojas followed with a single to left field. "I knew he'd come through," said manager McKeon. "That's the way he is."[28]

The Royals and New York Yankees were the first teams to win 40 games in the American League, both clubs accomplishing the feat with doubleheader sweeps on June 24. Both clubs held slim division leads, while in the AL West, there were remarkably four teams within one-and-a-half-games of first place.

Early the next month, Rojas went on a mini-RBI spree, driving home 10 runs in four games from July 4–7. On July 5, in his best offensive game of the season, he knocked home five runs with a home run and two doubles, leading the Royals to a 12–10 victory over the Minnesota Twins at Metropolitan Stadium. The infielder also stole his 10th base of the year, a career high.

Rojas had been pacing himself lately with respect to pre-game activities. The end result was reflected in his game-time hitting and running, he believed. In addition to his steals, he had accrued 43 RBI, only 16 from his best for one season. "I feel stronger for the game," he offered as an explanation. "I still get to the ballpark at 4:30. I'll go to the outfield, do some running and shag some fly balls. Then I rest until infield practice." He had also developed a further opinion about playing on his home turf. "The stuff is awfully fast," he said. "Balls go by you that you know you [normally] can get."[29]

Rojas collected his fifth three-hit game on July 14 in New York, when he tripled and homered; the eight total bases were a season-high. In the 4–2 Royals win, Rojas started the scoring with his four-base hit into the left field seats at Yankee Stadium. "After that early sounding off," described one reporter, "the 34-year-old native of Cuba with the magic glove singled and scored in the fourth and capped a 2-run burst in the seventh to chase home Kurt Bevacqua."[30]

The all-around good play landed Rojas on the All-Star team again, albeit losing out to batting champ Rod Carew, once more, in the fans' opinion poll. Amos Otis and John Mayberry joined their Kansas City colleague on the select AL squad. As MLB is prone to do, the game was played in baseball's, to borrow a phrase, "newest play-palace" on July 24.

Four-month-old Royals Stadium's largest crowd of 40,849 sat mostly on their hands as the National League defeated their younger rivals for the 10th time in the last 11 meetings, 7–1. Three senior circuit members clubbed home runs: the Reds' Johnny Bench, the Giants' Bobby Bonds, and Willie Davis of the Dodgers. The three home team favorites did provide the partisan throng some cause for cheering. Otis, starting in center, had two singles in a pair of trips to the plate, one of them driving in the lone AL run. He also stole a base before he was abruptly removed by manager Dick Williams for Milwaukee Brewers substitute Dave May. Playing the entire way at first base, Mayberry went one-for-three with a base on balls. Entering the game in the sixth inning, Rojas walked against Tom Seaver in his only time at bat. Rojas began the only twin killing in the contest, 4–6–3, doubling up speedy

Joe Morgan on a grounder, with Pete Rose forced out at second. The lack of competition seemed to have influenced participant involvement. The teams combined to use 54 players, a record, with NL manager Sparky Anderson utilizing 28. Both clubs also used seven pitchers, tied for most employed by any league in the four-decade-long annual gathering (AL, 1954, 1969, 1970; NL, 1949, 1967).

The Royals came out of the break sizzling hot, capturing 13 out of 17 games, to move into first place with a record of 68–50, two games better than the 65–51 Oakland A's at the close of play on August 11. Rojas had *three* more three-hit games in the span, as the team led by the main offensive contributions of Otis and Mayberry and bolstered on the mound by Splittorff and rookie Steve Busby, made everyone believers in Jack McKeon's team.

Other observers also pointed to the Royals' stellar, up-the-middle duo as an integral part of the club's success. "Cookie Rojas and Freddie Patek," read one print media report, "lead the American League in double plays and are a prime reason the Royals are on top in the American League West Division. Rojas may be the best in his position in the majors, everything considered. He is brilliant defensively despite his age, and he is a clutch hitter. More than that, however, he is a steadying influence."[31]

Surprising no one with the new ballpark and elevated play, the Royals went over the million mark in attendance for the first time since the formation of the franchise in 1969. (The Kansas City A's twice topped the seven-figure audience benchmark in 1955 and 1956.) The 18,047 local diehards that came out on August 14 helped turn the turnstile trick for the club. They were not disappointed in the home warriors, who defeated the Cleveland Indians, 8–5. The keystone duo of Rojas and Patek each had two hits. Rojas drove in a pair of runs, and Patek sent home one runner. Lou Piniella homered and dented the plate three times. Busby evened his record with his 11th win. The Royals maintained a tenuous half-game lead over Oakland.

Over the next two weeks, though, the Royals dropped out of first place and at the end of August faced a 5½-game deficit to the same Northern California team. McKeon's men got no closer than 3½ games over the final month. The Kaycee club reached that point on September 2, defeating the first-place A's, 6–5, at Royals Stadium. A big Sunday crowd of 35,466 witnessed the hard-fought win and saw Cookie Rojas twice clear the fences in a game for the second and last time in his career. Rojas victimized Vida Blue and Horacio Piña, leading off the fourth and fifth innings, respectively. Busby, who would be voted AL Rookie Pitcher of the Year by *The Sporting News*, gained his 14th victory.

At the finish, the Royals, at 88–74, were bested by six games by the 94-win A's. The shortfall may have reflected most the Kansas City pitching staff, which gave up almost a full run more in 1973 (4.19 ERA) than in 1972 (3.24). It was a point of concern to many, but not all, involved with the franchise. "People do not stop and think how much conditions changed when we moved from Municipal Stadium to our new ballpark," said Paul Splittorff, who became the Royals' first 20-game winner on September 26. "In Royals Stadium, the fences are shorter, the lighting is better, and you have artificial turf. The old ballpark was a pitcher's ballpark, the new park is a hitter's park. People should remember we're playing a different game now in our new stadium than in our old one."[32]

That different game, however, would be centered around speed, extra-base hits, and defense going forward.

Meanwhile, Rojas could be excused for not knowing whether he was coming or going, as he left the team in a harried state a week before the season ended to fly to Miami to be with his wife, who was about to undergo abdominal surgery. In 137 games—all at second base—and two other pinch-hitting appearances, Rojas hit .276. He set career-highs in doubles (29), RBI (69) and stolen bases with 18, and he was caught only four times—the best stolen base percentage in the circuit (81.2). His 77 runs were one fewer than his best mark in 1965. Only John Mayberry, with 13, had more game-winning hits than Rojas' 12. The Royals turned the most double plays in all of baseball with 192, of which 114, a personal best for any season, involved their Cuban second baseman.

The good numbers were tempered by the weight of his wife's pending operation. "My family must come first," Rojas said, explaining his absence. "Everything else is of no consideration. They don't know if the tumor is malignant and they won't know, they say, until they operate." So serious was the personal matter that Rojas contemplated retirement, expressing feelings of guilt sometimes common with many absent, professional ballplaying fathers. "I'm tired of being away from them so much. Nothing else seems important to me anymore next to them. My wife is a young woman, my kids are still young. I want to be together when they grow up. I can't think of anything they could say or do that would make it worthwhile enough to play one more year."[33]

The scare passed, and with no spoiler alert needed, Rojas and his wife were indeed together when their children grew up.

With one set of faithful priorities assured, Rojas set in motion another personal "pledge"—one of allegiance to the country that had taken in him and his family years earlier. In late October, Octavio Victor Rojas became a U.S. citizen in a naturalization ceremony in the U.S. District Court in Kansas City. Rojas said that until this year, his baseball travels had prevented him from living in one state for six consecutive months, as required by U.S. citizenship laws.

"Kansas City was the best U.S. city I ever lived in," assessed Candida Rojas. "We stayed in Stanley, Kansas, then a house on Melrose Drive in Overland Park."

All-Star Politics

Rojas was quickly back in the baseball saddle, accepting a managerial post in the Venezuelan Winter League with recent favorite Zulia. League results were not published that winter by *The Sporting News* as the periodical stepped away from its previous invaluable winter league coverage of the prior decades.

Getting Rojas into the Royals' fold for 1974 was another story. Unable to agree on salary figures, Rojas applied to be part of baseball's newest form of binding resolution between teams and players called "arbitration." An independent third party would have the final say in what an appealing player would make. As part of players' union head Marvin Miller's desire to make owners reveal more pages of their accounting books, current and asked-for salaries were disclosed for all involved parties. The eligible player made his demand, countered by another figure from the team. Rojas lost his case, but also came out ahead. The 12-year big leaguer asked for a big raise from $40,000 to $72,500. The Royals countered with $60,000 and "won." Five of the repeat World Series champion Oakland A's members won their arbitration cases, none bigger than Reggie Jackson. The polarizing outfielder's demand of a $135,000 salary, from $75,000 in 1973, was granted. Only 13 of the first-year class of 29 filing players won their cases—but all went to spring camp with substantial raises.

"They want a leader out on the field," responded Rojas with a touch of bitterness. "Leadership, however, is apparently a summertime commodity and perishable, expiring sometime around contract time. They didn't want to talk a lot about that."[34]

Always the professional, Rojas put the contract issue behind him and was one of the first Royals position players to arrive in Fort Myers. He was actually taking cuts in the batting cage before the end of February. So was a Kansas City hopeful who had "graduated" from the Kansas City Royals Baseball Academy, which opened in Sarasota, Florida, in July 1970.

The academy was promoted as an alternative for cultivating baseball talent apart from the minor leagues and teaching baseball fundamentals tailored to their club strengths. The Royals were the only major league team to have such a facility. One can speculate that when Rojas first heard about it, he was taken back to halcyon days in Havana when Cuban Sugar Kings owner Bobby Maduro instituted and ran a similar talent-seeking institution from his Gran Stadium complex.

"Frank White apparently will be the first cadet from the Royals' trailblazing academy to make it with the major league club for a full season in the majors," alerted one spring dispatch. A 23-year-old middle infielder, White was brought up the prior June to spell a banged-up Freddie Patek and appeared in 51 games. He filled in at second base for Rojas over the last week of the season as well. White viewed a similar role for himself in 1974. "If I could play four times a week, I'd like to stay," he said. "It's hot in Kansas City, so Cookie or Fred could use a rest once in a while. I could pinch hit. I could go in defensively if they hit for Fred or Cookie."[35]

White (who played winter ball for Zulia and was managed by Rojas) had to wait until the day after the Royals commenced the season to see action. The Kansas City Royals bid welcome to the new campaign on April 5, 1974, with their 20-game winner from last year, Paul Splittorff, on the mound at Royals Stadium. On a chilly evening, Splittorff battled Minnesota Twins pitcher Bert Blyleven to a stalemate after nine innings, each hurler reached for four runs, three earned. In the 11th inning, the road club scored twice off Royals reliever Lindy McDaniel to take home a 6–4 decision. McDaniel had been obtained by the Royals, from the New York Yankees, in December, for former Rookie of the Year Lou Piniella.

The following afternoon, the Royals battered six Twins pitchers for 23 runs on 16 hits. Coming into the blowout game in the fifth inning to replace Rojas, Frank White cracked his first big league home run. John Mayberry drove in five runs and scored four, and second-year Royal Hal McRae homered and knocked home four runs. A not-so-sharp Steve Busby benefited from the scoring output. The Sunday weekend finale was rained out.

Rojas hit in his first six games (9-for-24, .375). The Royals split the half-dozen assignments. On the 20th of April, Rojas displayed his offensive and defensive talents to assist the Royals to a 7–4 road victory over the Chicago White Sox. The second sacker crunched a four-bagger into the left field bleachers of Comiskey Park with two men on base, the most important of his two hits on the day. Knuckleballer Wilbur Wood was the victimized pitcher. "Before Rojas unloaded his first home run of the season he combined with Fred Patek for a dazzling double play in the second inning," wrote *Kansas City Star* staffer Sid Bordman.

"Eddie Leon sent a hot shot toward center field. Breaking to his right, Rojas backhanded the ball and flipped it from his glove to Patek. The little shortstop did the rest, completing Kansas City's first of three twin killings."[36]

"Defense is the beauty part of the game," remarked Rojas. "It's more important than hitting. I think hitting is overrated. When I get out there, I want to play the game right, make all the plays."[37]

A week hence at Royals Stadium, Rojas hit for three-quarters of the cycle. The six total bases (on three hits) came off Juan Marichal, who was making his second start of the season for the Boston Red Sox. The 36-year-old former master had been sold by the San Francisco Giants to the American League club in the off-season. The once-magnificent hurler was knocked around by Rojas and his teammates, surrendering nine hits and seven earned runs in the 10–3 setback.

From the opening of the campaign, Jack McKeon's crew had trouble getting their offense and pitching in sync. In May, as the team treaded water, struggling to stay above .500, Rojas came through with the bat in two big ways, a couple of weeks apart. In the first game of a twi-night doubleheader at the Oakland-Alameda County Coliseum on May 14, Rojas tagged Catfish Hunter for a sixth-inning, two-run, tie-breaking home run in the Royals' 4–2 victory over the two-time world champion A's. Paul Splittorff won his fourth game against three defeats.

When the team returned home from California, Rojas' glove work continued to receive attention in the press. "In Oakland Rojas saved the Royals' lone victory over the Athletics by making an incredible diving catch of a line smash by Deron Johnson with two runners on base," described one columnist. "Had the play come in a World Series or All-Star game it would have been equated with some of Brooks Robinson's heroics in the 1970 Series." Rojas categorized the defensive gem as follows: "Johnson is a pull hitter so I played him toward the middle. I broke with the ball, took two steps and dove. I had to be moving when the ball was hit or there is no way you could make the play."[38]

Back home, versus the Baltimore Orioles on May 28, Rojas delivered his only walk-off home run. The payoff blow came in the 11th inning of a 5–5 game, delivered against Orioles reliever Bob Reynolds. With one out and runners at first and third, Orioles manager Earl Weaver ordered Freddie Patek walked intentionally. "I was surprised they walked Patek to load the bases to get to me," Rojas said of the move.[39] The strategy-spoiling blast, landing in the left field seats, was the infielder's third (and final) career grand slam and stretched a Royals' winning streak to five games.

In June, Rojas collected his 1,400th hit. It came on the 11th of the month, a third-inning single at Royals Stadium, against the Brewers' Clyde Wright. The hit helped set up the only Royals run of the game as the home team's Al Fitzmorris outdueled Wright, 1–0.

In the Royals' visit to Milwaukee a week later, pitching history repeated itself. At County Stadium on June 19, second-year hurler Steve Busby threw his second no-hitter. In defeating the Brewers, 2–0, the hard-throwing right-hander faced 28 batters, one over the minimum (a second-inning walk to George Scott). A single by rookie George Brett accounted for the Royals' first run, and the second scored on an error. Clyde Wright suffered his second hard-luck loss in eight days. The 24-year-old Busby, who became the 25th man in baseball history with two no-hitters on his pitching ledger, was backed by a tight defense. "Cookie Rojas, Al Cowens, Fred Patek, George Brett all saved the no-hitter at one time or another," wrote one press box on-looker, "but it was Rojas, the ageless second baseman, who took away the ball that most looked like a hit."[40]

Another penned: "[Bob] Hansen's hard ground ball appeared headed to right field with two out in the eighth, but Rojas, after about three quick steps to his left, cut it off with a diving stab. The veteran second baseman sprang to his feet and threw out Hansen in plenty of time."[41] Fittingly, Rojas secured the final out on a pop-up. Busby received a standing ovation from the approximately 9,000 in attendance.

On the month's final day, Rojas was ticketed with the penultimate of his nine ejections as a player. In front of the home fans, Rojas clashed with second base umpire Armando Rodríguez over a tag play involving Bert Campaneris of the Oakland A's. Trying to stretch a single, Campaneris was tagged by Rojas at second, but the ball trickled free. "Rojas unloaded verbally on Rodríguez contending he held the ball long enough for Campaneris to be called out," explained a game account. The Cuban-born Rodríguez, who had made history at the start of the season as the major leagues' first Hispanic umpire, did not see it that way and ruled the speedy Campaneris safe. "McKeon joined in. 'I can't find out what's going on,' McKeon said, 'because they're all talking in Spanish.... Campy, Rojas, Rodríguez, all of them. I understood one thing—Rojas is out of the game for throwing his glove.'"[42]

Catcher Buck Martínez delivered a pinch-hit, tie-breaking single in the bottom of the ninth as the Royals rallied for a pair of runs for an 8–7 win, delighting a Sunday crowd of over 32,000. The Royals moved a game over break-even (37–36) and inched closer to first place, 2½ games behind the A's.

In the nationally televised Monday night game the next evening, Rojas put on a hitting display for the baseball-loving followers of the country. He drove in four runs with a single and a fence-clearing blast to lead the Royals over the Chicago White Sox, 9–0, at Comiskey Park. He added two other hits to raise his average to .305. Freddie Patek and Hal McRae also went deep in the blowout.

Rojas' next four-bagger came 12 days later, on July 13. Facing the Detroit Tigers at Royals Stadium, he lined a pitch toward the left field corner. Marvin Lane failed to cut the ball off, and it scooted back along the curve in the wall away from him. Rojas, with runner Kurt Bevacqua in front of him, raced around the bases for the second inside-the-park home run of his career and the third hit at Royals Stadium to date. It was the only scoring in the game for the Royals, who fell, 8–2.

In a scenario repeated over the past three Julys, Rojas finished behind Rod Carew in the spectator balloting for the All-Star Game. Carew, in his usual top spot for American League second baseman, raked in close to double the number of ballots cast for runner-up Rojas (2,402,968 to 1,269,585). Orioles second sacker Bobby Grich garnered 485,901 votes and was selected along with Rojas to back up Carew. Reggie Jackson received the most votes in either league with 3,497,358. The star-filled game was played at Three Rivers Stadium, July 23; the National League won rather easily, 7–2.

Carew afterward raised some objections to the way losing AL manager Dick Williams utilized his players. He insisted that he would not want to play in any more All-Star Games because Williams, who had skippered the Oakland A's to repeat World Series championships (1972–1973) and was now guiding the California Angels, removed him after 2½ innings. Williams' given reason was that the Twins' star had bruised himself during a steal of second base. The batting champion contested this and accused Williams of playing favorites. "It's all politics," Carew said. "Why did he put in Bobby Grich? Cookie Rojas was the second leading vote getter to me at second base, and he never got in the game. I was very disappointed. I didn't say anything to Williams. I just went up there, got a hit, stole a base and scored a run."[43]

Grich, the third-inning substitute, played the remainder of the game, gaining three at-bats to Carew's one. Jackson, teammate Bert Campaneris, and catcher Thurman Munson, along with National League write-in candidate Steve Garvey, were the select participants to play all nine innings.

Going into the break, Williams' former club had opened a five game lead on the second-place Chicago White Sox, while Kansas City had slipped into third, two games further back.

In early August, the Royals signed Orlando Cepeda, who was toiling in the Mexican League. The team's DH, Hal McRae, moved into left field so Cepeda could assume the strictly hitting duties. In his last hurrah as a major leaguer, Cepeda produced meagerly, slugging under .300, with one home run and 18 RBI in 33 games. The former National League slugger never forgot Rojas, however. He expressed in a 21st-century interview his feelings for his major league contemporary: "I have always considered my friendship with Cookie as a great honor. My last team was Kansas City in 1974.... Cookie was a big star on that team and there he treated me like few others in my career. That's something I'll never forget. I will always thank him for the way he has treated me ... my admiration for him is huge."[44]

During the same month of the Cepeda signing, the Royals, on the strength of Steve Busby's pitching and contributions from Al Fitzmorris (13–6) and Paul Splittorff (13–19), stayed in contention, regaining second place from the White Sox. But a terrible slide beginning August 26, in which McKeon's gang lost 19 out of 22 games, evaporated any hopes of challenging the A's for predominance in the division.

For the season, McRae was by far the team's best hitter, posting an .850 OPS with an accompanying .310 average. Busby became the second Royals hurler to enter pitching's charmed circle, September 17. He defeated the Oakland A's and Catfish Hunter, 2–1, at Royals Stadium. Both moundsmen went the distance. Allowing only three hits with an unearned run, Busby (22–14) won twice more before the close of the campaign.

But when all was said and done, the Royals had fallen under .500 (77–85) into fifth place, 13 games out of first, which was once more owned by the dynastic Oakland A's. Rojas played in 18 of 28 games in September for the Royals as McKeon rested both Rojas and Freddie Patek, using Frank White. The artisan second baseman still managed to play in 144 games, his most as a Royal. His final average was .271 with a reduced OPS of .648.

With the leather, Rojas led all peers in the league in fielding percentage (.987) for the third time in his career.

Seven

Playoff Disappointment and Bowing Out

Two days before the end of the 1974 season, the Royals fired first base and hitting coach Charlie Lau, much to the dismay of just about everyone on the Royals squad. Manager Jack McKeon was said to be behind the dismissal. The uproar was so great among the players that Lau was eventually rehired to work as a roving minor league hitting instructor within the Royals' organization.

"I loved Charlie Lau," said Tab Rojas. "Lau helped make George Brett the hitter he became. And Lau helped me when I was in high school. Right there on the field at Royals Stadium, hitting off a tee. He was a 'big' tee instructor. He worked everything off the tee."[1]

The loss of Lau notwithstanding, the Royal mentioned by Tab Rojas, under Lau's previous tutelage, would have a breakout season in 1975 and establish himself as the Royals' third baseman of the future. George Brett had not exactly torn the cover off the ball in his rookie campaign in 1974, hitting .282 with underachieving on-base (.313) and slugging (.363) figures. But as a sophomore, he hit .308, slugged .456, and led the league in hits (195) and triples (13), as well as accumulating the most at-bats with 634.

John Mayberry, who had slumped the previous campaign due to injuries, bounced back to lead the circuit in RBI again (119). The offensive infusion from these two players, plus another solid season by Hal McRae, along with improved pitching, helped the Royals achieve their first 90-win season.

Hoping to add more offensive punch, the six-year-old franchise signed former home run king Harmon Killebrew on January 24, 1975, eight days after his release by the Minnesota Twins. The "Killer" was signed to be a DH, which transitioned McRae to left field. The genial slugger, entering his age 39 season, would not be the run-producing stimulus that had been hoped for, knocking only 14 balls out of the park in 106 games and failing to hit his weight.

Brett, outfielders Jim Wohlford and Tony Solaita, and Cookie Rojas were spotted at the Royals' camp in Ft. Meyers, engaging in workouts several days ahead of the official full squad report date of February 28.

In early spring, shortly after his 36th birthday had come and gone, Rojas discussed his future. "I know my legs are not as good as they used to be," he admitted, "but I'm not hobbling yet. I feel I can play at least two more seasons." After that, Rojas said, "I tried managing in the winter leagues. And that's what I'd like to do, stay in baseball and manage." He also mentioned the comfort level he had attained with his double play partner of several seasons. "Freddie and I have been playing together for four years. We have gotten to know what each of us is going to do in any given situation. Freddie has such great range and is very quick, he's very easy to play with." As far as predictions for the upcoming season: "With the material we have, we should be in the race."[2]

The Royals engaged the new crusade on April 7 in Anaheim, California. Steve Busby faced the Angels' Nolan Ryan. The expected pitchers' duel developed. Ryan surrendered only three hits and two runs, while striking out a dozen. One of the hits was an RBI-single by Rojas which plated George Brett, who had singled and stolen a base. The other hit was a sixth-inning long ball by John Mayberry. Busby took a 2–1 lead into the bottom of the ninth inning but could not close out the win. After allowing a leadoff hit, he was replaced. Two Royals relievers could not prevent the Angels from rallying for two runs, resulting in a 3–2, opening night setback.

In their second game, McRae and Amos Otis homered to lead the visitors to a 7–6 win. After splitting the two-game opening set with the Angels, the Royals began their home campaign on April 11. Al Fitzmorris faced down the Minnesota Twins, 8–3, in a complete-game victory. Rojas had three hits, including a double; he scored twice and knocked in as many. Rojas hit in 18 out of his first 20 games; the Royals won 13 out of 25 games in the span.

The Royals, as a base-stealing club, had been led in tandem, with few exceptions, by their shortstop and center fielder. In Freddie Patek's initial season in 1971, he swiped 49 bases, three fewer than team leader Otis. Since then, the diminutive shortstop had headed the club in steals every year. The flashy pair had earned their own nickname, as evidenced in a write-up following a hard-earned, 13-inning, 11–10 win versus the Angels, at Royals Stadium, on May 1:

Cookie Rojas doubled in the tying run and scored on Buck Martinez's single for the difference in this wild shootout but it was the "Golddust Twins" who had a lot to do with keeping the Royals in the battle.

That would be Amos Otis and Fred Patek. Otis stole four bases and Patek two. Patek got three hits and Otis two, and each scored twice.[3]

Patek and Rojas, this time, received additional press notice, involving their patented "flip play," in a game against the New York Yankees on May 21 at Shea Stadium. "Demonstrating a kind of creativity that's rarely seen," wrote *Newsday*'s Steve Jacobson, "[Rojas] went far to his right to backhand a grounder hit by Chris Chambliss. Rojas had no chance to plant himself and throw out Chambliss, so he flipped the ball with his glove to shortstop Fred Patek, who did throw Chambliss out. 'We've done that five or six times,' Patek said. 'Once we did it in Milwaukee and they did it to us in the same game. Other than that, I've never seen it done.'"[4] The game, eventually won in the 10th inning by the Royals on a three-run home run by catcher Fran Healy, was scoreless at the moment of the razzle-dazzle exhibition.

In the media capital of the world, Rojas elicited a humanized back-story reminder from Jacobson that only a limited number of professional ballplayers could relate to.

> If Rojas is named to his sixth all-star game this season, it will be his second as an American citizen. "I'm an American citizen and I'm proud of it," Rojas said. "But I'm still a Cuban at heart. It's painful when you have to leave your country. I left the land which gave birth to me. I left the palm trees, the coconuts, the rum, the women, and the freedom. The shame is that we could be back playing in our country. One of the first expansion cities would have had to be Havana."
>
> He said the life he remembered as the son of a middle class worker did not exist anymore. "They were a great people in Cuba," Rojas said. "A happy people. There was not a spot in the whole island that was not happy."
>
> There have been reports from journalists who have visited Cuba saying that some of Cuban life has improved under Castro. "I don't have to agree," Rojas said. "That's politics. My politics is sports."[5]

When the Yankees visited Kansas City the following week, the Cuban exile had a good day in the opener of a three-game set on May 26, up to a point. Rojas' second hit of the contest was obtained in the bottom of the ninth inning, and he came around to score the game-tying run. In the top of the 10th, Rojas took a throw from outfielder Hal McRae and applied the tag to the Yankees' Craig Nettles, trying to turn a single into two bases. Nettles' knee smacked against Rojas' head, knocking the infielder unconscious. Rojas held on to the ball to register the out. He had to be taken off the field on a stretcher after regaining consciousness.

Seven—Playoff Disappointment and Bowing Out 145

Rojas was sidelined for nine days. Less than a week following his return, he smacked his first home run of the year. It came on June 11, with two men on base, versus the visiting Cleveland Indians. Killebrew also joined Rojas in circling the bases, his for the eighth time. The Royals, behind rookie right-hander Dennis Leonard, cruised to a 7–1 win. Indians manager Frank Robinson was ejected for arguing a check swing ruling by first base umpire Ron Luciano. It was the second of three expulsions on the year for Robinson, who became the first Black manager in the major leagues on Opening Day.

As the month of June closed, both the Oakland A's and Royals had played 75 games; seven games separated the respective first- and second-place teams with more than half the season to play.

In the early days of July, with All-Star Game balloting rushing toward counted conclusion for the July 15 scheduled contest, Rojas made an unusual plea to Alvin Dark, manager of the junior circuit by virtue of his World Series victory over the Los Angeles Dodgers the past October. As in past years, Rojas methodically trailed batting wizard Rod Carew as runner-up in the second baseman balloting. He asked publicly for Dark not to choose him for the squad, feeling that Jorge Orta of the Chicago White Sox, for one, was having a superior season and deserved selection over himself.

"I'd rather just take the three days off and spend it here with my family," Rojas asserted. Even though the managers were different, apparently Rojas had not forgotten about his "exclusion" from last year's Mid–Summer Classic. "I have nothing against any ballplayer, but Carew played three innings and Grich played the rest of the way. It was embarrassing to me. I had my wife, kids and father there and didn't get into the game. I personally think every player selected should get into the game as a pinch hitter, pinch runner, something."[6]

Rojas received his wish, as Dark chose Orta (who *was* having a better season than Rojas) as the second base substitute over Grich and Sandy Alomar, who received the third-most votes, behind Carew and Rojas. Perhaps trying to make amends for last time, Carew was permitted to play the entire way at second for the AL All-Stars, as did third baseman Craig Nettles. The Americans continued their losing ways in recent head-to-head competitions, falling to the older circuit, 6–3, at the former National League venue of County Stadium in Milwaukee.

Nine days after the starry encounter, on July 24, the Royals, still in second place with a record of 50–46, fired Jack McKeon and replaced him with Whitey Herzog, who was working as third base coach of the California Angels. Apparently, McKeon had problems communicating with his players. "There was really no rapport between the team and

Jack or between Jack and the team," said Royals general manager Joe Burke, the orchestrator of the change. At his introductory news conference, one of the first things Herzog said he would do was bring back Charlie Lau. "Lau's return is certain to be popular with the players," read one print analysis. "They vigorously denounced his dismissal last year."[7] Lau was in Waterloo, Iowa, with the Royals' Double A club. The other coaches, Harry Dunlap, Galen Cisco, and Steve Boros, would remain with the team through the end of the campaign, Herzog indicated.

"Whitey was a laid-back manager," remembered Rojas. "He always strolled to the mound, never seemed to be in a hurry. Jack McKeon, he was tobacco man. Loved to puff on those cigars. Used to smoke them in the tunnel to the dugout."

On August 7, Rojas accrued a three-hit game against Minnesota, as the Royals lashed out 13 hits in a 10–3 paddling of the Twins at Royals Stadium. With the safety trifecta, Rojas raised his average to .292. Immediately after that, Rojas inexplicably fell into a 0-for-43 batting drought. He broke the horribly wretched streak with a fourth inning, two-run double off Cleveland's Fritz Peterson on August 22 at Royals Stadium.

In September, Rojas started only seven games as Frank White appeared more and more ready to take over the keystone bag from the veteran.

Under Herzog, the Royals went 41–25. They trimmed the deficit behind Oakland from 11 at the time of the managerial change seven. At 91–71, it was the best Royals finish yet. The Texas Rangers finished a distant third, 19 games behind the division champions. Steve Busby had another excellent season, going 18–12, with a career-best ERA of 3.08. Al Fitzmorris won 16 games, three more than last season, and rookie Dennis Leonard gained an impressive 15 victories, with seven setbacks, in 30 starts. Marty Pattin added 10 more to the win column and Paul Splittorff nine. It was the second down season in a row for the left-hander, following his 20-win campaign in 1973.

10/5 Man

The 1975–1976 off-season was one of reassessment for the veteran second baseman. Rojas himself was not blind to the writing on the wall. He knew White had to play. But he also felt he could still contribute to the team as a backup infielder. At the end of the 1974 season, he had made clear that he wanted to finish his career in Kansas City.

A couple of weeks after the conclusion of the exciting and dramatic

World Series between the Cincinnati Reds and Boston Red Sox, the Royals released 39-year-old Harmon Killebrew, ending his Hall of Fame career. In December, the team cut ties with 37-year-old Vada Pinson, former star outfielder of the Reds, who had been obtained by the Royals in a trade prior to the 1974 season.

The same month, at the annual baseball winter meetings, held in Hollywood, Florida, Rojas exercised his 10/5 status and refused a trade that would have sent him to the Pirates. The Royals were prepared to send Amos Otis and Rojas to Pittsburgh for Al Oliver. A 10-year veteran who had five years or more of service with one team had the right to approve all trades, as part of the collective bargaining that had been negotiated between owners and players. Sometimes the trades you don't make are the best ones, goes the old baseball saying. Oliver, a future batting champion, hit .323 with an .839 OPS for the Pirates in 1976.

The nixed deal also helped solidify Otis, a speedy defender and offensive mainstay, as one of the most appreciated faces of the Royals' early years. There were also extenuating circumstances causing Rojas to decline. Apart from not wanting to uproot his family again, he was branching out into the sports shoe business and needed his name to remain relevant in the Kansas City area. His store, named Cookie Rojas' Royal Pair, with the promo tag line of "Footwear for Active People," opened in June at the Indian Hills Shopping Center. Rojas also opened a restaurant in the area.

Luis Rodríguez-Mayoral, a most accomplished Latin American baseball writer and historian, had the opportunity to visit the eating establishment. "Covering the 1985 World Series in Kansas City, I bumped into Victor Pellót [Power]," wrote Rodríguez-Mayoral, who for many years was the Spanish language radio voice of the Texas Rangers. "Given his friendship with Victor, one night we were invited to dinner at Cookie's restaurant on the outskirts of Kansas City and we spent several hours chatting about this and that, but mostly reminiscing about his experiences in baseball. During that visit I immediately realized what an intelligent and forthright person Cookie was. He was poised and reflected a great self-confidence. Also, it comes to my mind that his wife was a very nice lady! They treated us like royalty."[8]

Though manager Whitey Herzog had already named Frank White as the Royals' new second baseman, he played White at shortstop in half of the Royals' spring training games, while penciling in Rojas and Dave Nelson at White's supposedly inherited position the other half of the time. (Nelson had been acquired in a trade with Texas in November.) "The job is his," said Herzog, referring to White and second base. "I told him not to let this bother him."[9]

In early April, Random House came out with a baseball book called *Unsung Heroes of the Major Leagues*, comprised of profiles of 10 big leaguers. Three Hispanics, all Cubans, were featured among the group: Joe Rudi, Doug Rader, Phil Niekro, Thurman Munson, Cookie Rojas, Billy Williams, Mike Cuéllar, Bill Melton, Ron Fairly and Tony Pérez. "Each man has made major contributions to the game of baseball—and each has failed to receive the kind of attention his fine play deserves," read part of the book's Introduction by author Art Berke.

The same month, All-Star ballots were previewed. The Royals had six players on the voting register: Mayberry, Patek, Brett, Healy, McRae, and Otis.

Demolition began on Municipal Stadium on the morning of the Royals' night home opener, April 13, 1976—the eighth season inaugural for the Royals in the 22nd season of big league baseball in the City of Fountains. The Royals downed the California Angels, 7–4. The more than 25,000 in attendance received their first look at the new double play combination of Patek and White. The shortstop had two hits and scored twice, while the second baseman went hitless. With help from two other pitchers, Al Fitzmorris picked up the first win of the year. In the clubhouse, manager Herzog proclaimed that his team had 95 more to go, speculating that it would take 96 victories to capture the division.

Four days earlier, the Royals had played their initial game and were blanked, 4–0, by the White Sox's Wilbur Wood in Chicago. Both Patek and White booted balls as the visitors committed four errors. In the top of the eighth, Rojas pinch-hit for White without result. The remaining games of the set were postponed due to cold weather.

On Saturday, April 24, the Royals played the Yankees in the NBC Game of the Week at newly renovated Yankee Stadium. In an exciting game, especially for the home team's rooters, Chris Chambliss singled home the winning run in the bottom of the 11th inning to give the Yankees a 9–8 victory. Rojas did not participate in the game. It would be one of two walk-off hits the Yankees first baseman produced against the Royals—the other coming in October.

Through April and May, and for the remainder of the season, Herzog found a few starting assignments for Rojas, but mostly the veteran was relegated to part-time offensive and defensive duties. Rojas also received several opportunities at DH. "You know I wondered how he would take it sitting on the bench this year," Herzog said in late May. "But you know Cookie hasn't caused one problem. He just minds his business and doesn't say anything. When I need him to pinch hit, he's ready. He's always ready to do anything I want him to do."[10]

Case in point—in the second game of a doubleheader on May 26 in Arlington, Texas, Herzog used up John Mayberry and back-up Tony Solaita in a close game versus the Rangers, and had to rely on Rojas to finish up the last two innings at first base. Rojas recorded one putout as the Rangers came out on top, 5–4, in 10 innings. The contest was suspended due to curfew after nine innings and completed the next day.

Perhaps stirring up memories of his multi-positional, Philadelphia days, Rojas started at third base on June 18 for George Brett. The adaptable player keyed a 5–3 road win over the Cleveland Indians, notching a single, double, and sacrifice fly to drive in three runs. Dennis Leonard pitched the distance for his seventh win. At this stage of the campaign, Herzog guided a first-place club that had built a five-game lead over their nearest chasers, the Texas Rangers.

Games like this for Rojas probably did not make it easier for Frank White to receive the fan acceptance he desired. The transition to full-time player had not been a totally smooth one for him. Even though White, in his youth, had grown up near Municipal Stadium, the hometown crowd readily dismissed the connection with little hesitation. "Early in the season, there was a lot more pressure on Frank," his manager conveyed. "The fans were on him because he was playing instead of Cookie. One series they were booing him and throwing coins at him."[11]

When Rojas pinch-hit at home, he typically received loud cheers. For his part, in the awkward situation, the young infielder graciously acknowledged his elder. "Cookie's a great guy," said White, whose average in late July was around .200. "People are used to seeing him play the last six years. They've grown to like him. It's like having something really good in your life. It's hard to let go."[12]

During White's struggles at the plate, the Royals lost the pitching services of Steve Busby. The team's most intimidating and winningest pitcher the past three years, Busby was lost after making only 13 starts and compiling a 3–3 mark. A rotator cuff injury, which inevitably caused a premature end to his career, had struck the hard-throwing hurler. Picking up the slack for Busby, sophomore slinger Dennis Leonard won 17 games and the steady Al Fitzmorris another 15. Former reliever Doug Bird, pressed into starting duties this year, was the next-winningest pitcher on the club with 12, while Paul Splittorff added 11. Fifth starter Marty Pattin and fireman Mark Littell each brought home eight wins.

The frontline pitching totals provided the bulk of the Royals' 90 total victories. It was not the 96 Herzog had predicted that were necessary to win the division, but it turned out to be sufficient for the Royals to capture their first Western Division title.

Following an 8–3 win over the Boston Red Sox on August 28, the

78–50 Kansas City Royals were riding high atop the division, nine games better than the Oakland A's. The front-runners won only 12 more times—but it was enough to hold off the A's over the last week of the season to win the race by 2½ lengths.

In a crucial three-game series at the Oakland Coliseum from September 27–29, Herzog opted to start Rojas at his familiar keystone spot in all three games, over his younger heir.

A key victory was provided by Larry Gura on Wednesday, September 29. Gura, a left-hander obtained in a mid–May trade with the Yankees for catcher Fran Healy, handcuffed the A's on four hits. The 4–0 whitewash came after four straight losses (the last two to the A's) and guaranteed no worse than a tie for the division with three games left. Rojas knocked in the first run of the game with a two-out, RBI bunt single that caught A's third baseman Sal Bando completely by surprise. When the count ran 2–0, Rojas noticed that Bando moved back a few steps, and he took advantage and laid one down. All agreed in the following day's newspaper accounts, in particular the manager, that the heads-up play gave the Royals the spark they needed. Amos Otis later homered and drove in two runs, and Brett knocked home the fourth run on a ground out. Rojas played with six stitches in the inside of his mouth, the result of an on-field brawl between the teams the prior night.

Rojas surprised the author when he placed the bunt RBI-hit among his two biggest thrills on the baseball diamond as a player. "That home run in the [1972] All-Star Game in Atlanta was huge because it put us ahead and I thought it was going to hold up," said Rojas. "My wife and parents were there.... And the bunt that got us going in Oakland that helped bring the first championship of any kind to Kansas City, that's why it was so significant to me."

The Royals returned to home base after the game, arriving just ahead of the first light of day. An enterprising reporter was there to greet the plane, and found he was not alone. He wrote about the early morning encounter:

> For 17 years Mrs. Candy Rojas has been meeting her husband, Cookie Rojas, at airports at the end of team trips. At 5:31 o'clock this morning at Kansas City International Airport it was different. She greeted the second baseman as both husband and star of last night's 4–0 victory in Oakland.
>
> Deep in her heart had been the fear that something would happen like the infamous fade-out that deprived the Philadelphia Phillies of a pennant at the end of the 1964 season. Her husband was part of that team. After the long wait, it was only proper, perhaps, that no one among the 60 fans and family members was more excited, more animated, more joyous than she at the airport.[13]

"The perfect way to describe Mom is that she wore 20 hats," expressed eldest son Tab. "Back then the pay was not a lot for a major leaguer, so my Dad played year round. It was spring training to the season, to the winter leagues and back to spring training. Growing up basically without a father, Mom was responsible for the discipline, homework, and taking us everywhere."[14]

Both top-tiered teams, the Royals and A's, were off Thursday. On Friday, October 1, the Royals backed into the division crown despite a 4–3 loss to the Minnesota Twins. Rojas had two hits and an RBI as a seventh-inning substitution for White. Later in the evening, the visiting California Angels suppressed the bats—and all hopes—of the Oakland A's for a sixth consecutive division title by taking a 12-inning, 2–0 victory. With 11 shutout stanzas, the Angels' Frank Tanana was credited with the win, his 19th. Vida Blue took the complete-game loss. The five-year reign of the mighty Oakland A's over the AL's Western Division was over.

Because of the late conclusion of the Oakland game Friday night, it was not until the end of the game Saturday afternoon (a 3–2 loss to the Twins) that the Royals could mark their championship with a locker room celebration. Two particular Royals joyously got the party started in front of the hometown crowd. "Fred Patek and Cookie Rojas initiated the festivities by waiting for the game's conclusion," described one report, "then strolling out to the centerfield wall display at Royals Stadium and taking a bath with their uniforms on."

"I'm just glad they turned the electricity off out there," sighed GM Joe Burke.[15]

According to Rojas, the "big splash" was not spontaneous: "Back in 1973 when we were contending, I told Freddie that if we ever became champs, I was going to dive into the waterfalls. Freddie agreed to do it with me."

Candida Rojas recalled the celebratory day: "We the wives bathed ourselves in champagne. We stood on the roof of the dugout and poured champagne all over each other. We were a close-knit group. Times have changed. You don't see that type of comradery among players' wives anymore. We were like a family."

While the Royals had clinched, another race of sorts was being played out between teammates Hal McRae and George Brett. McRae was enjoying his best season ever, while Brett had emerged as the sweet-swinging, extraordinary hitter for which he came to be known. The two were battling for the batting title. An 0-for-4 at the plate by McRae in the 4–3 loss to the Twins on Friday dropped his league-leading average to .331. A perfect 3-for-3 by Brett raised his average to .330, setting up a unique batting title showdown on the last day of the season, Sunday, October 3.

Herzog gave both players the day off on Saturday, after clinching the previous night. Although it is not unusual for a manager to rest his starters after a clinching game of a long season, it could be considered odd that Herzog would deny the two a chance to continue their head-to-head hitting battle. The focus of the day clearly weighed one-sidedly on the team and not any individual.

It could also be said that by sitting McCrae and Brett as he did, Herzog set up a more dramatic finish to the batting race on the season's final day. That end was not without controversy, however. Brett duplicated his three-hit performance from Friday to win batting laurels from McRae, who collected two hits, with a final .333 hitting mark to .332.

After eight-and-a-half innings, the Twins were ahead, 5–2. Both players had two hits, and both were due to bat in the bottom of the ninth. McRae was hitting .3326, Brett .3322. Hitting third with one out, Brett hit a ball the opposite way that left fielder Steve Brye misplayed. The ball bounced past him, and the Royals third baseman circled the bases for an inside-the-park home run. In the clean-up spot, the Royals DH now needed a hit to take the hitting crown. He grounded out. After being thrown out at the bag, McRae, who, like many, thought the ball to Brye should have been caught, shouted angrily at Twins manager Gene Mauch in the dugout. The frustrated player accused Mauch of having ordered his outfielder to permit the ball to drop in favor of Brett, who scored the last run of the game.

Although McRae happily shook Brett's hand after his inside-the-park home run, he later indicated he thought racial factors were behind the disputed event. "This is America," McRae, who is Black, said. "Not much has changed."[16]

Brett agreed with his teammate with respect to Brye's effort. "I thought he let it drop."[17]

Rojas apprised the author that he came out on the field, with Whitey Herzog and others, during the heated accusations, which stopped the game. He said Gene Mauch turned to him in front of the umpires and asked, *Am I the type of manager to tell my players to purposely not catch a ball?* Rojas said he answered for all to hear: *Absolutely not.*

The 90–72 Royals lost nine of their final 11 contests of the season. Thankfully for Royals fans (and Cookie Rojas), the A's went 6–5 down the same stretch. Herzog's troop went into their first Division Series competition against a team that was no stranger to the post-season, but one that had been absent in recent years. After a 12-year October drought, the New York Yankees, as winners of the AL Eastern Division, faced the Kansas City Royals for the privilege of advancing to the World Series. "The Yankees are a very good club," assessed Rojas, who finished the season with a .242/.280/.288 slash line in 63 games. "They hit for more power than we do, but our defense is better than theirs."[18]

The power aspect would end up tipping the hard-fought, best-of-five series to the Yankees in a most thrilling fashion for their many backers.

The teams split the first two contests in Kansas City on October 9 and 10. Catfish Hunter five-hit the Royals, 4–1, in the opener, but the Royals bounced back, 7–3, on the strength of Paul Splittorff's 5⅔ innings of scoreless middle relief the next day. Rojas saw action in the first game as a substitute and did not play in the Royals' series-evening victory.

Chris Chambliss hit the first home run of the series as the Yankees took Game Three on October 12, on their home turf, 5–3. The Royals forced a deciding Game Five the next night, knocking out Hunter after three innings and coming away with a 7–4 victory. Rojas started his first post-season game and went 2-for-3; he scored once and added a sacrifice fly to plate another run. Graig Nettles hit two home runs in the Yankees' loss.

At Yankee Stadium, in the fifth and final encounter on October 14, the Royals hit their first two home runs in the series as Rojas was again in the starting lineup. John Mayberry clubbed a two-run shot in the opening frame; the Yankees answered with two runs of their own in their first turn at-bat, sending starter Dennis Leonard to the showers after only facing three batters, all of whom reached safely. In the second inning, Rojas singled, stole second, and scored on a Buck Martínez single. (Rojas had been picked off first by Yankees hurler Ed Figueroa but managed to slide into second base while avoiding second baseman Willie Randolph's tag attempt.) The Yankees outscored the visitors from there and held a 6–3 lead with six outs to go when George Brett went deep against reliever Grant Jackson, with two men aboard, to knot the game at 6–6.

Leading off the bottom of the ninth with the score unchanged, Chambliss deposited a first-pitch fastball from Royals reliever Mark Littell over the right-center field wall to propel the Yankees to a 7–6 win and a trip to the World Series for the first time since 1964. Hundreds of frenzied fans rushed the field following the stadium-quaking blow, preventing Chambliss from rounding the bases completely and touching home plate.

Rojas went 3-for-9 in the series with two runs scored and one batted in. "We lost, but we left Yankee Stadium with our heads held high."

Hanging Up the Spikes

The Royals punctuated their ninth year of spring training in Fort Meyers by reaching a deal with Lee County for extended use of Terry Park, their home park, until 1987. The current 10-year lease was set to expire in 1981. Celebrating his 38th birthday prior to the agreement being reached, Cookie Rojas knew his longevity as an active player would have nowhere near the same life span.

Kansas City improved by 12 wins in 1977, in Whitey Herzog's second full year with the team, and more easily captured their second consecutive Western Division crown, outdistancing the second-place Texas Rangers by eight games. In fact, the team's 102 wins were the most in baseball. A trade in December that brought pitcher Jim Colborn and catcher Darrell Porter from Milwaukee to the Royals for outfielders Jaime Quirk and Jim Wohlford and reliever Doug McClure, proved key to the team's upgrade. Colborn won 18 games, and Porter became an All-Star catcher beginning in 1978.

The Royals opened their home schedule against the team that dramatically defeated them six months earlier, on April 11, attracting almost 40,000 patrons. Kansas City obtained a small measure of revenge with a 5–4, extra-inning victory over the New York Yankees, as did reliever Mark Littell. John Mayberry singled home the walk-off run in the bottom of the 13th inning as Littell pitched four hitless frames, retiring Chris Chambliss once, to earn the win.

Rojas and wife Candy wave to fans at his retirement ceremony in Kansas City, September 30, 1977. At their side, the four nattily dressed Rojas boys (from left, Bobby, Tab, Victor and Mike) take in the special event (courtesy Cookie Rojas).

SEVEN—*Playoff Disappointment and Bowing Out*

Herzog's club came out of the gate strong, winning 13 of its first 21 games. Frank White was the undisputed Royals second baseman as Rojas received only one start, at DH, in the opening stretch of games. But during the second week of May, Rojas filled in for an injured George Brett at third base for a two-week period. The veteran collected the final four-hit game of his career on May 20 in the role against the Cleveland Indians. The three singles and a triple came at Royals Stadium as Paul Splittorff blanked the visitors, 4–0, scattering eight hits. But, surprisingly, by the close of May, the Royals' record had dipped below .500.

That overall record certainly did nothing to spare certain underachieving players from the wrath of impatient Kaycee fans. One such player was the Royals' young second baseman, who was batting in the .220s. "Frank White realized his dream last year," earmarked one report, "but the man he replaced, aging Cookie Rojas, was then and remains one of the most popular athletes to wear a Kansas City uniform." In a 13–3 laugher over the Seattle Mariners at Royals Stadium on June 21, White boosted his average to .230 with a couple of hits and "stilled, at least for the night, the steady chorus of boos from the hometown crowd."[19]

On July 10, in walk-off style, Rojas registered his final game-winning RBI. A Rojas single capped a three-run, bottom-of-the-ninth-inning rally to lift the Royals to a 5–4 victory over the Oakland A's. The 45–37 Royals trailed the division-leading Chicago White Sox by four games at the close of the day's play.

It wasn't until early August that Herzog's men hit their stride. The 56–45 Royals won 20 games in the month and another 25 in September to pull away from the field. The Kansas Citians split their two final scheduled games, gaining their 102nd win on October 2. Dennis Leonard tossed a six-hit shutout over the California Angels to become the franchise's third 20-game winner (Busby, 1974, and Splittorff, 1973). Behind Leonard (20–12) and Colborn (18–14), Splittorff went 16–6. Marty Pattin and Doug Bird gained 10 and 11 wins, respectively.

Brett hit .312 in 139 games, and so did Al Cowens, a fourth-year outfielder the Royals had originally drafted in 1969. Hal McRae was again a big offensive contributor, hitting .298 and slugging .515. Cowens, who did not miss a game, posted a 5.3 WAR, behind Leonard's 5.6 and Brett's team-leading 7.6.

As the Royals were streaking in mid–September, one of their more popular players announced that he was retiring as an active player. "I figure why take the chance of going to spring training and getting cut at the end," said Cookie Rojas. "I'd rather step away now with a winning ballclub that has a chance to win the World Series. It's always a hard decision for a professional athlete to make. I said back in 1970 when I came to Kansas City this was going to be my last stop. I owe a lot to the fans of Kansas City for all the support they have given me. It has really been a privilege to play for them."[20]

The news was accompanied by a co-announcement that the Royals would hold a night of tribute for Rojas on Friday, September 30, two days before the end of the season.

The special evening was reminiscent of the appreciation night the Philadelphia Phillies had given Rojas years earlier but, under the circumstances, this one had to be more emotional for the honoree. Considering the occasion, the booty was greater, as well. Rojas received a television set, stereo, and easy chair among the higher-ticket items. Mrs. Rojas was presented with a fur stole. The prize that elicited the most reaction from the big crowd was the rolling out of a brand-new Plymouth Volare station wagon. Also gifted to the retiring player were plaques, proclaiming "Cookie Rojas Night in Jackson County," "Cookie Rojas Day in Kansas City" and one from the Hispanic Chamber of Commerce with a congratulatory inscription written in Spanish. Certainly most gladdening for Rojas was the fact that his entire family, including wife, four children, parents, and in-laws, were present on the field with him.

That night brought a clearer understanding of the extent of his father's importance to third son Victor.

> In my fourth-grade year, we moved up to KC. I was in fifth grade when dad retired. Royals Stadium was a unique place during those two years with Dad being a veteran player. It was cool. Seeing an expansion team like the Royals progress to a playoff team in '76 and '77. Those were fun years, fun but tough years because the Yankees unfortunately were in the way.
>
> I never thought of my dad as being famous. Baseball was just his job to me. Then one day my teacher in fifth grade, Mrs. Sheets, read to our class from a book. It might have been because the retirement ceremony for my dad was coming up. She started reading from a book called *Unsung Heroes*—and that's when it first dawned on me, oh, my dad might be famous—he's in a book. I thought it was the coolest thing in the world. Joe Rudi was in the book. So that's when it first hit me that what my dad had been doing for a lot of years was significant and it impacted lives, both locally and nationally and internationally having come from Cuba. And as I've grown older, I've come to appreciate all that.[21]

"My father is my hero," added Mike Rojas, the second-born son of the Rojases. "Everything I know is thanks to him. Everything I've learned in the game is through my father. Watching my dad prepare himself on a daily basis to be a professional was the best instruction I could have had for a life inside of baseball. He and Freddie Patek were the best double play combination I ever saw."[22]

Patek, along with Frank White, spoke a few words on behalf of their teammates, all lined up on the field behind Rojas. White's brief remarks were particularly resonating, saying he had never inherited anything, but that he was proud to have inherited second base from Rojas.

"The amount of appreciation the fans showed was indescribable," stated Tab Rojas. "I know what my father was feeling ... when you come from where he came from, to go through what he went through ... [emotional pause] ... to make it to the big leagues, to know he had put his stamp on history, so to speak, and the fans appreciated *all* of that."

Bobby, the youngest of the Rojas boys, had this recollection of the heart-tugging night: "I remember the fans, how they showed their appreciation for my father as an athlete and seeing how the players appreciated him as a teammate, and all of baseball, really, that was paying him tribute. I remember Freddie Patek and Frank White hugging my dad. Seeing how close they were was special."[23]

"This is beyond my comprehension," a humbled Rojas told the large audience. "To be rewarded for just playing a game. I regret I couldn't have given you more."[24]

The 16-year veteran had to put his emotions aside rather quickly as Herzog had penciled Rojas into the starting lineup. "The 38-year-old filled in at third base for George Brett," catalogued one writer, "rapped one single and turned in a pair of exceptional defensive plays as the Royals dumped the California Angels, 8–5, for their 25th win in 30 games."[25] The single would be the 1,660th and final base hit of Rojas' career, in his 1,821st regular season major league game. The 101st victory for the team set a record for most wins by an expansion club, topping the 100 of the 1969 New York Mets. (Rojas would appear as a pinch-hitter without result in one more game.)

Rojas concluded the night with a splash—literally. After the final out of the game was recorded, in an encore performance from last season—but this time without his double play partner—Rojas strolled out to behind the left-center field wall. He raised his hands to the cheering crowd of 33,285 and jumped into the water works. "I said a few years back whenever we won the division title, I'd jump in," the endearing ballplayer reminded. "I asked Freddie if he wanted to go, but he said, 'No, this is your night.'"[26]

Another of the newspaper reports quipped that "in view of his latest performance, the scouting report on Rojas can only be: good field, good hit, good swim."[27]

A few days later, the team with the best record in baseball entered a playoff rematch with the New York Yankees. The best-of-five series, scheduled in a 2–3 format, this time around would be played without a day off. The opening games were on New York's home field. The Royals split the pair of contests at Yankee Stadium on October 5 and 6. In a strong opening assignment, Paul Splittorff easily got the best of the Yankees' Don Gullett, 7–2, in Game One. The Royals clubbed three home runs (McRae, Mayberry, and Cowens), accounting for five of the runs. Another Yankees left-hander, Ron Guidry, spun a three-hitter in Game Two for a 6–2, series-evening victory. Rojas did not play in either game.

Back home for the final three games, things looked promising for the Royals when they upended the repeat AL Eastern Divisional champs, 6–2, in the third encounter on October 7. Dennis Leonard, the Royals' top winner, held the Yankees to just four hits, one walk, and one earned run in the superlative, nine-inning effort.

Herzog had strategized to negate the Yankees' left-handed power bats of Chris Chambliss, Graig Nettles, and free agent signee Reggie Jackson by starting two southpaws, Splittorff and Andy Hassler, a nine-game winner, at Yankee Stadium. But Herzog also passed up his second-best pitcher, Jim Colborn, electing to start lefty Larry Gura, in Game Four. Used mostly as a reliever during the season, Gura was lifted after two innings, with four runs permitted. The Royals got the runs back against Yankees starter Ed Figueroa. But entering the game in the *fourth* inning, reliever Sparky Lyle shut the door on home team scoring with 5⅓ scoreless relief frames. Marty Pattin gave up two runs in long relief. The final 6–4 Yankees win set up another series-deciding Game Five on Sunday night, October 9.

In the pennant-deciding game, Herzog came back with Splittorff, and Yankees manager Billy Martin opted to start Ron Guidry on two days' rest. Herzog inserted Rojas at DH, the first action for the retiring player in the series. A far more controversial move than starting Guidry on short rest was Martin's decision to bench slugger Jackson in the winner-take-all contest. Jackson was not having a good series, 1-for-14, so far.

Guidry did not have it and was removed in the third inning with three runs charged. Trailing 3–1, Martin made another payoff move to the bullpen, bringing in Mike Torrez to relieve his southpaw starter. Torrez, who had been the starter and loser, tossing 5⅔ innings in Game Three just two days earlier, hurled 5⅓ innings of shutout ball to keep the Yankees in the ballgame. Pinch-hitting in the DH slot in the eighth inning, Jackson singled home the Yankees' second run. There was no further scoring for either team in the frame, and the 3–2 game entered the ninth inning with the Royals three outs away from their first World

Series and another sellout crowd of more than 41,000 on the brink of euphoric celebration.

In the fifth game, Splittorff had followed up his eight-inning, two-runs allowed, series-opening performance at Yankee Stadium with an almost identical outing of seven innings and two runs charged to his ledger. Two relievers got the Royals through the eighth with the one-run lead intact. Herzog chose Dennis Leonard, the complete-game winner from the day before yesterday, to obtain the final three outs. In the ninth, when the first two Yankees reached on a hit and walk, Herzog pulled Leonard in favor of Larry Gura—who started yesterday's game and lasted only two innings. Left-handed hitting Mickey Rivers greeted Gura with a game-tying single. With the go-ahead run at third with no one out, Herzog replaced Gura with right-hander Mark Littell. Willie Randolph brought home the Yankees' fourth and go-ahead run with a sacrifice fly. Following the second out, a fifth run scored when George Brett threw wildly to first base after fielding a ground ball hit by Lou Piniella. Jackson grounded out to White at second to end the nightmarish half-inning for Kansas City partisans.

Sparky Lyle picked up his second win in as many nights, securing the final four outs of the 5–3 Yankees victory. Freddie Patek hit into a game-ending double play to seal the disappointing, last-inning turn of events for the Royals.

In his last major league game, DH Rojas went 1-for-4 with a stolen base. But he blamed himself for not coming through in the clutch. Rojas fanned against Lyle, who had relieved an obviously tiring Torrez, late in the contest, following two consecutive walks with two outs. "I came up there in the eighth inning with men on first and second," he said. "I could have broke it open with a base hit or double. It might have been a different story. I would have liked to go out with a World Series, but it just wasn't meant to be. They played a hell of a game. You have to give them all the credit in the world. They came back from behind twice and won, but I don't think this club has anything to be ashamed of."[28]

Of the back-to-back playoff losses, Rojas today still considers the second one to have been the hardest to absorb. "We had the lead going into the ninth in the deciding game...."

Perhaps swayed too much by the purported Yankees' weakness against left-handed hurlers, Herzog was left to contemplate a series loss without his second-best pitcher and 18-game winner Jim Colborn having thrown a single pitch.

Eight

From the Coaching Lines and Beyond to Contented Retirement

Cookie Rojas was the sixth-oldest player in the league at the announcement of his retirement in 1977. He did not stay unemployed for long, however. He was hired by the Chicago Cubs to become their first base coach a week after the disappointing defeat to the Yankees. Joey Amalfitano and Mike Roarke were also announced as coaching additions to the team for 1978.

Rojas wanted to stay in Kansas City. He and his wife had decided to make their full-time home in the Blue Valley district of Overland Park. But the Royals had no openings at the major league level. "I talked to Preston Gómez, who has always been my adviser," outlined Rojas. "Preston had talked with the Cubs and found out they were looking for a coach. I wanted to stay in the major leagues, especially because I want to get 20 years in on the pension plan."[1]

The job in the Windy City would start a new baseball trajectory for Rojas, which would take him, over the next nearly 40 years, from the coaching lines to scouting, back to the dugout (as manager), to scouting again, back to coaching, to the broadcast booth, to finally, contented retirement. "The Chicago fans are special," recalled Rojas of his time back in the National League. "The way they treat their players is a thing apart."

The 1978 Chicago Cubs had a handful of Hispanic players on their squad, including their keystone pairing of second baseman Manny Trillo and shortstop Ivan De Jesús. The Cubs that Rojas joined were a .500 ball club in 1977, finishing fourth in the NL East. For the North Siders, Trillo was arguably the league's top glove man at his position. The Venezuelan led the league in assists four straight campaigns

(1975–1978) and three times scored the highest range factor/game at second base, 1977, 1978, and 1980. (The latter season's accomplishment came with the Philadelphia Phillies, with whom he won two of his three Gold Gloves, in 1981 and 1982.) The Santurce-born De Jesús topped all peers in assists in 1977 and 1978 and in putouts in 1981, Rojas' last season with the Cubs.

While the up-the-middle play was no doubt appreciated by the pitching staff, the Cubs lacked the overall talent to contend with the division's top teams in 1978, finishing in third place, 11 games behind the first-place Philadelphia Phillies.

In mid–June, with barely two months on the job, Rojas took up a public cause for fellow Hispanic player and former teammate Orlando Cepeda, who had run afoul of the law. Cepeda was facing the commencement of a five-year prison term for marijuana trafficking, the bust having occurred at San Juan International Airport in December of 1975. A week before the former NL star was set to start serving his sentence, Rojas began a public campaign for clemency for the former NL MVP. "Baseball owes something to Cepeda," voiced Rojas, "because every man deserves to go to bat a second time."[2] Rojas had first run across Cepeda in the 1960 Caribbean Series in Panama City and played with the retired slugger for a time with the Royals in 1974.

Rojas asked every MLB player rep to write letters on behalf of their teams to U.S. congressmen and to the commissioner of Puerto Rican Affairs in Washington, D.C. Among the high-profile players Rojas received promises of cooperation from were a Cincinnati Reds trio, Pete Rose, Joe Morgan and Davey Concepción. Rojas contacted Ron LeFlore, who had been incarcerated before reaching the major leagues with the Detroit Tigers, as his American League liaison on the matter. The Cubs coach also reached out to César Cedeño, the Astros' star outfielder who been involved in a fatal shooting three years earlier. Cedeno had escaped severe consequence in what could be viewed as having received another opportunity toward becoming a productive member of society.

"We all make mistakes in life," wrote Rojas, in an open letter to the people of San Juan, "and a lot of us are given a second chance. I say that if a man accepts his mistakes and can straighten out a few young lives, he is more valuable to teach others than to sit behind the walls of confinement. How can we forget all the things this man has done for his country?"[3] Cepeda had been vilified and ostracized in Puerto Rico over the incident. He ended up serving 10 months in a minimum-security facility in Florida.

On September 1, the 66–65 Cubs sat in third place, 5½ games out of first. As part of the annual roster expansion, Chicago activated their first base coach to player status. "I'll do anything to help the Cubs," Rojas said. "I can give them a little experience in September. I'll still coach first, too. Anything to help us win the division. I want to see the Bleacher Bums wearing dinner jackets one of these days."[4]

The fitting for the dinner jackets would have to wait another nine years and the grand World Series tailoring even longer, as any Cubs follower can attest. Rojas, it turned out, did not receive any playing time, as the Cubs were unable to muster a stretch drive and fell to their eventual double-digit deficit in the final standings.

Rojas left for Venezuela to manage over the winter but resigned (or was forced to because of player conflict) from the Magallanes club after only one month at the helm. The team was in next-to-last place. The Tigers' Willie Horton took over. "They begged me to manage the team the rest of the way," said Horton when he returned. "I really wasn't interested but they were in a spot, so I decided to help them."[5] Horton guided the team to a first-place finish and an eventual Caribbean Series victory in San Juan.

One of the pitchers on the turned-around squad was Pittsburgh Pirates prospect Benny Wiltbank, who tossed a five-hit shutout against the Mexican champions on the third day of the championship tournament. "The fans over there [Venezuela] are very excitable, very emotional," he described shortly upon his return to the States. "They get totally involved. When they get upset they start pulling on the fences, they litter the playing field and toss out firecrackers. We always had armed guards at the playoff games, guys armed with machine guns."[6]

Like his father, Mike Rojas has had managing experience in the Latin American leagues. He managed his father's old team, the Caracas Lions, in 2017–2018. "I would say Venezuela has the best baseball fans," said the Rojas offspring, who was also bench coach for Santo Domingo's Escogido franchise in 1998–1999.

> Dominican Republic, second, and USA, third. Venezuelan fans are so knowledgeable about the game. Dominican fans root passionately, but at a more local level, for their teams. Baseball is a break to whatever is going on in their countries. In Venezuela, I never encountered anything political having to do with the game and I never involved myself with anything political. It's strictly baseball. Also, I managed in Mexico for a year in Monclova. There's pressure on the clubs to win in all those countries, but there's no player development like the minor leagues.[7]

"All things being equal, I think Puerto Rican fans had the edge," Mike's father said. "Then I would say the Caracas fans, followed by Dominican rooters."

EIGHT—From the Coaching Lines and Beyond   163

Player development breeds mixed results, even at the major league level, as the Cubs found out with an underperforming 80–82 season in 1979, Rojas' second with the team.

No matter what a club's record, often a big league player's community work goes unnoticed. During the Cubs' final homestand in September, several team members found time to give back. Their efforts were praiseworthy enough for one fan to write a letter to the editors of the *Sporting News*, which published its contents:

> Despite having stood in the sun for more than an hour for Camera Day at Wrigley Field and having played a full game, the following members of the Chicago Cubs donated their time for the clinic which raised money for worthy charities: Cookie Rojas, Steve Dillard, Larry Bittner and Bruce Sutter. The example set by these gentlemen for the kids who attended was tremendous and their instructions were well received. They received no fees and were delighted to work with the kids.—Ron Van Raalte, Arlington Heights, Ill.[8]

A week before the 1979 season ended, Cubs skipper Herman Franks suddenly quit. Franks, who was expected to step down due to the Cubs' fifth-place showing in the six-team division, decided to leave early following a newspaper story in which he criticized some of his players. He said he was misquoted. Joey Amalfitano directed the team to a pair of wins and five losses in the seven remaining games. The Cubs named a replacement rather quickly.

On October 1, the day after the season concluded, Cubs general manager Bob Kennedy named his new hire: "We are delighted to be able to obtain someone with the baseball experience of Preston Gomez. He fits the mold of the type of manager we are looking for."[9]

Two days after the campaign, the axe fell on another field strategist. The Royals fired Whitey Herzog. After three straight division titles (1976–1978), but no World Series trips to show for them, and a second-place finish in 1979, the Royals' front office obviously wanted more.

Speculation arose that Cookie Rojas, who had several years of winter league piloting duties under his belt, could be considered for the post. But Rojas' name as a viable candidate was quickly squashed by Royals general manager Joe Burke. "I can tell you that Cookie doesn't have the experience to be a major league manager," Burke said. "That's why, I'm sure, he didn't get the job in Chicago."[10]

Rojas actually garnered the most support for the post from fans in a poll conducted by the *Kansas City Star*. Charlie Lau, former batting coach of the Royals and now with the New York Yankees, came in second. Rojas, for his part, did not think he was ready. "I've managed seven years in winter ball. Someday, yes I'd like to manage in the major leagues. I don't want to rush it. When the right time comes along, when the right team comes along, I'll jump at it."[11]

The Royals hired Jim Frey, who never played in the major leagues but managed in the minors and winter league in Venezuela. Frey would lead the Royals to the World Series in 1980.

In Chicago in 1980, the Cubs got worse. The backslide dropped the club to last in the division with 98 losses. As often occurs, the manager paid the price. Trying to salvage the season, GM Bob Kennedy ousted his managerial selection shortly after the All-Star break. The Cubs' record was 38–52, trailing every team in the division. Gómez was replaced by Joey Amalfitano, who steered the team along the same bottom depths until the end of the campaign. The 57-year-old Gómez, who had become the first Latin American hired to pilot a major league team (the 1969 expansion San Diego Padres), never managed again in the big leagues. (He had also skippered the Houston Astros for parts of four seasons in the mid–1970s.) But Gómez found work as a coach with the California Angels in 1981.

Rojas moved over to the third base coaching box, replacing Amalfitano. He stated he was going to be aggressive with runners in scoring

A gladsome Gene Mauch (right) hands over the managerial reigns of the California Angels to Rojas in spring training 1988. Mauch decided to step aside due to ill health (author's collection).

position: "I watch the runner out of the corner of my eye, because I'm looking at the fielder. If the outfielder is bending for the ball before my runner reaches third, I can't send him. If he's at third, he goes."[12]

Following the Cubs' 64–98 last-place finish, Rojas went back to Puerto Rico over the winter of 1980–1981 to manage the capital city team of Santurce. His three coaches were island legends Orlando Cepeda, Juan Pizarro, and Rubén Gómez.

Amalfitano was retained as Cubs manager for 1981, and he kept Rojas on, as well as hitting coach Billy Williams and first base coach Gene Clines. Amalfitano brought in a new pitching instructor in Less Moss. But the team's play did not improve. In a truncated season, due to the first elongated players' strike in history, the Cubs posted the poorest record in the National League: 38–65.

In Charge in the Dugout

Following the work stoppage season of 1981, a new manager, Lee Elia, was hired for 1982; he overhauled the Cubs' coaching staff with the exception of Williams, whom he retained. Victor Rojas picked up on his father's trail: "We spent the summers in Chicago when Dad was with the Cubs. He was then hired as an advanced scout with the Angels in 1982. When the Angels came to play the Royals, my brother Bobby and I would serve as bat boys for the Angels because of the connection my dad had."[13]

It's not surprising Rojas landed in Southern California. His most influential mentors were with the Angels in prominent capacities. Gene Mauch was the club's manager, while Preston Gómez manned the third base coaching lines. The same year Rojas joined the California Angels, he was elected to the Cuban Hall of Fame in Exile. Also selected for the 1982 honor were Tony Oliva and Cuban executive and team owner Emilio de Armas.

In September, the Angels and Kansas City Royals battled for the Western Division's top laurels. As the teams clashed that final month, a KC reporter gave fans a peek at the end result of an advance scout's labor. "When Angels manager Gene Mauch opens his scouting report this morning," wrote Mike Fish, "he'll find a detailed evaluation by Cookie Rojas of each Royal: everything from the location of pitches Frank White has hit for power lately to information on Bob Tufts' sinker."[14]

A month earlier, Rojas had been instrumental in the Angels signing a former star pitcher who, due to age, was now relegated to a castoff veteran pitcher's role in a lower league. Angels vice president and general manager Mike Port identified the hurler: "Our scouting reports were very good on Tiant. Cookie Rojas, our special assignment coach saw Luis pitch for Tabasco [Mexican League] and recommended we acquire him."[15] In his last year in the major leagues, Tiant went 2–2 in five starts, while the Angels outdistanced the Royals to win the division by three games. But the Gene Mauch–led squad lost in the Division Series to the AL East champ Milwaukee Brewers, after winning the first two games of the five-game set.

In January 1983, the Hall of Fame inducted into its hallowed corridors Brooks Robinson and Juan Marichal, the first Dominican player enshrined in Cooperstown. Along with nearly two dozen other players who retired in 1977, in his first year of eligibility, Rojas' name was ushered off future balloting consideration for failing to receive a minimum percentage of the sportswriters' vote.

The following winter (1983–1984), the Toros del Este entered the Dominican Winter League, along with another franchise in San Cristobal. With a home base in La Romana, the franchise was originally known as the Azucareros del Este. Rojas became the team's second manager during the 1984–1985 hibernal season.

Two years later, on May 30, 1987, Rojas and Paul Splittorff were elected to the Kansas City Royals Hall of Fame. The Royals' place of honor had been initiated the prior year with Steve Busby and Amos Otis as inaugural inductees. Splittorff had been the first Royals player drafted and signed by the expansion team in 1968. The Hall of Fame section of the Kansas City Royals' website recognizes Rojas in this way: "His experience and professional demeanor had a profound influence on his teammates, especially younger players, helping the early Royals teams grow into champions. Bringing both veteran presence and leadership, Rojas played a vital part in the Royals first championship teams."[16]

Rojas managed several winters in La Romana, the last in 1987–1988. Less than two months after the Toros' season concluded, in the middle of spring training, Gene Mauch asked for a two-week leave of absence as Angels manager. Mauch had left the Angels following the playoff disappointment in 1982 but returned in 1985, only to experience another devastating playoff loss a year later against the Boston Red Sox. The team sank to sixth place in the seven-team AL West in 1987. Cookie Rojas was asked to step in for his longtime instructor. "Mauch was ailing, he smoked a lot," recalled Rojas. "I accepted the Angels managerial job on Mauch's recommendation."

Becoming the 11th manager in the 27-year history of the franchise, Rojas was initially named on an interim basis until Mauch's leave expired. But on March 26, 1988, Mauch called it quits for good, and Rojas was permanently elevated 10 days before the start of the season. "This is the second shock I received this spring," said Rojas. "The first was when Gene stepped aside in Arizona."[17]

Rojas dismissed any questioning notions that he did not work his way up from a lower-level dugout post. "I played for 16 years in the big leagues," he stated. "I coached four years. I scouted for nine years. I also managed in the winter leagues for 20 years, and that's an advantage because you're taking veterans and rookies from different organizations and trying to mold them into a winning team in a shorter amount of time. I don't think I missed anything by not managing in the minors."[18]

With the passage of time, Rojas added: "I told Gene, don't resign yet. Let me be your bench coach for a few months. Then if you still want to step away, okay. That way it will help me, too. I should never have accepted the job without a managerial contract of more than one year."

The singular experience for Rojas also left an indelible mark on one of his children. "When he managed the Angels in 1988, Dad convinced me to come out there and I stayed the whole summer," said Victor. "I was in college at the time. I remember working with Marcel Lachemann, pitching coach. I was a pitcher in college. Being in the clubhouse. Soaking all that in, the good and the bad. It was really cool. The team played really well over the summer, then cooled off."[19]

On April 4, 1988, Rojas became the fifth Latin American and eighth minority manager to hand in lineup cards for a major league game.[20] In his first Opening Day as manager, Rojas was the only minority pilot in the big leagues. It was a sensitive topic at the moment as baseball was two days away (April 6) from the one-year anniversary of Dodgers vice president Al Campanis publicly saying that Blacks perhaps "lacked the necessities" to occupy high-level jobs in the sport. The severe backlash produced by the comments prompted Commissioner Peter Ueberroth to launch a minority hiring initiative throughout baseball. At Comiskey Park, a five-run seventh inning by the White Sox spoiled the occasion for Rojas. The home team won, 8–5.

Two evenings hence, Rojas notched his keepsake managerial win with a 4–2, 10-inning decision. Rojas put the right pieces in place, in particular in the final frame, inserting Bill Buckner as a pinch-hitter with the bases loaded. Buckner delivered a single for the decisive runs. Reliever Donnie Moore handed Rojas the ball after the final out, and Wally Joyner made a clubhouse presentation of the baseball to his manager in front of the entire team. A bit over 7,000 fans braved the windy and frigid 40-degree night. Rojas showed off the ball briefly but preferred to defer the occasion of his first win to his team. "It was presented to me by all the guys," he said in visiting manager's office, "but don't talk about me, let's talk about the Angels."[21]

For hometown fans, the talks, at least positive ones, about the Angels were limited to a 76-game run in the summer in which the team earned 20 wins over .500 ball (48–28). The rest of the season, the club was not competitive, although that could be, at least in part, attributed to the dynamic Oakland Athletics team that ran away with the division. Led by "Bash Brothers" José Canseco and Mark McGwire, the crunching club won 104 games and cruised to a 13-game winning cushion over their closest pursuers.

In late August, as the Angels' good stretch was nearing an end, a local news story surfaced that Rojas might *not* be returning to the helm in 1989: "Mike Port, Angels general manager, met with Rojas Monday [August 29], and told him a decision will be reached during the off-season, a policy the club has followed for years. 'I reminded Cookie today that back in July we had discussed the fact, that, barring some unforeseen scenario, we would approach matters on a post season basis,' Port said."[22]

Port did not live up to his word. With the team having lost 10 of 12 contests, he dismissed Rojas on Friday, September 23, with eight games left in the season. "His firing may have been triggered by an incident in Thursday night's game when Rojas mistakenly made a second mound visit without intending to change pitchers," attributed one report of the move. "Pitching coach Marcel Lachemann had already gone out to talk to reliever Rick Monteleone. First base umpire Jim McKean forced a change of pitchers."[23]

The Angels, 75–79 under Rojas, lost all their remaining games under third base coach Moose Stubing, who replaced his former manager. "I'm still glad they lost those last eight games," said Victor Rojas.

> My father didn't deserve to get fired in that manner. The team could have easily ridden it out to the end of the year. He was put in a difficult position because Gene retired a few days prior to the opening of the season. With that roster, to be able to do what he did for an extended period of time over the summer was just awesome. But those were some of the kind of things, without him saying the words, that helped me become aware of the reality of the business of baseball. It has served me well. At the end of the day, it's always a business.[24]

Rojas remembered this about his firing: "I was called up to the office and told. Mrs. Autry called a talk radio show, asking why had they fired Cookie." In an interview the following spring with the *Los Angeles Times*, Mrs. Autry's husband, Gene, the Angels owner, said pointedly that the decision to oust Rojas was strictly the general manager's and that, at the time, he agreed with it.

A sports reporter from the same newspaper eventually viewed the distasteful episode in this manner: "The Angels dumped Rojas as if he were the evening garbage. Rojas was there when the Angels needed a last-minute replacement for Gene Mauch. He was there when they needed someone to guide a team headed for double-digit injuries. He was there when they congratulated themselves on a remarkable 48–28 run from mid–June to early September. Then, on September 22, he was gone. Poof."[25]

Rojas joined a group of seven other managers who lost their jobs in 1988: the Phillies' Lee Elia (let go on the same day as Rojas), Baltimore's Cal Ripken, Sr., Atlanta's Chuck Tanner, Larry Bowa in San Diego, Dick Williams in Seattle, John McNamara in Boston, and Billy Martin of the Yankees.

Briefly Back to Scouting and Then Coaching Again

In January 1989, Rojas was rehired by the Angels as an advanced scout, a post he previously held from 1982 to 1987. His first assignment came in spring camp in Florida, checking out the Chicago White Sox; the team would be the Angels' Opening Day opponent. To his credit, Rojas seemed to hold no bitter feelings. "It's water under the bridge," he said later from Winter Haven, spying the Red Sox. "I'm back with the Angels in my old job, and everything is fine."[26] An old job he held for just short of three more years.

In October of 1991, Rojas was contracted by the Florida Marlins, one of two expansion teams approved to begin play in the National League in 1993. His official title was assistant to the general manager. He would provide input in the areas of scouting and player development.

"I was hired as a scout with the expectation of coaching with the expansion Marlins," Rojas said. "The Marlins front office was headed by Dave Dombrowski. I was responsible for scouting the National League East. This was the season before the expansion draft. I had to see one player one day, fly to a different city and see a pitcher. These were the players that we thought were going to become draft eligible."

Rojas interviewed for the new team's managerial opening in September 1992. There was certainly no dearth of applicant names bandied about in the press throughout the process. High on the speculative list were Bill Virdon, Jimy Williams, Dave Duncan, and Rene Lachemann, all of whom were current major league coaches who could make the easy

Cookie and Candy, pictured here in the early 2020s, are still going strong after almost 65 years of marriage (courtesy Cookie Rojas).

transition. Former big league skippers Davey Johnson, Bobby Valentine, Dallas Green, and Bucky Dent were often mentioned as candidates. Minor league pilots Bob Boone, Tony Muser, and Clint Hurdle were said to be ready if the Florida team decided to go in a younger direction. The long-shot job-seekers were all minorities: Chris Chambliss, Don Baylor, Hal McRae, and Cookie Rojas.

In the end, it was Lachemann who walked up the lineup cards in the Marlins' inaugural game, on April 6, 1993, at Joe Robbie Stadium. Rojas was named third base coach. The Marlins beat the visiting Los Angeles Dodgers, 6–3. After many years as a scout on the road, the field appointment was of added convenience. Remaining in Kansas City until 1987, Rojas and family had relocated to Miami years earlier. The New York Mets, with 103 losses, kept the 64–98, first-year Marlins out of the cellar in the National League's Eastern Division.

The following season, one of infamy for the sport, the Marlins dropped to last place. During a year in which realignment branched out 28 teams from two divisions into three, across the imaginary baseball landscape of both leagues, baseball failed to play a World Series for the first time in more than 90 years due to another players' strike. Initiated at the close of play, August 11, 1994, the work stoppage wiped out more than one-third of the remaining schedule and canceled the Fall Classic.

A "walkout" of a much more serious nature also began that summer 90 miles from U.S. soil. On August 5, many residents of Havana took to the streets to protest more than three decades of totalitarianism, and in particular the recent years of exacerbated hardships brought on by the collapse of the subsidizing Soviet Union. To alleviate the pressure on the boiling pot of social discontent, Fidel Castro unleashed a wave of illegal immigration upon U.S. shores by permitting Cubans unregulated, perilous egress from the island across the Florida Straits. It was an exodus that eventually saw 35,000 Cubans escape communism on makeshift rafts and inner tubes. Seeing an opportunity to come to America in the pell-mell conditions, thousands of Haitian migrants also fled their poverty-stricken country under similar precarious means. U.S. President Bill Clinton ordered all asylum seekers intercepted at sea to be transferred to the American Naval Base at Guantanamo, Cuba.

On November 30, a "humanitarian relief effort organized by Marlins third base coach Cookie Rojas, the Kiwanis Club of Miami and the Puente de Jovenes Profesionales Cubanos visited 23,000 Cubans and 6,000 Haitians living on the base."[27] Accompanying Rojas on the trip was Rene Arocha, the first Cuban ballplaying defector in 1991, Tony Pérez, who was the Marlins' director of international operations, and Puerto Rican slugger Rubén Sierra. The group delivered $60,000 worth of basic supplies, including recreational baseball equipment. "I organized the effort," recalled Rojas. "It was a phenomenal experience. Arocha, Sierra and Pérez joined us. We played a pickup baseball game with some of the detainees." The day technically marked the first time since Rojas left his native land more than three decades earlier that he had returned.

Baseball returned in 1995, with grievances sufficiently addressed between players and management to allow for the signing of a new collective bargaining agreement. The protracted resolution to the frustrating (for fans) impasse shortened spring training and delayed by a fortnight the usual start of the season. Most clubs played a 144-game schedule as a result.

From an entertainment aspect, at least, the first baseball action since the players' walkout came on February 25, 1995, at the Joe DiMaggio Children's Hospital Legends Game. The annual charity exhibition occurred at its usual Ft. Lauderdale Stadium locale, winter home of the New York Yankees. Rojas and Pérez competed on opposite teams. Bert Campaneris, Warren Cromartie, Steve Yeager, George Foster, Tony Oliva, and Rennie Stennett were some of the former big league players who lent their time to raise money for the pediatric hospital. The expected heavy Yankees participation was reflected with the presence of Mickey Rivers, Gene Michael, Willie Randolph, and Buck Showalter. "This isn't just a one-day event for a lot of us," commented Rivers. "Most of us out here play in fantasy camps and other charity games."[28]

During these same "nostalgically athletic" times, the 50fifty-something Rojas and Pérez and other contemporary Cuban stars often suited up in the uniforms of Cuban Winter League teams for remembrance charity games in Miami. The usually off-season occurrences were designed to raise money for the local Cuban Baseball Federation and the Cuban Baseball Hall of Fame in Exile organizations. "I'm very proud to be part of this game," Rojas said at the 1995 exhibition. "It's a great thing to remember all those great players and for us to be reunited."[29]

With labor issues settled, baseball also returned to the minor leagues. Thirty-two-year-old Mike Rojas became manager of the Double A Hickory Crawdads of the South Atlantic League's North Division. "Beginning in 1992, I managed in rookie ball for the Chicago White Sox," said Rojas, recapping his baseball journeys. "Then I was promoted in 1995. I went on to manage in the minor league systems of four other major league clubs, for a total of 14 years—Cincinnati, Houston, Detroit Tigers and Kansas City Royals." Rojas, who graduated high school in Kansas City, had tried traveling the same early baseball path as his father. "I played semipro ball out of high school and then played at Mesa Community College. I signed professionally as a catcher and spent two years in the Blue Jays' organization and another two in Oakland's. But I was put in to pitch and injured my arm and that was the end of my career."[30]

Rojas, who spoke to the author as he was awaiting arrival of his visa to travel to Venezuela to manage in the summer league, was also the bullpen coach with the Detroit Tigers from 2010 to 2013, when Jim Leyland was the manager. The 2012 club reached the World Series but were defeated by the San Francisco Giants. "Then I spent two years with Seattle as the bullpen coach under Lloyd McClendon, a great guy, until new management sent most of us packing."[31]

In the initial years of the Rojas Sr.–coached Marlins, they did not have the same success as their expansion counterpart Colorado Rockies. In 1995, the Rockies made the playoffs as a wild card team, while the Marlins languished in fifth place with a 67–76 divisional record.

However, the fortunes of the Marlins franchise would change in just two short years, as the team not only became the first wild card club to win the World Series but also the quickest, in terms of years as an expansion franchise, to win it all—topping the 1969 New York Mets. The Marlins captured the brass ring in just their fifth year of existence in 1997.

No one could have seen that coming in 1996 when Rene Lachemann took the reins of the team for the fourth year. Perhaps in light of the success of the Rockies the prior season, the Marlins' front office wanted to see more progress. On July 6, after six straight losses and a club-record nine consecutive road defeats, the Marlins' record stood at 39–47. General manager Dave Dombrowski made a change and fired the only manager the Marlins had known.

Cookie Rojas was asked to step in as interim skipper. He did so and halted the bad run, the next day, with a 7–4 win in 10 innings over the Philadelphia Phillies. Guiding his men from his third base coaching box, Rojas employed 20 players and a successful suicide squeeze to help bring about the win on a hot day in Philadelphia. It happened to be the Sunday before the All-Star break.

Rojas made it clear that he did not want the dugout job, that his job was as the third base coach. That left the Marlins with other organizational talent from which to choose: Tony Pérez, now with the title of assistant to Dombrowski, Sal Rende, the club's Triple A manager, and Carlos Tosca, the Marlins' Double A pilot. A host of outside aspirants with experience existed, many of whom were known to the Marlins from the big job search of 1992. The Marlins' head of player development, John Boles, was the ultimate Dombrowski pick. Boles had never managed a major league baseball game. Boles guided the team to a

40–35 record over the remaining two and a half months and to an overall mark of 80–82, their best record to date.

A handful of days after the 1996 season concluded, the Marlins hired Jim Leyland to be their manager. Leyland, who had spent the last 11 years at the helm of the Pittsburgh Pirates, brought in new coaches, with the exception of Larry Rothchild, who was retained to keep handling the pitchers. "I left for the Mets in 1997 to coach under Bobby Valentine, a man with a tremendous baseball mind," said Rojas. "The first time I met with Valentine in his office, I wanted to make one thing clear. I am not a 'yes man,'" I told him. Bobby responded, "that is *not* what I'm looking for."

The local South Florida community certainly missed Rojas' presence among them. "I have no idea how many public appearances I have made since I joined the Marlins," he told an interviewer. "It is great to get out and meet all the fans. Parents will come up to me and introduce their children, telling the children how much they enjoyed watching me play when they were the child's age. Many of the grandparents even remember me from when I played in Cuba."[32]

The New York team Rojas joined had finished 10 wins below break-even in 1996. As a team, they did not pitch well, and they committed the most errors in the majors. A season-ending report, however, capsulized the club's improvement in Valentine's first full year at the helm in 1997: "Entering the final weekend, the Mets have trimmed their season total of errors to 115 from a major league–leading 159 last year. They likewise cut their staff ERA to 3.99 from 4.22 in 1996. Bobby Valentine frequently cited the work of pitching coach Bob Apodaca and third base coach Cookie Rojas, the de facto infield instructor, for the turnaround."[33]

In 1998, the Mets duplicated their 88–74 record from the prior campaign, finishing one position higher in the division, in second place. In the off-season, Rojas accompanied an MLB team's goodwill tour of Japan. "It was great," said Rojas. "The Japanese are a people with a great sense of purpose. They're such a respectful people. And they play the game right. I was really impressed."

In 1999, a balanced pitching staff and three players who knocked in more than 100 runs helped the Mets make the playoffs for the first time since 1988. A single-contest, wild card playoff game was pitched and won by Al Leiter, who suppressed the Cincinnati Reds on two hits, winning 5–0. The October 4 shutout earned the Mets, who finished the season in a 96–66 tie with the Reds, the NL's fourth playoff spot and a Division Series matchup with the 100-win Arizona Diamondbacks, only a two-year-old expansion entry in the league. New York downed the

Diamondbacks in four games but were toppled by the Atlanta Braves in the LCS in six games, after dropping the first three games of the series.

Rojas received a second dose of Japan's unique culture when the Mets opened the 2000 season against the Chicago Cubs in the Tokyo Dome. Valentine's Mets were not only again ready to compete for the National League title—but for baseball's ultimate crown.

During the early stages of the campaign, politics intruded on the sport. On April 25, a few days after the United States government forcibly removed Elián González, referred to as the "Cuban rafter boy" by news outlets, from the home of relatives in Miami with the intent of returning the boy to Cuba, many Hispanic major leaguers protested the action with a boycott of their services for the day. González, six years old, had been part of a group of 14 Cubans who tried to cross the Florida Straits in search of freedom. His mother died in the attempt, as did all but the child and two others.

On the Mets, Rojas and shortstop Rey Ordoñez were two such dissenting participants. "They came in and they both had a look of conviction in their eyes," stated their manager. "I wasn't surprised. I support my coaches and players in just about everything they do. Rey's teammates are behind him."[34]

José Canseco of the Tampa Bay Devil Rays sat out his game, while Rafael Palmeiro played for his Texas Rangers. The Florida Marlins, with the most Hispanic players in the majors, experienced the most withdrawal of talent for the day; the short-handed club fielded 19 players for its game against the San Francisco Giants and lost, 6–4, in 11 innings.

A year earlier, North American baseball and Cuba had also been in the news. In March 1999, a big league baseball team visited Havana for the first time in 40 years when the Baltimore Orioles played the Cuban national team at Estadio Latinoamericano, the baseball complex co-built by Bobby Maduro and partner Miguel Suárez and originally called Gran Stadium del Cerro de la Habana. The stadium was expropriated by Castro's Communist government and renamed. Opened in 1946 as testament to the men who built it, the stadium still stands as the principal venue for baseball in Cuba nearly 80 years later. The exhibition contest was part of a home-and-home series, with the second game conducted at Camden Yards in Baltimore in July. The teams split the encounters, with the road clubs coming out on top.

"I don't like it. I don't think it's right," Rojas said of the engagement at the time. "Castro has never given anything back. It's just take, take, take. Where are the human rights, the freedom of the Cuban people? I'm 60 years old now and I haven't been able to go to my land. I'd rather die without seeing it and remember it when it was free."[35]

As the seven-month-long grind of the 2000 season reached its climax, the Mets were one of the two teams left standing as they faced the New York Yankees in the World Series, the first Subway Series since 1956. After more than four decades in organized baseball, Cookie Rojas had made it to the World Series. (Every time I saw Rojas, he had his Mets 2000 National League Championship ring on one finger.) The Yankees took home the gleaming October hardware, beating their Queens borough rivals in five games.

In 2001, new Toronto Blue Jays manager and former Royals teammate Buck Martínez hired Rojas away from the Mets to be his bench coach. "It's a small, small universe in baseball," Martínez said during his first spring encampment with the club. "Cookie brings enthusiasm, experience, knowledge of baseball, ability to handle people, and a relationship that is 100% trustworthy."[36] Martínez had no coaching or managing experience in the major or minor leagues.

In late May, Rojas got a chance to manage at the big league level again—for three games. Martínez left the team to attend his mother-in-law's funeral. The Blue Jays lost the first two games with Rojas at the helm, scoring a total of one run. In the third contest, on May 26, Rojas and the Jays pocketed a victory. Hurler Chris Michalak spun eight shutout innings, leading to a 5–0 win over the Boston Red Sox.

Heading into September, the Blue Jays were five wins below .500, in third place with no real chance of catching the first-place New York Yankees. Then the foreign terrorist attacks on the 11th of the month were perpetrated. "It was a dark time not only for baseball but for the nation," Rojas recollected. MLB halted operations for a week and, intent on completing the entire 162-game schedule for all teams, finished the regular season a full week into October. Remaining in third place, the Jays lost two more games than they won.

On Opening Day 2002, the Blue Jays outslugged the Red Sox at Fenway Park, 12–11. Rojas was ejected from the game after coming out of the dugout to argue a tag play at third base involving a Red Sox runner. It was Rojas' sixth and final expulsion as a coach. He had received four ejection slips as a manager in 1988 (and nine as a player).

After 53 games and a poor 20–33 record, their worst start in two decades, Blue Jays management lost faith in Buck Martínez and relieved him of his duties—curiously, after sweeping a three-game series against the Detroit Tigers. Third base coach Carlos Tosca, who had managed over 1,700 games in the minors, was named the replacement field general. Martínez became the fifth pilot already to receive a pink slip from his major league club.

Blue Jays general manager J.P. Ricciardi met with the coaching staff after the June 2 firing. He informed them (all except first base coach Garth Iorg, who had been let go with Martínez) that they could stay for the remainder of the season. He wanted everyone's answer by 10:00 a.m., June 5. Rojas stayed on the bench for two more games before deciding. Rojas and pitching coach Mark Conner then resigned from the Blue Jays over the abrupt firing of Martínez. Not even the Cuban-born Tosca could dissuade Rojas.

"It was very unfair to make the change," said Rojas, offering injuries to key players that had befallen the club as a reason for the team's poor showing so far. "Jose Cruz missed most of the spring, and we haven't had Chris Carpenter or Esteban Loaiza."[37]

Years on, Rojas recalled, "Toronto gave us [coaches] a chance to stay. Buck himself told me to stay. My position was, *Buck Martinez brought me here. If he's leaving, I'm leaving, too.*"

After witnessing two more Blue Jays victories over the Tampa Bay Devil Rays on June 3 and 4, Rojas never put on a major league uniform again.

Transition Into the Broadcast Booth and Retirement

Armando Mendez started his South Florida business, Dynasty Apparel, with his two brothers in 1980. It supplies branded apparel to national sports teams and corporations. His perspective of Cookie Rojas is not only one of a fan but a personal acquaintance.

> I grew up in the Cerro district. I used to walk to Gran Stadium. I used to bike to Ciudad Deportiva [indoor sporting arena]. I arrived from Cuba in 1970 when I was ten years old. I started following Cuban players, those that my father had told me about that were major leaguers—Luis Tiant, Mike Cuéllar, Tony Pérez, and I came across Cookie.
>
> He became my favorite player in the American League, along with Tony Oliva. I watched Cookie and Freddie Patek, and that was a defensive wall on the infield. In my house the women didn't watch novelas, they watched baseball with me.
>
> My first baseball coach was Borrego Alvárez. He operated a baseball academy near the grounds of the old army base in Opa Locka. My father signed me up. I learned baseball, the fundamentals, understanding the game situations there, with coaches like Sandy Valdespino and José Tartabull. And that's where I met Cookie for the first time.
>
> And then I became friends with Cookie later in life, and business associates. I watched a baseball game once with Cookie. It was an education. Seeing Cookie at third base coaching with the expansion Marlins in 1993 was

very exciting. Cookie had a mantra: When you think a young player knows what to do in a certain situation, you have to remind him 100 more times.

I then got to go to spring training and watch Cookie hit ground balls to the Mets' infield of [John] Olerud, Edgardo Alfonzo, [Rey] Ordoñez and Robin Ventura.

I live in Miami Lakes now. I see Rey Ordoñez jogging around the neighborhood. I beep the horn and he comes over. And every time I mention Cookie Rojas, he lights up. He valued Cookie's instruction.

Cookie's career is unblemished on and off the field. You won't find a player or person that has ever had a negative thing to say about Cookie. He played baseball year-round, most always with his wife and kids in tow.[38]

In 2003, Rojas tried his hand at broadcasting, taking a post with Fox Sports Net to do color commentary for Marlins home games in Spanish. "We did an audition tape and I got the job," Rojas recalled. "I maintained a good working relationship with the players and coaches, and the opposition as well." There was a limitation of games broadcast that initial year, 46, but the 2003 season was no less special to Rojas and Marlins fans as the team captured its second World Series trophy. They upset the New York Yankees in six games, with Marlins right-hander Josh Beckett hurling a 2–0 shutout in the deciding contest at Yankee Stadium.

Rojas spoke out against the treatment that the Marlins' regular Spanish-language announcers received in the first two games played in New York. The radio team of 80-year-old Rafael "Felo" Ramírez and color analyst Luis "Yiky" Quintana were assigned exposed seating at Yankee Stadium. "What they did to Felo was wrong," voiced Rojas. "I don't think that's the way you treat a Hall of Famer [sic]. It was freezing out there."[39]

Rojas was offered a chance to reprise his role as third base coach with the Marlins in 2004. But he and the team could not come to a financial agreement. "I've been in the game for 47 years, 20 of them in the coaching lines," Rojas commented. "For what they offered me, there's no way I'm going to go back to the field."[40] (Rojas coached 14½ years in the big leagues.)

In 2004, Rojas did playoff games for the first time with ESPN Deportes, and in 2005, he teamed up with announcer Raúl Striker, Jr., for the FSN Marlins games in Spanish. After three years behind the mike, Rojas evaluated his transition from the field to the booth as follows: "I've seen so many things in this game, little can surprise me. I try to tell the fans what is occurring in the moment and explain the variants that can occur from a particular play. It's like analyzing a chess game with living pieces."[41]

EIGHT—From the Coaching Lines and Beyond 179

In 2006, Rojas teamed up with son Victor to broadcast the Caribbean Series in Venezuela for the YES Network. (An encore genealogical pairing for the same event and network followed from San Juan in 2007.) The broadcasts were done in English. Rojas did a couple more games in English in the summer of 2006. Over the weekend of July 28–30, he jumped to the Marlins' TV booth with lead announcer Rich Waltz to fill in for analyst Tommy Hutton, who was attending a brother's wedding. The games were played in Rojas' old stomping grounds, Philadelphia.

Over another weekend the following summer, Rojas was immortalized in collectible form. The first 20,000 fans entering Royals Stadium in their matchup against the Toronto Blue Jays, August 10, 2007, received a Cookie Rojas bobblehead. The bespectacled figurine, in a Royals uniform, is half-bent on one knee with a baseball in hand in an action pose.

In September 2008, room on the Rojas mantle was made for another Hall of Fame honor. The Miami Sports Hall of Fame inducted the former ballplayer, along with all-pro Miami Dolphins linebacker John Offerdahl, LPGA champion Christie Kerr, and executive Curtis Gray of the Homestead-Miami Speedway.

During this time, Rojas returned to Cuba, now the longest-lasting dictatorship in the history of the Western Hemisphere. He went by himself to see his half-brother, José Luis, and his family. "It was sad to see everything destroyed, the places I had grown up around in such bad shape, unrecognizable. There's a scarcity of everything for the people. It was depressing."

The Hispanic Heritage Baseball Museum Hall of Fame was established in San Francisco in September of 1998. In 2011, as part of a large class of eight inductees, Cookie Rojas was honored as a select international member.

In 2012, Rojas began his tenth season as color commentator in a new booth. He did not leave South Florida, rather the Marlins opened a new, state-of the-art stadium complete with retractable roof on the site of the former Orange Bowl. Barely a week into the season, Marlins manager Ozzie Guillén made sympathetic comments about Cuban dictator Fidel Castro. Guillén was suspended by the team for five games. Guillén issued a formal news conference apology in front of a packed press conference room with two dozen TV cameras. "It affects all of us Cubans," said a present Rojas afterward. "It opens a wound. The wound is going to bleed, then it will cure. But it is going to stay there to remind you."

"We all make mistakes," Rojas magnanimously added. "There is a space in baseball with an 'E' for error."[42]

Elected to the National Baseball Hall of Fame in 2000, Marlins executive Tony Pérez indicated that the front office punishment may not have been sufficient. "People want to get Ozzie fired," Pérez stated. "A lot of people do not think five games is enough. I don't blame them because a lot of people have been hurt here by Castro for more than 50 years. When something like that comes up, with the new stadium opening here in Little Havana, that's something people don't forget."[43]

In February 2013, Rojas returned to La Romana—not as Toros manager but one of a group of exalted members of the Latino Baseball Hall of Fame, established in the Dominican Republic city in 2010. Rojas was one of eight contemporary inductees (post–1970), including Mike Cuéllar, Tony Armas, Teddy Higuera, Matty Alou, and Juan "Igor" González. A veteran's committee selected eight other pre–1970 individuals for enshrinement. The honored South Florida broadcaster mentioned the two founders of the modern Hall in preliminary comments related to his election: "It is a great honor for me to receive this award that represents the greatest source of pride in the life of a Latino baseball player who has performed in the major leagues and in Caribbean baseball. The work created by Rafael Avila and Roberto A. Weill is immense, as it does justice to the Latino players who have dedicated their lives to the sport of balls and strikes."[44]

In June 2016, Rojas returned to Kansas City for the first time in 10 years. He was invited back to be part of MLB's "Viva Baseball" campaign that was adopted by all major league clubs years earlier. Rojas' appearance was part of the "Viva Los Reales" weekend at Kauffman Stadium.

There had been many "Vivas!" shouted at Marlins Park for pitcher José Fernández since 2013, the year he debuted as a rookie. Fernández, a talented and charismatic hurler with a backstory worthy of a movie script, won the NL Rookie of the Year Award in 2013. Not since Mark "The Bird" Fidrych had a pitcher displayed more joy and infectious enthusiasm pitching from a major league mound than Fernández did. In September of 2016, Fernández and two others were killed in a tragic boating accident; the pitcher's blood alcohol level was found to have been above the legal limit, and his system contained cocaine. He was 24 years old. Though his short career was staggered by Tommy John surgery, he was still able to post a 38–17 record, with an ERA of 2.58 in four seasons. He registered 589 strikeouts in 471⅓ innings; his ERA+ was 150. The loss to the franchise was felt for years.

"Sadly, the brightest lights are often the ones that extinguish the fastest," said Marlins owner Jeffrey Loria. "Jose left us far too soon, but his memory will endure in all of us."[45]

The Marlins franchise had to deal with the loss of another beloved individual in 2017. Felo Ramírez, a giant behind the microphone for Latin American sports fans and the longtime Spanish radio voice of the Marlins, died in August. The passing of the 94-year-old Ramírez did not carry the same shock value as Fernández' death, but his loss was heartfelt among the Marlins and the Hispanic broadcast community throughout the U.S. and Latin America. Honored as a winner of the Ford Frick Award at the National Baseball Hall of Fame in Cooperstown in 2011, Ramírez, despite his advanced age, was remarkably still calling Marlins games, at home and on the road. He suffered a fall from the team bus in April in Philadelphia, which led to his decline and ultimate death a few months afterward.

At 77, Rojas left the Marlins after the 2016 season and moved to Naples, Florida, where he lives today with his wife. "I would do it all over again, change nothing," said Candida Rojas. "I always liked baseball and eventually came to love it. I was Cookie's biggest cheerleader and probably the loudest among the wives. I always loved watching Cookie and his teams play."

Son Victor recalled his mother's passion for the game: "My mom was the louder one of the two [parents]. She was more intense about the games. My mom was famous in KC for being a fan, being involved in every pitch. Rob Nen came over to the Marlins in a trade in 1993. I was the bullpen catcher with the Marlins. Nen's wife at the time, Jendy, was 22 years old. To this day, whenever I see her, she always mentions the impact of my mother on her on how to act like a major leaguer's wife. She always asks how my mom is doing."[46]

"My mom was our baseball coach," said brother Bobby. "She knew the game better than most men I knew."[47]

Mike Rojas resides in the same west coast Florida development as his parents. He lauded his mother's dedication, especially during the early years: "Having to raise four boys was not easy, managing our age differences and all. Driving us everywhere we had to go. I remember when we were young, the four of us were playing on different fields at Flagami Park in Miami. The four fields were cornered against the others and she sat in the center field middle so she could watch all four of our games."[48]

"They are just great people," added Victor. "I was fortunate to have grown up around them. I learned a lot from them."[49]

Jim Murray, the longtime *Los Angeles Times* columnist and BBWAA Career Excellence Award recipient, dedicated a column to Rojas in 1974. In it, he quoted Kansas City broadcaster Buddy Blattner as saying, "If you were to get out an instructional film on fielding second base, Cookie would have to be your man." Murray closed the written piece with perhaps the quintessential description of Rojas as a player: "There isn't a pitcher on the staff who doesn't keep Cookie's picture close to his heart. Especially with one out and the bases loaded."[50]

The same reliable characterization pervades the entire, exemplary life of Cookie Rojas.

Chapter Notes

Chapter One

1. Frederick C. Mills, "Prices in a War Economy: Some Aspects of the Present Price Structure of the United States," accessed October 31, 2021, https//www.nber.org/system/files/chapters/c5535/c5535.pdf1943.
2. Amity Shlaes, *The Forgotten Man: A New History of the Great Depression* (New York: MJF Books, 2007), 12.
3. *Ibid.*
4. After divorcing, Octavio Gregorio remarried and had another son, José Luis Rojas. "I was able to visit José Luis a few years ago," adds his half-brother. Rojas' mother also remarried and had two other daughters, Raisa and Alina.
5. In contrast, Felipe Alou's first trip to the United States occurred the same year as Rojas,' 1956. The 21-year-old Alou was assigned to the Lake Charles Giants of the Class C Evangeline League, which resisted integration attempts by the San Francisco Giants' and Chicago Cubs' (Lafayette Oilers) affiliates. The Giants' conscript, Alou, was therefore reassigned to the Cocoa Indians, part of the same Florida State League as Rojas' Sun Chiefs. Alou spent the three-day Greyhound bus ride from Louisiana to Florida (in the back of the bus with African American riders) eating only peanuts and other snacks bought from vending machines during stops along the way, due to the language barrier stymieing his ability to order food. Exceptionally, 18-year-old Tony Taylor, an Afro-Cuban, spent the entire season in the Evangeline League, two years earlier, as posted in the player's SABR online biography, leading the circuit in triples with 12. In 1954, Taylor courageously suited up with the Texas City Pilots and the Thibodaux (Louisiana) Pilots. The Texas franchise relocated to the Cajun State in mid-June, according to several sources.
6. Phone conversation with Jose Padilla, November 12, 2021.
7. *Ibid.*
8. *Ibid.*
9. "Rojas Is Hero in Redleg Win," *Wilson Daily Times*, July 11, 1958. The referenced All-Star Game was the 14th in the league's history. The first-place team (Savannah) played a squad of composite talent from the rest of the circuit. Rojas tripled in three runs, following an intentional walk to Alberto Alvarez, to give Savannah a 4–2 triumph. Candido Andrade was the victor with six shutout innings in relief. Savannah's slide to the bottom had begun with a 10-game losing streak prior to the All-Star Game.
10. Terry Sloope, "Curt Flood," sabr.org/bioproject.
11. Lou Hernández, *Bobby Maduro and the Cuban Sugar Kings* (Jefferson, NC: McFarland, 2019), 35. The Cuban Winter League, although an "unclassified affiliate" of organized baseball, was considered, talent-wise, equal to the U.S. Triple A leagues.
12. The official team name was *Cubanos Reyes del Azucar*, best translated as Cuban Sugar Kings. But many North American writers and their newspapers, perhaps with the Havana Cubans fresh in their minds, often mistakenly called the club the Havana Sugar Kings.

There was nothing on the team's uniform that referred to Havana. The official caps during the team's six-and-a-half-year existence were imprinted with the letter "C" and emblazoned across the uniform chest was "Cubanos" (home and away). An alternate 1955 road and home uniform with "Sugar Kings" scripted on the front was briefly used.

13. John Phillips, *The Story of the Havana Sugar Kings, 1954–1960* (Kathleen, GA: Capital, 2003), 53.

14. *Ibid.*, 57.

15. Sean Lahman, "Rochester Team Made Baseball History in Cuba," *Bradenton Herald*, December 26, 2014, C5.

16. Hernández, *Bobby Maduro*, 113.

17. *Ibid.*, 122.

18. Conversation with Jorge Maduro, February 13, 2022.

19. Hernández, *Bobby Maduro*, 129.

20. "Fidel Castro Speaks to Reporters on January 10, 1959, a Week After the Cuban revolution," accessed February 27, 2022, http://www.bbc.com/news/av/world-latin-america-388115309.

21. Ada Ferrer, *Cuba: An American History* (New York: Scribner's, 2021), 321.

22. Phillips, *The Story of the Havana Sugar Kings*, 100.

23. Ferrer, *Cuba*, 340.

24. Tommy Devine, "IL Boss Explodes on Cuba," *Miami News*, April 17, 1960, 26.

25. Tommy Devine, "Baseball No Exception to Cuban Crisis," *Miami News*, July 3, 1960, 26.

26. Cy Kritzer, "Sugar Kings Jolt IL by Asking for Loan of $20,000," *Buffalo News*, June 27, 1960, 14.

27. Sean Lahman, "Rochester Team Made Baseball History in Cuba," *Bradenton Herald*, December 26, 2014, C5.

28. "Havana Shift Only Reasonable Action," *The Sporting News*, July 20, 1960, 14.

29. "Jersey City Falls Heir to Havana Franchise," *Herald-News* (Fall River, MA), July 8, 1969, 12.

30. "Reds to Retain Pact with 'Kings,'" *Cincinnati Enquirer*, July 11, 1960, 12. The "official transfer" was approved in a special meeting in New York on July 13 by International League team directors.

31. The late edition of Rochester's *Democrat and Chronicle* listed Bobby Tiefenauer as closing out the game. But a line score of the same game in the *Miami News* has pitcher Tom Hurd spelling Tiefenauer in the ninth inning. A box score in the July 6 *Sporting News* coincides with the latter.

32. Gaspar González, "When They Were Kings," *Miami Herald*, July 22, 2005, 18.

33. George Beahon, "In This Corner…," *Rochester Democrat and Chronicle*, August 18, 1960, 41.

34. Ferrer, *Cuba*, 348.

35. David E. Hoffman, *Give Me Liberty: The True Story of Oswaldo Paya and His Daring Quest for a Free Cuba* (New York: Simon & Schuster, 2022), 126.

36. "Cuban Players Slash Pay, Gate Dip Threatens Loop," *The Sporting News*, November 16, 1960, 21. The four CWL teams were the Almendares Scorpions, Habana Lions, Cienfuegos Elephants, and Marianao Tigers.

37. Hoffman, *Give Me Liberty*, 134.

38. "Ike Breaks Off Ties with Castro Regime," *Pittsburgh Post-Gazette*, January 4, 1961, 1.

39. "Cuban Baseballers Await U.S. Ruling," *Fort Lauderdale News*, January 12, 1961, 45.

40. *Ibid.*

41. Lou Hernández, *The Rise of the Latin American Baseball Leagues, 1947–1961* (Jefferson, NC: McFarland, 2011), 227.

42. Rubén Rodríguez, "Elephants Grab Crown with Win in Final Contest," *The Sporting News*, February 15, 1961, 22.

Chapter Two

1. Sam Zygner, *The Forgotten Marlins: A Tribute to the 1956–1960 Original Miami Marlins* (Lanham, MD: Scarecrow, 2013), 323.

2. https://www.history.com/this-date-in-history/castro-declares-himself-a-marxist-leninist, accessed September 28, 2022.

3. Thomas E. Van Hyning, "Ed Bauta," sabr.org/bioproject.

4. Lou Hernández, *The Rise of the Latin American Baseball Leagues, 1947–1961* (Jefferson, NC: McFarland, 2011), 180.

5. Tony Oliva with Bob Fowler, *Tony O! The Trials and Triumphs of Tony Oliva* (New York: Hawthorn, 1973), 7.

6. Thomas E. Van Hyning, *Puerto Rico's Winter League: A History of Major League Baseball's Launching Pad* (Jefferson, NC: McFarland, 1995), 151.

7. Ibid.

8. Ibid. The PRWL consisted of six clubs. The Santurce Crabbers and San Juan Senators were based in the capital city. The Mayagüez Indians, Ponce Lions, Caguas Criollos, and Arecibo Wolves were other metropolitan circuit representatives.

9. Phone conversation with Tab Rojas, June 10, 2023.

10. Earl Lawson, "Otero High on Rojas, Rookie Second Sacker," *Cincinnati Post & Times-Star*, February 21, 1962, 25.

11. Pat Harmon, "This Cookie Never Crumbles," *Cincinnati Post*, March 30, 1972, 20.

12. "Reds Familiar Problem," *St. Louis Post-Dispatch*, March 4, 1962, 25.

13. Cárdenas became a starter, but instead of transitioning Kasko, who was far from a star, the Reds chose to keep the 31-year-old infielder and send Harper to the minors. Playing the entire 1962 season with San Diego in the PCL as a third baseman, Harper hit .333 with an eye-popping on-base percentage of .450 and 120 runs scored in 144 games. Harper returned to the big leagues in 1963 as a regular outfielder, the position at which he would shine. Kasko played only one more year as a starter with the expansion Houston Colt .45s (1964). The Harper demotion is reminiscent of Tony Oliva, who hit .444 and .429 in two September call-ups for the Minnesota Twins in 1962 and '63, nine and seven games, respectively. Even though he excelled in both seasons in the minors, Oliva wasn't brought up by the big club permanently until 1964. In between, Oliva won the 1963–1964 PRWL batting title with a .365 mark. The two situations harken to Minnie Miñoso in 1949, when the Cleveland Indians optioned him, also to San Diego in the PCL, nine games after his major league debut. Miñoso would not return to the majors until 1951. The cases illustrate the uphill climb players of color faced during the initial decades of integration. Finally, it should be noted that with Cárdenas in 1962, the Reds did showcase three Black players as starters, a departure from the norm at the time. In 1963, with the return of Harper, the Reds fielded a regular starting lineup with four men of color, including an all-Black outfield. The great Frank Robinson and the underappreciated Vada Pinson returned to roam the two other outfield spots.

14. Earl Lawson, "Lawson's Notes: 'Dad Schools Rojas,'" *Cincinnati Post & Times-Star*, March 9, 1962, 20.

15. Hugh Brown, "Cuqui Hits .307, Endears Himself," *Evening Bulletin* (Philadelphia, PA), July 2, 1965 (Cookie Rojas Hall of Fame File).

16. Earl Lawson, "Lawson's Notes: 'Moe Drabowsky Pitches Tonight,'" *Cincinnati Post & Times-Star*, April 11, 1962, 25.

17. "Phillies Sign Cookie Rojas to Contract," *Daily Times* (Salisbury, MD), February 7, 1963, 7.

18. Conversation with Mike Rojas, April 24, 2022.

19. The September 18 Phillies-Mets finale was not quite the end of professional baseball at the Polo Grounds. On October 12, one more contest was played as a first-of-its-kind showcase for Latin American players. Dubbed the Hispanic All-Star Game, the nine-inning game featured a majority Hispanic cast of standout players from both leagues. Five future Hall of Famers (Juan Marichal, Orlando Cepeda, Luis Aparicio, Roberto Clemente, and Tony Oliva) participated in the event, won by the National League's Iberian best over their rival league counterparts, 5–2. Attendance was slightly over 14,000. The 24-year-old Rojas did not participate. No similar event has been staged since.

20. John Vorperian, "Gene Mauch," sabr.org/bioproject. Wes Covington and Tony González were identified as the two players whose suits were caught in the culinary crossfire. They had to have their luggage pulled from the equipment truck heading to the airport so they could change clothes. Mauch promised to reimburse the pair with new threads and did so.

21. "Mauch Goes on a Food-Tossing

Tear," *Tucson Daily Citizen*, September 23, 1963, 40.

Chapter Three

1. Joe Reichler, "Jim Bunning Is Happy, and So Is Gene Mauch," *Morning Call* (Allentown, PA), December 6, 1963, 45.
2. Sandy Grady, "Cookie Keeps Swingin' Sweet," *Philadelphia Bulletin*, June 3, 1964 (Rojas HOF File).
3. Rory Costello, "1964 Phillies: What to Do with Two Gold Glove Shortstops?" 1964 Philadelphia Phillies essays, sabr.org.
4. In 1880, two NL pitchers tossed perfect games within five days of each other: June 17, John Montgomery Ward of the Providence Grays against the Buffalo Bisons, 5–0, and June 12, Worcester's John Lee Richmond versus the Cleveland Blues, 1–0. Cy Young hurled no-hitters in both the National and American leagues. Bunning had no-hit the Boston Red Sox in 1958 as a Detroit Tiger. The last regular season perfect game in baseball, before Bunning's, was pitched in 1922 by the White Sox' Charlie Robertson over the Tigers, April 30, 2–0. In his perfecto, Bunning's Game Score was 97, bested by only eight of the 24 perfect game hurlers through 2023. Among the eight, Matt Cain and Sandy Koufax have the highest Game Score of 101. Game Score is a Bill James analytic designed to measure a pitcher's performance from the hill in a single outing, normally balancing innings, hits, runs, strikeouts and walks.
5. Allen Lewis, "Bunning Pitches Perfect Game, Phillies Sweep," *Philadelphia Inquirer*, June 22, 1964, 26. Fifty Father's Days later, the Phillies commemorated Bunning's perfect game at Citizens Bank Park with the pitcher as guest of honor. Dick Allen and Cookie Rojas were on hand as the only other players who participated in the eventful game. Tony Taylor was unable to attend due to an illness, but Bunning, 82, distinctly remembered his second baseman for saving his historic effort: "It was a play directly in the hole and Taylor made a diving stop and then got the ball and from his knees threw Gonder [the hitter] out"; Jake Kaplan, "Still Memorable Fifty Years Later," *Philadelphia Daily News*, June 16, 2014, 63–64. As a member of the Pittsburgh Pirates, Jesse Gonder, incidentally, was Bunning's 2000th career strikeout victim on June 24, 1966, at Connie Mack Stadium.
6. "Dive—Do Something, Jim Asks Phillies For Help," *Philadelphia Inquirer*, June 22, 1964, 1. To their credit, the hometown newspaper probably polished the quote by Taylor, as opposed to renowned New York sportswriter Dick Young, who quoted Taylor phonetically in his game story: "I deedn't know I saved no-hitter. I deedn't know he pitch no-hitter until eighth inning"; "Phils Bunning Hurls Perfect 6–0 Game," *New York Daily News*, June 22, 1964, 46. Viewing it through the more culturally sensitive lens of today, such quotations were a tactless practice that trapped the most gifted baseball writers of the period. Young certainly was one of the best and best-known at his craft. Sportswriter and novelist Frank Deford did the same thing to Chico Ruíz on a piece on the Cincinnati Reds' season in an October 1964 *Sports Illustrated*. Some of the earliest curt and phonetic quoting of Hispanic players in newspapers began with Shirley Povich, like Young, a BBWAA Career Excellence Award recipient—the sport's highest journalistic honor. In the late 1930s, when the Washington Senators first began promoting Latin American ballplayers to their clubs on a consistent basis, Povich covered the teams for the *Washington Post*. The advent of sound motion pictures and Hollywood's marginalized treatment of minorities during its early decades, through ethnic sight gags and stilted dialogue, cannot be discounted as a correlating influence in this regard upon the bygone men of the press box.
7. Ray Kelly, "Rojas' Knockout Crash Catch Saves Phils," *Evening Bulletin* (Philadelphia, PA), July 3, 1964 (Rojas HOF File).
8. *Ibid*.
9. *Ibid*.
10. "'Hot' Cookie Rojas Phillies' Hero in a 9–1 Romp Over Cards," *Sentinel* (Lewiston, PA), Saturday July 25, 1964, 7.

11. "Allen's Home Runs Pace Phils," *Progress Bulletin* (Pomona, CA), August 24, 1964, 16. The game was on a Sunday, and it gave the Phillies a four-games-to-one series victory over the Pirates, which began with a Thursday, August 20, twi-night doubleheader sweep that drew 35,814 fans—the Phils' largest crowd of the year (a couple of thousand over Connie Mack Stadium's capacity of 33,608). The Phillies went over the million mark in attendance on the evening.

Philadelphia won the first game (2–0) on a ninth-inning, walk-off home run by Johnny Callison, and took the nightcap (3–2) by scoring two runs in the eighth inning on a sacrifice fly by Callison. Baserunners Rick Wise and Tony González, from second, scored on the deep fly to center by the Philles right fielder. In the top of the ninth, Callison threw out Bill Mazeroski at third base as the tying run, attempting to tag up from second on a fly. The seemingly charmed events prompted Gus Triandos to provide the press with a whimsical quote that has now been linked to the fateful squad. "It's the year of blue snow," said the back-up backstop, who did not play in either game (Clay Dalrymple caught both ends of the double dip); Larry Merchant, "The Year of Blue Snow," *Philadelphia Daily News*, August 21, 1964, 50. Capitalized, as in "The Year of the Pitcher," the meaning entertains rare or unusual occurrences.

12. "Top Rookie Honor Means Little—Allen," *Progress Bulletin* (Pomona, CA), August 24, 1964, 16.

13. John Dell, "Wandering Rojas Just Wants to Play," *Philadelphia Inquirer*, August 31, 1964, 29.

14. Frank Bilovsky, "Rojas Was 2d Baseman, 'Now I Am Everything,'" *Philadelphia Sunday Bulletin*, August 2, 1964 (Rojas HOF File).

15. John Dell, "Wandering Rojas Just Wants to Play," *Philadelphia Inquirer*, August 31, 1964, 29.

16. Costello, "1964 Phillies."

17. Harry Grayson, "Mauch Catches Foes in Switches," *Morning News* (Florence, SC), September 1, 1964, 22.

18. Fred Hartman, *Baytown Sun* (Baytown, TX), September 17, 1964, 26.

19. Stan Hochman, "What Colts Did to Bunning Just Didn't Figure," *Philadelphia Daily News*, September 17, 1964, 58, 60.

20. Josh Moyer, "Phillies' Collapse of 1964 Is Still on Mahaffey's Mind," *Morning Call* (Allentown, PA), July 7, 2007, 32.

21. For success rate probabilities, see Rory Costello, "1964 Phillies: In Defense of Chico Ruiz's 'Mad Dash,'" 1964 Philadelphia Phillies essays, sabr.org.

22. *Ibid.*

23. *Ibid.*

24. "Mauch Says They'll Win," *Bangor Daily News*, September 24, 1964, 30.

25. Ralph Bernstein, "For Phils Latest Loss," *Greeley Daily Tribune*, September 26, 1964, 8.

26. *Ibid.*

27. Stan Hochman, "Volunteer Bunning Can't Kill Pain," *Philadelphia Daily News*, September 28, 1964, 46.

28. Larry Merchant, "Calm Panic," *Philadelphia Daily News*, September 28, 1964, 46.

29. "Restrained Mauch Won't 'Blow Top' Despite Late Slump," *Daily Press* (Newport News, VA), September 30, 1964, 17.

30. *Ibid.*

31. "Mauch Blamed for Collapse," *Morning News* (Florence, SC), September 30, 1964, 27. Reference is to Mauch's infamous overturning of a post-game spread following a loss to the Houston Colt .45s late in the 1963 season.

32. Joe Reichler, "Phils in Greatest Collapse in History?" *St. Cloud Times*, September 29, 1964, 22.

33. Joe Reichler, "Pitching Key Factor in Cards' Drive," *Evening Sun* (Hanover, PA), September 30, 1964, 18.

34. Stan Hochman, "Bunning: It's All Our Own Fault," *Philadelphia Daily News*, October 1, 1964, 59. Bunning was used as a reliever twice during the season, saving both games. The day after a subpar start in Chicago, June 18, he was called to the hill by Mauch to get the final two outs of a game against the same club and did so with minimal effort. On July 13, two days after hurling eight innings in a 3–2 loss to the Cincinnati Reds, Bunning saved a 3–2 game for Ray Culp, versus the Milwaukee Brewers, by getting the final three outs against the visitors.

He walked one batter in doing so. Warren Spahn took the complete-game loss.

35. Larry Merchant, "An Incredible Horror Story," *Philadelphia Daily News*, October 1, 1964, 59.

36. *Ibid.*

37. "Mauch Says Phils Alive; Reds Angry," *Courier-Post* (Cherry Hill, NJ), October 3, 1964, 15.

38. Earl Lawson, "Lawson's Notes," *Cincinnati Post*, October 3, 1964, 9.

39. George Crudden, "The Observer," *Sunday News* (Lancaster, PA), October 4, 1964, 33.

40. Bob Sullivan, "The News of Sports," *Springfield News*, October 4, 1964, 24.

41. Frank Dolson, "Cards Win Pennant by Crushing Mets," *Philadelphia Inquirer*, October 5, 1964, 33.

42. Ralph Bernstein, "Why Did Phils Collapse, Mauch, Injuries, Schedule," *Express* (San Antonio, TX), October 5, 1964, 13. "A bulldozer sat by the third-base dugout at Connie Mack Stadium, ready to move dirt to make room for additional field boxes"; Steve Wulf, "The Year of Blue Snow," *Sports Illustrated*, September 25, 1989, accessed May 10, 2023, The Year of the Blue Snow—Sports Illustrated Vault | SI.com.

43. "Bunning Unhappy Despite Shutout," *News Journal* (Wilmington, DE), October 5, 1964, 28.

44. Wulf, "The Year of Blue Snow."

45. Bryan Soderholm-Difatte, "Beyond Bunning and Short Rest: An Analysis of Managerial Decisions That Led to the Phillies Epic Collapse in 1964," *SABR Baseball Research Journal* (Fall 2010), sabr.org.

46. José I. Ramírez and Rory Costello, "Tony Taylor," sabr.org/bioproject.

47. Jake Kaplan, "Phillies Veteran Rojas Focuses on the Good Things About 1964," *Philadelphia Inquirer*, July 19, 2014.

48. Ralph Bernstein, "Why Did Phils Collapse, Mauch, Injuries, Schedule," *Express* (San Antonio, TX), October 5, 1964, 13.

49. *Ibid.*

50. Costello, "1964 Phillies."

51. Charles Karmosky, "The Sportscope," *Daily Press* (Newport News, VA), September 30, 1964, 17.

52. John Vorperian, "Gene Mauch," sabr.org/bioproject.

53. Bran Soderholm-Difatte, "Beyond Bunning and Short Rest."

54. Sandy Grady, "Gene Wouldn't Alter Strategy, Denies Overworking Bunning," *The Sporting News*, October 17, 1964, 6.

55. *Ibid.*

56. "'Wait 'til '65,' 7,000 Phils Fans," *Express* (San Antonio, TX), October 5, 1964, 13.

57. John Dell, "Wandering Rojas Just Wants to Play," *Philadelphia Inquirer*, August 31, 1964, 29.

58. Mel Marmer and Ralph Berger, "Art Mahaffey," sabr.org/bioproject.

Chapter Four

1. Thomas E. Van Hyning, *Puerto Rico's Winter League: A History of Major League Baseball's Launching Pad* (Jefferson, NC: McFarland, 1995), 235.

2. Jack Hand, "Phillies Hoping to Bounce Back," *Portsmouth Herald*, April 12, 1965, 9.

3. "Mauch Says Phils, Dodgers, Most Improved," *Lebanon Daily News*, March 8, 1965, 13.

4. Al Cartwright, "A La Carte," *News Journal* (Wilmington, DE), March 18, 1965, 43.

5. Al Cartwright, "Mauch Purrs Over Rojas; May Be Starting Shortstop," *Morning News* (Florence, SC), April 5, 1965, 19.

6. Al Cartwright, "Riding Bench Miffs Phils Cookie Rojas," *Morning News* (Florence, SC), April 13, 1965, 21.

7. Al Cartwright, "A La Carte," *News Journal* (Wilmington, DE), February 25, 1965, 29.

8. Richard Riis, "April 12, 1965: Phillies Win First Game at Astrodome," sabr.org game project (Gary Cartwright of the *Dallas Morning News* is being quoted).

9. Murray Chass, "Luis Tiant Stops Twins Four-Game Win Streak," *Indiana Gazette*, June 8, 1965, 14.

10. Wendell Smith, "Richie Allen Loves His Bats," *Pittsburgh Courier*, June 27, 1964, 15. The young Allen did not help his cause when he made poorly thought-out comments about Southern Whites to

nationally syndicated columnist Milton Gross. It was through Gross that Allen first voiced his racially-influenced mistreatment at Little Rock.

11. Gregory H. Wolf, "Rob Gardner," sabr.org/bioproject. The game marked the fifth and last time since 1920 that two pitchers each tossed 15 innings and allowed one run or less, according to the same article.

12. "Phils Should Have Won Pennant, Says Covington," *Sunday News* (Lancaster, PA), October 3, 1965, 41. Covington had been part of the 1957–1958 back-to-back pennant-winning Milwaukee Braves.

13. "Cookie Rojas a Good Spare Tire," *Daily Times* (Salisbury, MD), April 15, 1966, 10.

14. Ray Kelly, "Allen Socks 520-Foot HR," *Philadelphia Bulletin*, June 17, 1966 (Rojas HOF File).

15. "Cookie Rojas a Good Spare Tire," *Daily Times* (Salisbury, MD), April 15, 1966, 10.

16. Mel Durslag, "Usual Dodger Exodus—Koufax," *San Francisco Examiner*, October 4, 1966, 64.

17. José I. Ramírez and Rory Costello, "Tony Taylor," sabr.org/bioproject.

18. "Castoff Ferguson Jenkins Come Back to Haunt the Phils," *Delaware County Daily Times*, April 12, 1967, 30.

19. "Phillie Boo Birds Perplex Uecker," *The Sporting News*, June 10, 1967, 19.

20. Harmon, "This Cookie Never Crumbles," 20.

21. Bill Conlin, "As Midnight Tolls, Cookie Turns into—Pitcher?" *Philadelphia Daily News*, July 1, 1967, 30, 32.

22. Ibid.

Chapter Five

1. Phone conversation with Victor Rojas, April 10, 2022.

2. Ibid.

3. Ross Newhan, "Crunch Time for Cookie," *Los Angeles Times*, May 23, 1988, 1,17.

4. "Bunning Is Swapped To Pirates," *Sacramento Bee*, December 16, 1967.

5. Bill Conlin, "Whiff Kids Stagger in for Home Opener," *Philadelphia Daily News*, April 17, 1968, 57.

6. Dick Couch, "When Wind Is Right, 'Lil Cookie Rojas Blows up Storm," *Town Talk* (Alexandria, LA), April 18, 1964, 8. The well-traveled Catholic High School Band won the World Music Festival competition in Kerkrade, Holland, in 1966 and became the first U.S. school to perform in the Vatican for Pope Paul VI in the same year.

7. Dwight Chapin, "Boyer Carefully Handles Slow Hopper for Record," *Los Angeles Times*, June 9, 1968, 50. Prior to the game, Dodgers shortstop and former AL MVP Zoilo Versalles was recognized by Cuban exiles for his 10 years of major league service.

8. "Don Within Another Mark," *Cincinnati Enquirer*, June 9, 1968, 44.

9. Ralph Bernstein, "Phillies Fire Gene Mauch, Hire Bob Skinner as Pilot," *Sacramento Bee*, June 16, 1968, 84.

10. Ibid., 77.

11. "Phillies Fire Gene Mauch," *Atlanta Constitution*, June 16, 1968, 45. Also that summer, Allen's name made the papers following a physical altercation with a Philadelphia barroom owner on Saturday, August 17. Both involved parties presented opposite arguments as to the reason for the fight. The barkeep ended up dropping the assault and battery charges he originally wanted levied upon Allen. The lightning rod player was in the lineup on Sunday and collected three hits.

12. Range Factor, a Bill James analytic, is computed by dividing putouts plus assists by the number of games played at a position. A secondary Range Factor analytic adjusts for nine innings per game, which typically inflates the statistic.

13. George Langford, "Pinch Homer by W. Smith Ends Thrilling Opener, 7–6," *Chicago Tribune*, April 9, 1969, 74.

14. Tiny Parry, "The Sportfolio," *Lebanon Daily News*, August 8, 1969, 14.

15. Milton Richman, "Richie Allen Leads Phillies Managers, 2–0," *Delaware County Daily Times*, August 8, 1969, 17.

16. "Phillies Trade Allen to Cardinals," *Detroit Free Press*, October 9, 1969, 63.

17. "Flood Intends on Retirement," *Springfield News-Leader*, October 9, 1969, 31.

18. Phone conversation with Tab Rojas, June 10, 2023.
19. Bob Broeg, "New Cardinal Cookie Caught Fans' Fancy in Philly," *St. Louis Post-Dispatch*, March 23, 1970, 30.
20. Ibid.
21. Ralph Bernstein, "Rich Allen Hears Same Philly Song," *Lebanon Daily News*, May 22, 1970, 14.

Chapter Six

1. Hal Bodley, "Rojas Gets KC's Royal Treatment," *News Journal* (Wilmington, DE), July 13, 1971, 31.
2. Sid Bordman, "Cookie Rojas Proves Baseball Men Wrong," *Kansas City Star*, June 21, 1970, 25.
3. "Cookie Rojas Plays Steady Ball at 2nd for KC Royals," *Salina Journal*, August 23, 1970, 18.
4. Hal Bodley, "Rojas Gets KC's Royal Treatment," *News Journal* (Wilmington, DE), July 13, 1971, 31.
5. The all-minority starting nine consisted of five African Americans and four Afro-Hispanics. The lineup order: Rennie Stennett, 2B (Panama), Gene Clines, CF, Roberto Clemente, RF (Puerto Rico), Willie Stargell, LF, Manny Sanguillén, C (Panama), Dave Cash, 3B, Al Oliver, 1B, Jackie Hernández, SS (Cuba), and pitcher Doc Ellis.
6. Allen Siefert, "The Wise Owl," *St. Joseph News-Press*, June 18, 1971, 12.
7. Phone conversation with Tab Rojas, June 10, 2023.
8. "Rojas Finds Himself," *Kenosha News*, May 1, 1971, 14.
9. Dick Wade, "Rojas Providing Royals' Glue," *Kansas City Star*, May 9, 1971, 134.
10. Allen Siefert, "The Wise Owl," *St. Joseph News-Press*, June 18, 1971, 12.
11. Hal Bodley, "Rojas Gets KC's Royal Treatment," *News Journal* (Wilmington, DE), July 13, 1971, 31.
12. Ibid.
13. Other players, to that point, previously selected to All-Star squads who played in both leagues: Mike Cuéllar, Frank Robinson, Ray Culp, Jim Bunning, Schoolboy Rowe, John Roseboro, Johnny Mize, and Johnny Temple.
14. "Rojas' Hot Bat Paces 7–1 Win," *Daily Times* (Salisbury, MD), July 21, 1971, 16.
15. Harmon, "This Cookie Never Crumbles," 20.
16. Sid Bordman, "Royals Won Wrong Way," *Kansas City Star*, April 16, 1972, 153.
17. "Cookie Rojas Is Almost the Hero of 43rd All-Star Contest," *Danville Register*, July 26, 1972, 9.
18. The All-Star pinch-hit homers, to date, came off the bats of Mickey Owen, Gus Bell, Larry Doby, Willie Mays, Stan Musial, Harmon Killebrew, George Altman, Pete Runnels, and Reggie Jackson.
19. Phone conversation with Tab Rojas, June 10, 2023.
20. "A Dream Game for Four Players," *Kingston Daily Freeman*, July 26, 1972, 26.
21. Bill Lee, "With Malice Toward None," *Hartford Courant*, July 26, 1972, 66.
22. "KC Players Disagree with Lemon's Dismissal," *Star Gazette* (Elmira, NY), October 5, 1972, 47.
23. "Royals Dismiss Lemon; Promote Jack McKeon," *St. Joseph News-Press*, October 4, 1972, 23.
24. Randy Galloway, "Tip-Top Toby Receives Titanic Texas Hurrah," *The Sporting News*, March 10, 1973, 41.
25. Joe McGuff, "Otis Has Elevated Plans for Both Royals and Himself," *The Sporting News*, March 31, 1973, 40.
26. Joe McGuff, "Sporting Comment," *Kansas City Star*, April 11, 1973, 30.
27. Gib Twyman, "Royals Real Dazzlers in Show," *Kansas City Times*, April 11, 1973, 39, 44.
28. "A Big Pinch Hit by Bevacqua," *Chillicothe Constitution-Tribune*, May 29, 1973, 21.
29. Sid Bordman, "No Practice Makes Perfect," *Kansas City Star*, July 8, 1973, 137.
30. Sid Bordman, "Hot Rojas Bat Picks Up Royals," *Kansas City Star*, July 15, 1973, 139.
31. "McKeon Predicts First Place for KC," *Jefferson City Post Tribune*, August 15, 1973, 17.
32. John DiFonzo, "Paul Splittorff," sabr.org/bioproject.
33. Gib Twyman, "Cookie Rojas

Contemplates Retirement," *Kansas City Times*, September 25, 1973. 20.
34. Gib Twyman, "Cookie Wants Royals' Dough to Rise," *Kansas City Times*, February 3, 1974. 146.
35. "White Should Be First Cadet to Stay Full Year in Majors," *Paducah Sun*, March 15, 1974, 35.
36. Sid Bordman, "Rojas Worth Two in Glove," *Kansas City Star*, April 21, 1974, 156.
37. *Ibid.*
38. Joe McGuff, "Sporting Comment," *Kansas City Star*, May 19, 1974, 150.
39. "Rojas Sinks O's with Grand Slam," *Sedalia Democrat*, May 29, 1974, 24.
40. Gib Twyman, "No-Hit Hurler 'Not Me!' Says Busby," *The Sporting News*, July 6, 1974, 13.
41. Mike O'Brien, "'My Biggest Thrill of All,'" *Journal Gazette* (Fort Wayne, IN), June 20, 1974, 6.
42. "Martinez' 'Biggest Hit' Lifts KC," *Leavenworth Times*, July 1, 1974, 12.
43. "Little-Used Carew: No More All-Star Games," *Orlando Sentinel*, July 26, 1974, 35.
44. Luis Rodríguez-Mayoral, "Mis Memorias: Recordando y Hablando De Cookie Rojas con Orlando Cepeda!" Facebook profile page post, February 24, 2022, accessed December 10, 2022, MIS MEMORIAS: RECORDANDO Y HABLANDO DE...—Luis Rodriguez-Mayoral | Facebook, translated from Spanish.

Chapter Seven

1. Phone conversation with Tab Rojas, June 10, 2023.
2. Bill Chronister, "Veteran Cookie Rojas Takes Work Seriously," *St. Joseph News-Press*, March 8, 1975, 53.
3. "Royals in Wild 11–10 Victory," *Salina Journal*, May 2, 1975, 18.
4. Steve Jacobson, "Rojas, a Bargain at Second, or Third," *Newsday* (Melville, NY), May 25, 1975, 249. Yankee Stadium was being renovated.
5. *Ibid.*
6. "Cookie Rojas to Al Dark: 'Don't Make Me an All-Star,'" *Palladium Item* (Richmond, IN), July 6, 1975, 25.
7. "Herzog New Royal Boss," *Omaha World Herald*, July 25, 1975, 27.
8. Rodríguez-Mayoral, "Mis Memorias."
9. "Rain Dampens Royals, Expos," *St. Joseph News-Press*, April 7, 1976, 25.
10. Ken Leiker, "Reserve or Not, Cookie Rojas Still Valuable to Kansas City," *Maryville Forum*, May 29, 1976, 6.
11. Mike DeArmond, "Frank White Can't Escape Shadows," *Kansas City Star*, July 19, 1976, 13.
12. *Ibid.*
13. William L. McCorkle, "Heroes Welcomed at Early Hour," *Kansas City Star*, September 30, 1976, 1.
14. Phone conversation with Tab Rojas, June 10, 2023.
15. "Royals Celebrate Pennant Win," *Park City Daily News*, October 3, 1976.
16. Fred Rothenberg, "Brett Is AL Batting King," *Rocky Mount Telegram*, October 4, 1976, 10.
17. *Ibid.*
18. Ed Boswell, "Cookie Glad He Could Contribute," *Olathe News*, October 1, 1976, 6.
19. "Home Town Boos Are Tough," *Columbian* (Vancouver, WA), June 22, 1977, 12.
20. "Cookie Rojas to Call It Quits," *Salina Journal*, September 16, 1977, 15.
21. Phone conversation with Victor Rojas, April 10, 2022.
22. Phone conversation with Mike Rojas, April 24, 2022.
23. Phone conversation with Bobby Rojas, May 22, 2023.
24. George Koppe, "Fans Tell Cookie He's Their Champ," *Kansas City Times*, October 1, 1977, 1, 14.
25. Dan George, "Rojas Hits, Swims," *Courier News* (Sommerville, NJ), October 1, 1977, 9.
26. *Ibid.*
27. "Rojas Celebrates Night With Splash," *Emporia Gazette*, October 1, 1977, 25.
28. "Rojas Career Ends," *Salina Journal*, October 10, 1977, 14.

Chapter Eight

1. "Cubs to Use Rojas as Coach," *Springfield News-Leader*, October 18, 1977, 10.
2. Richard Dozier, "Rojas Goes to Bat

for Convicted Cepeda," *Chicago Tribune*, June 21, 1978, 79.

3. *Ibid*.

4. "Cubs Add Rojas, 38, to Active Roster," *Chicago Tribune*, September 2, 1978, 59.

5. "Horton Tired of Shuffling Around," *Bennington Banner*, March 10, 1979, 12.

6. Mike Zabitka, "Wiltbank Pitches Well in Venezuela," *News Journal* (Wilmington, DE), February 12, 1979, 14.

7. Conversation with Mike Rojas, April 24, 2022. Unlike Cuba, the Venezuelan Socialist Government is not involved and, therefore, does not interfere with the baseball operations of its country.

8. Voice of the Fan, "Cooperative Fans," *The Sporting News*, October 6, 1979, 8.

9. Randy Minkoff, "Cubs Pick Dodger Coach," *Kenosha News*, October 2, 1979, 15.

10. "Herzog Successor? People Want Rojas," *Fort Worth Star-Telegram*, October 4, 1979, 74.

11. Randy Brown, "Rojas Has Exactly What It Takes to Be a Manager," *Wichita Eagle*, November 19, 1979, 88.

12. "New Leadership Hopes to Keep Cubs on the Run," *Chicago Tribune*, August 19, 1980, 39.

13. Phone conversation with Victor Rojas, April 10, 2022.

14. Mike Fish, "The Shadow Knows What the Angels Lack in Race: A Quisenberry," *Kansas City Times*, September 20, 1982, C2.

15. "Angels Sign El Tiante," *Bangor Daily News*, August 3, 1982, 12.

16. http://www.mlb.com/royals/hall-of-fame, accessed April 24, 2023.

17. Jon Heyman, "Cookie Jumps at Promotion," *Daily Breeze* (Hermosa Beach, CA), March 27, 1988, 36.

18. Ross Newhan, "Crunch Time for Cookie," *Los Angeles Times*, May 23, 1988, 1, 17.

19. Phone conversation with Victor Rojas, April 10, 2022.

20. In 1938, on an interim basis, Cuban Mike González assumed the role of the majors' first manager from Latin America with the St. Louis Cardinals. He was followed by Preston Gómez in 1969. In 1984, Dominican native Ozzie Virgil skippered the San Diego Padres for nine games, and Havana-born Orlando "Marty" Martínez piloted one game for the 1986 Seattle Mariners. African Americans Frank Robinson, Larry Doby, and Maury Wills rounded out the list.

21. "Rojas Has Ball Over First Win," *Indianapolis News*, April 7, 1988, 27.

22. John Weyler, "Port Denies He's Already Decided Rojas Won't Manage Angels in 1989," *Los Angeles Times*, August 30, 1988, 74.

23. "Cookie Crumbles for Rojas," *Tampa Tribune*, September 24, 1988, 29.

24. Phone interview with Victor Rojas, April 10, 2022.

25. Mike Wojciechowski, "Through It All Rojas Is Still a Loyal Angel," *Los Angeles Times*, March 11, 1989, CC14.

26. Larry Whiteside, "Horn's Chances Increase with Two Good Showings," *Boston Globe*, March 14, 1989, 71.

27. Ronnie Ramos, "Arocha Sees Friend in Guantanamo Visit," *Miami Herald*, December 1, 1994, 43. Similar visits, involving relief aid, were made by other ballplayers, including José Canseco. Iconic, exiled Cuban singers Gloria Estefan, Willy Chirino, and Celia Cruz all performed at the base during the humanitarian crisis.

28. George Richards, "A Tag at the Plate, but Rivers Says He Ran Through It," *Miami Herald*, February 26, 1995, 54.

29. Mike Phillips, "Cuban Legends to Star Again Sunday," *Miami Herald*, July 23, 1995, 6D.

30. Phone conversation with Mike Rojas, April 24, 2022.

31. *Ibid*. *Liga Mayor de Béisbol Profesional*, known as the LMBP, is a current summer league operating in Venezuela. In English, it is the Venezuelan Major League.

32. Chuck Greenwood, "Things Worked Out Well in Florida," *Sports Collector's Digest*, March 29, 1996, 101.

33. Thomas Hill, "Valentine's Way Worked Wonders," *New York Daily News*, September 28, 1997, 65.

34. Barry Stanton, "Players Make America Look Good," *Journal News* (White Plains, NY), April 26, 2000, 27.

35. Murray Chass, "O's Foes Speaking Out," *York Dispatch*, March 25, 1999, B5.

36. Tom Maloney, "He's Touched All the Bases," *National Post* (Toronto), February 26, 2001, 22.
37. Bob Elliot, "Tosca Has Been a Winner Before," *Kingston Whig-Standard*, June 5, 2002, 24.
38. Conversation with Armando Méndez, January 26, 2022.
39. "Florida Notebook," *Miami Herald*, October 22, 2003, 55.
40. Juan C. Rodríguez, "Neu Will Return to Familiar Turf," *South Florida Sentinel*, December 18, 2003, 58.
41. Jorge Ebro, "'Cookie' del diamante al micrófono," *El Nuevo Herald* (Miami, FL), February 2, 2006, 27. Translated from Spanish.
42. Greg Cote, "Team Is Ready for Guillen's Absence," *Miami Herald*, April 11, 2012, 7D.
43. Steven Wine, "Guillen Returns from Suspension," *Daily Chronicle* (DeKalb, IL), April 17, 2012, 14.
44. Marino Martínez Peraza, "Cookie Rojas a la inmortalidad," *El Nuevo Herald* (Miami, FL), February 9, 2013, C1, translated from Spanish. The Latino Hall's website (latinbaseball.org) presents the player eligibility eras as pre– and post–1970.
45. Tom D'Angelo, "Shocking Death Feels Like Losing Family," *Palm Beach Post*, September 26, 2016, C5.
46. Phone conversation with Victor Rojas, April 10, 2022.
47. Phone conversation with Bobby Rojas, May 22, 2023.
48. Phone conversation with Mike Rojas, April 24, 2022.
49. Phone conversation with Victor Rojas, April 10, 2022.
50. Jim Murray, "Cookie's Specialty: Not Hitting, It's Fielding," *Pensacola News Journal*, August 29, 1974, 32.

Bibliography

Books

Berke, Art. *Unsung Heroes of the Major Leagues*. New York: Random House, 1974.
Cresconi Benítez, José A. *El Béisbol Profesional Boricua*. San Juan: Aurora Comunicación Intregal, 1997.
Ferrer, Ada. *Cuba: An American History*. New York: Scribner's, 2021.
Figueredo, Jorge S. *Who's Who in Cuban Baseball, 1878–1961*. Jefferson, NC: McFarland, 2007.
Hernández, Lou. *Bobby Maduro and the Cuban Sugar Kings*. Jefferson, NC: McFarland, 2019.
_____. *The Rise of the Latin American Baseball Leagues, 1947–1961*. Jefferson, NC: McFarland, 2011.
Hoffman, David E. *Give Me Liberty: The True Story of Oswaldo Paya and His Daring Quest for a Free Cuba*. New York: Simon & Schuster, 2022.
Oliva, Tony, with Bob Fowler. *Tony O! The Trials and Triumphs of Tony Oliva*. New York: Hawthorn, 1973.
Phillips, John. *The Story of the Havana Sugar Kings, 1954–1960*. Kathleen, GA: Capital, 2003.
Shlaes, Amity. *The Forgotten Man: A New History of the Great Depression*. New York: MJF Books, 2007.
Van Hyning, Thomas E. *Puerto Rico's Winter League: A History of Major League Baseball's Launching Pad*. Jefferson, NC: McFarland, 1995.
Zygner, Sam. *The Forgotten Marlins: A Tribute to the 1956–1960 Original Miami Marlins*. Lanham, MD: Scarecrow, 2013.

Articles

Barrouquere, Elizabeth. "Evangeline League Archives Provide Glimpse of Past." houmatoday.com, accessed April 30, 2022.
Breen, Matt. "The Legend of Dick Allen's 42-Ounce Bat/Extra Innings." *Philadelphia Inquirer*, December 10, 2022, inquirer.com, accessed February 8, 2023.
Costello, Rory. "1964 Phillies: In Defense of Chico Ruiz's 'Mad Dash.'" 1964 Philadelphia Phillies essays, sabr.org.
Francis, Bill. "Cookie Rojas' Glove Made It to Cooperstown." April 1, 2020, accessed January 23, 2023. https://www.mlb.com/news/phillies-alumni-cookie-rojas-glove-in-hall-of-fame.
Hochman, Stan. "Retelling the Story of the Phillies' Collapse of 1964." *Philadelphia Inquirer*, July 19, 2014.
Kaplan, Jake. "Phillies Veteran Rojas Focuses on the Good Things About 1964." *Philadelphia Inquirer*, July 19, 2014.

Krell, David. "April 6, 1973: Nolan Ryan Whiffs 12 on Opening Day; Vietnam War POW Throws Out First Ball." sabr.org/gamesproject.
Riis, Richard. "April 12, 1965: Phillies Win First Game at Astrodome." sabr.org/gamesproject.
Soderhold-Difatte, Bryan. "Beyond Bunning and Short Rest: An Analysis of Managerial Decisions That Led to the Phillies Epic Collapse in 1964." *SABR Baseball Research Journal* (Fall 2010), sabr.org.
Sweetman, Jim. "1964 Phillies: Building the Not-Quite Perfect Beast." 1964 Philadelphia Phillies essays, sabr.org.
Wolf, Gregory H. "October 4, 1964: Reds Pennant Hopes Dashed on Last Day of Season." sabr.org/gamesproject.

Newspapers

Atlanta Constitution, Bangor Daily News, Baytown Sun (Baytown, TX), *Benington Banner, Boston Globe, Bradenton Herald, Buffalo News, Chillicothe Constitution-Tribune, Cincinnati Enquirer, Cincinnati Post, Cincinnati Post & Times-Star, Columbian* (Vancouver, WA), *Courier News* (Sommerville, NJ), *Courier-Post* (Cherry Hill, NJ), *Daily Breeze* (Hermosa Beach, CA), *Daily Chronicle* (DeKalb, IL), *Daily Press* (Newport News, VA), *Daily Times* (Salisbury, MD), *Danville Register, Delaware County Daily Times, Detroit Free Press, Emporia Gazette, Evening Bulletin* (Philadelphia, PA), *Evening Sun* (Hanover, PA), *Express* (San Antonio, TX), *Fort Lauderdale News, Fort Worth Star-Telegram, Greeley Daily Tribune, Hartford Courant, Herald-News, Indiana Gazette, Indianapolis News, Jefferson City-Post Tribune, Journal Gazette* (Fort Wayne, IN), *Journal News* (White Plains, NY), *Kansas City Star, Kansas City Times, Kenosha News, Kingston Daily Freeman, Kingston Whig-Standard, Leavenworth Times, Lebanon Daily News, Los Angeles Times, Maryville Forum, Miami Herald, Miami News, Morning Call* (Allentown, PA), *Morning News* (Florence, SC), *National Post* (Toronto), *New York Daily News, News Journal* (Wilmington, DE), (*Newsday* (Melville, NY), *El Nuevo Herald* (Miami, FL), *Olathe News, Omaha-World Herald, Orlando Sentinel, Paducah Sun, Palladium-Item* (Richmond, IN), *Palm Beach Post, Park City Daily News, Pensacola News Journal, Philadelphia Bulletin, Philadelphia Daily News, Philadelphia Inquirer, Pittsburgh Courier, Pittsburgh Post-Gazette, Portsmouth Herald, Progress Bulletin* (Pomona, CA), *Rocky Mount Telegram, Sacramento Bee, St. Cloud Times, St. Joseph News-Press, St. Louis Post-Dispatch, Salina News Journal, San Francisco Examiner, Sedalia Democrat, Sentinel* (Lewiston, PA), *South Florida Sentinel, Springfield News, Springfield News-Leader, Star Gazette* (Elmira, NY), *Sunday News* (Lancaster, PA), *Tampa Tribune, Town Talk* (Alexandria, LA), *Tucson Daily Citizen, Wichita Eagle, Wilson Daily Times, York Dispatch.*

Periodicals

The Sporting News, Sports Collector's Digest.

SABR Bioprojects

Allen, Malcolm. "Roberto Peña." sabr.org/bioproject.
Armour, Mark. "Orlando Cepeda." sabr.org/bioproject.
Berger, Ralph. "Jim Bunning." sabr.org/bioproject.
Bloss, Bob. "Bobby Wine." sabr.org/bioproject.
Corbett, Wayne. "Gabe Paul." sabr.org/bioproject.
Costello, Rory. "Wayne Simpson." sabr.org/bioproject.
D'Ambrosio, Rich. "Dick Allen." sabr.org/bioproject.

Bibliography

DiFonzo, John. "Paul Splittorff." sabr.org/bioproject.
Even, Dan. "Bob Oldis." sabr.org/bioproject.
Gordon, Peter M. "Cookie Rojas." sabr.org/bioproject.
Green, John F. "George Myatt." sabr.org/bioproject.
Hawthorne, Tom. "Charlie Metro." sabr.org/bioproject.
Kuehl, Steve. "Don Money." sabr.org/bioproject.
Nowlin, Bill. "Tommy Harper." sabr.org/bioproject.
Puerzer, Rich. "Vida Blue." sabr.org/bioproject.
Ramírez, José I. "Pancho Herrera." sabr.org/bioproject.
Ramírez, José I., and Rory Costello. "Jackie Hernández." sabr.org/bioproject.
Ramírez, José I., and Rory Costello. "Miguel de la Hoz." sabr.org/bioproject.
Ramírez, José I., and Rory Costello. "Tony González." sabr.org/bioproject.
Ramírez, José I., and Rory Costello. "Tony Taylor." sabr.org/bioproject.
Sloope, Terry. "Curt Flood." sabr.org/bioproject.
Van Hyning, Thomas. "Ed Bauta." sabr.org/bioproject.
Vorperian, John. "Gene Mauch." sabrbioproject.org.
Wancho, Joseph. "Cal McLish." sabr.org/bioproject.
Wancho, Joseph. "Dick Groat." sabr.org/bioproject.
Wolf, Gregory H. "Al Widmar." sabr.org/bioproject.
Wolf, Gregory H. "Rob Gardner." sabr.org/bioproject.

Websites

Baseball-reference.com.
Eventshistory.com.
Newspapers.com.
PaperofRecord.com.
Retrosheet.org.
Sabr.org.
Wikipedia.org.
Wikiwand.com.
YouTube.com.

Index

Numbers in ***bold italics*** indicate pages with illustrations

Aaron, Henry 12, 126
Águilas Cibaeñas 123
Alfonso, Edgardo 178
Allen, Dick 42, 47–49, 52–55, 57–59, 61, 64, 66, 68, 74–75, 80, 82–83, 85–86, 88–90, 92, 94–99, 102–113, 115, 124–125
Almendares Alacranes (Scorpions) 28–29
Alomar, Santos "Sandy" 125, 132, 145
Alonso, Reinaldo 11
Alou, Mateo "Matty" 36, 180
Alston, Walter 81, 91
Altman, George 51
Alvarez, Alberto 11
Alvarez, Rogelio "Borrego" 25–26, 34, 177
Amalfitano, Joey 160, 163–165
Amaro, Rubén 45, 48, 55, 60, 65, 71, 74–75, 78–80, 87
American Association 17
American League 33, 47, 116, 118, 120–121, 126–127, 130, 132, 134, 138, 140, 161, 177
Anaheim Angels 101
Anderson, George "Sparky" 134
Andrade, Candido 12
Aparicio, Luis 121, 129
Apodaca, Bob 174
Aragua Tigres (Tigers) 100–101, 123
Arecibo Lobos (Wolves) 35, 36, 43–44, 76–77, 86–87, 93
Arias, Rodolfo "Rudy" 34
Arizona Diamondbacks 174–175
Arizona-Mexico League 12
Arkansas Travelers 48, 57, 83
Armas, Tony 180
Arocha, Rene 171

Arroyo, Luis 21, 36
Ashburn, Richie 110
Astrodome 98, 103
Atlanta Braves 96, 98, 175
Atlanta Stadium 126–127
Autry, Gene 168–169
Autry, Jackie 168
Avila, Rafael 180
Ayón, Andrés 11, 25
Azcué, José 21, 34
Azucareros del Este 166

Bailey, Bob 48
Bailey, Ed 53
Baldschun, Jack 58, 62, 66, 80, 81, 83
Baltimore Orioles 38, 79, 82, 112, 119–120, 122, 125, 138, 175
Bando, Sal 150
Banks, Eddie 109
Banks, Ernie 105, 108
Batista, Fulgencio 32
Bauta, Eduardo "Ed" 32
Baylor, Don 171
Beahon, George 22
Beckert, Glenn 107
Beckett, Josh 178
Bécquer, Julio 10, 30
Belinsky, Bo 78, 80, 88
Bench, Johnny 125, 133
Bengochea, Arturo 20
Bennett, Dennis 55, 63, 72, 78
Benson, Vern 32
Berdette, Lew 82, 88
Berke, Art 148
Berra, Yogi 68, 82
Bevacqua, Kurt 132–133, 140
Biittner, Larry 163
Bird, Doug, 155

199

Blasingame, Don 39–41
Blasingame, Wade 59
Blattner, Buddy 181
Blomberg, Ron 130
Blue, Vida 121, 127, 134, 151
Blyleven, Bert 119, 137
Boer Indians 43
Boles, John 173
Bonds, Bobby 133
Boone, Bob 170
Boozer, John 43
Bordman, Sid 137
Boros, Steve 146
Boston Red Sox 78, 102, 116, 120, 125, 130, 138, 147, 149, 166, 169, 176
Boullón, Luis 10, 21
Boullón, Luis Roberto 21
Bowa, Larry 112, 169
Bowsfield, Ted 19
Boyer, Ken 53, 74
Bracho, José "Carrao" 35
Bragan, Bobby 60
Brandt, Jackie 192
Brett, George 38, 114, 139, 142–143, 148–153, 155, 157, 159
Briggs, John 52, 75, 78, 88, 90
Bristol, Dave 9, 11
Brock, Lou 115
Broeg, Bob 114–115
Browne, Byron 112
Brye, Steve 152
Buckner, Bill 167
Buffalo Bisons 17
The Buffalo News 23
Buhl, Bob 87, 93
Bunning, Barbara 51
Bunning, Jim 38, 47–52–56, 58, 61, 64–65, 67–68, 70, 72–73, 80, 85, 87–88, 90–92, 94–95, 98, 102–104
Bunning, Mary 51
Burgmeier, Tom 124
Burke, Joe 151, 163
Busby, Steve 132, 134, 137, 139, 141, 143, 146, 149, 155, 166
Busch Stadium 51, 88, 109

Caguas-Guayama Criollos 34
California Angels 43, 80, 117, 120, 125, 129–130, 132, 140, 143, 145, 148, 151, 155, 157, 164–169
Calixto García Hospital 2
Callison, Johnny 44, 47, 52–55, 59, 61–63, 74, 80–81, 83, 86–87, 104, 106
Calviño, Wilfredo 34
Camden Yards 175
Campaneris, Dagoberto "Bert" 139–140, 172
Campanis, Al 167
Campanis, Jim 119
Candlestick Park 103
Cannizzaro, Chris 25
Canseco, José 168, 175
Caracas Leones (Lions) 35, 39, 100, 122, 129
Cardenal, José 34
Cárdenas, Leo 12–13, 15, 34, 40, 66, **89**, 121
Cardinal Dougherty High School Band 104
Cardwell, Don 81, 104
Carew, Rod 57, 114, 120–121, 123, 125–126, 128, 133, 140, 145
Caribbean Professional Baseball Federation 29, 35
Caribbean Series 20, 29, 35, 43, 118, 123, 161–162, 179
Carlton, Steve 105
Carolina League 13
Carpenter, Bob 73, 94, 106–107, 110
Carpenter, Chris 177
Carty, Rico 60
Cash, Norm 122
Castaño, Antonio "Tony" 22, 26, 76, 77
Castro, Fidel 12, 19, 21, 23–25, 28, 30, 32–33, 144, 171, 175, 179–180
Cater, Danny 43
Cedeño, César 161
Cepeda, Orlando 86, 140–141, 161, 165
César, José 28
Chacón, Elio 13, 15, 18, 39
Chambliss, Chris 144, 153–154, 158, 171
Chicago Cubs 48, 53, 66–67, 81, 87–88, 94, 102, 105, 107–108, 110, 160–165, 175
Chicago White Sox 11, 28, 117, 123–125, 137, 140–141, 145, 148, 155, 167, 169, 172
Chiriqui-Bocas Farmers 43
Cienfuegos Elefantes (Elephants) 18–19, 20, 29–30
The Cincinnati Enquirer 24
The Cincinnati Post 39
Cincinnati Reds 9, 11–12, 21, 34, 37, 39–42, 44, 52–54, 56–59, 60, 62, 64–66, 68, 70, 72–73, 88, 91–92, 98, 102, 125, 128–129, 133, 147, 161, 172, 174
Cinco Estrellas (team) 34
Cisco, Galen 146
Ciudad Deportiva 177
Clem, Harold 102

Index

Clemente, Roberto **89**, 98, 125
Cleveland Indians 68, 76, 145, 149, 155
Clines, Gene 165
Clinton, Bill 171
club Artesano 10
club Fortuna 8
Cobb, Ty 57
Colburn, Jim 154–155, 158–159
Colegio La Luz 8, 9, 21
Colorado Rockies 173
Colt Stadium 45
Columbus Jets 17, 26
Comiskey Park 137, 140, 167
Concepción, Davey 129, 161
Conner, Mark 177
Connie Mack Stadium 44–45, 48, 51, 57–58, 60–61, 81–82, 91, 95–98, 100, 107–108, 110, 115
Contón, Alfredo 11
Cordeiro, Reinaldo 18
Corrales, Pat 82–83, 87
Covington, Wes 47, 51, 55, 68, 75, 80, 85–86
Cowens, Al 139, 155, 158
Crawford, Shag 60
Cromartie, Warren 172
Crosley Field 41, 53, 66, 68, 89
Cruz, José 177
Cuban Sugar Kings 8–9, 11, 13–14, 16, 19, 21–23, 25, 29–30, 76, 137
Cuban Winter League 10, 14–15, 19–20, 27, 30–31, 33
Cuéllar, Miguel Angel "Mike" 24–25, 76, 98, 122, 148, 177, 180
Cuéllar, Mike (Mrs.) 26, 122
Cueto, Dagoberto "Bert" 35
Culp, Ray 47, 53, 72, 86, 88, 102
Culver, George 77

Dal Canton, Bruce 119
Dallas-Fort Worth Rangers 41
Dalrymple, Clay 47, 52, 55, 57, 59, 66, 81, 83, 88, 96, 105
Dark, Alvin 145
Davalillo, Vic **89**, 100, 118
Davis, Willie 41, 45, 57, 92, 133
de Armas, Emilio 165
De Jesús, Iván 160–161
Demeter, Don 45, 47
Dent, Bucky 170
DeRosa, Mark 101
Detroit Tigers 47, 76, 125, 132, 140, 161–162, 172–173, 176
Devine, Bing 113
DeWitt, William O. 39
Dillard, Steve 163

Dodger Stadium 40, 45, 56, 81, 96, 103, 105
Dolson, Frank 69
Dombrowski, Dave 169, 173
Dominican Winter League 166
Donatelli, Augie 106
Doubleday Field 38
Doyle, Denny 112
Drago, Dick 120, 122, 124, 132
Dressen, Charlie 47
Drysdale, Don 49, 71, 80, 104, 106, 107
Duluth Dukes 10
Duncan, Dave 169
Dunlap, Harry 146
Durocher, Leo 94
Dustal, Bob 32

Easter, Luke 21
Easterly, Ted 128
Eckert, William 93
Ed Sullivan Show 51
Edwards, Johnny 53
Eisenhower, Dwight D. 23, 27–28
Elia, Lee 165, 169
Ellis, Sammy 88
Ellsworth, Dick 102
Ennis, Del 110
Escogido Leones (Lions) 162
Estadio Latinoamericano 175

Fairly, Ron 57, 148
Farrell, Turk 97, 104, 105
Fenway Park 125, 130, 176
Fernández, José 180
Ferrer, Ada 20, 27
Fidrych, Mark "The Bird" 180
Figueroa, Eduardo "Ed" 153, 158
Fish, Mike 165
Fisher, Jack 86, 95
Fisk, Carlton 126
Fitzmorris, Al 139, 141, 143, 146, 148–149
Flood, Curt 12–13, 51, 112, 113
Florida Instructional League 34, 123, 128
Florida International League 14
Florida Marlins 32, 169–171, 173, 175, 177–178
Florida State League 9
Forbes Field 95, 108
Ford, Ted 124
Forman, Al 60
Ft. Lauderdale Stadium 172
Forte, Dominic 84
Forte, Fabian 84
Foster, George 172

Index

Foy, Joe 118
Franks, Herman 162–163
Frazier, Joe 97
Freehan, Bill 47, 132
Freese, Gene 39
Frey, Jim 164
Frick, Ford 28
Frisco Roughriders 101
Fryman, Woody 102–104
Fuentes, Rigoberto "Tito" 97

Gagliano, Phil 84
García González, Caridad 21
Gardner, Rob 85
Garner, Horace 12
Garvey, Steve 140
Ghandi, Mahatma 61
Gibson, Bob 51, 62, 64, 67–68, 76
Giles, Warren 66
Gómez, Pedro "Preston" 16, 18, 34, 77, 116, 160, 163–165
Gómez, Rubén 86, 165
Gonder, Jesse 50
González, Andrés Antonio "Tony" 11, 33, 36, 45, 47–48, 50, 55, 66, 68, 75, 79–80, 85, 90, 95, 98
González, Elián 175
González, Juan "Igor" 180
González, Miguel Angel "Mike" 28
Gotay, Julio 34
Grady, Sandy 73
Gran Stadium (del Cerro de la Habana) 10, 15, 19, 21–22, 37, 137, 175
Gray, Curtis 179
Green, Dallas 61, 170
Grich, Bobby 140, 145
Groat, Dick 87, 89, 95–96
Guasave Cotton Growers 122
Guerra, Fermín 10
Guerra Matos, General Felipe 29
Guidry, Ron 158
Guillén, Ozzie 179
Gullett, Don 158
Gura, Larry 150, 158–159

Habana Leones (Lions) 28, 30
Hall, Dick 104
Haller, Tom 97
Hamilton, Jack 43, 47
Hamner, Granville "Granny" 109
Hannan, Jim 117
Hansen, Bob 139
Harmon, Pat 39
Harper, Bryce 80
Harper, Tommy 39–40
Harrah, Toby 129

Harrison, Chuck 98
Hassler, Andy 158
Havana Biltmore 8
Havana Cubans 14
Healy, Fran 144, 148, 150
Hernández, Jackie 117, 119
Herrera, Francisco "Panchón" 18, 34
Herrnstein, John 55, 59, 87
Herzog, Whitey 145–149, 152, 154–155, 157–159, 163
Hickory Crawdads 172
High Point-Thomasville Hi-Toms 13
Higuera, Teddy 180
Hiram Bithorn Stadium 42
Hisle, Larry 103–104, 109
Hispanic Heritage Baseball Museum Hall of Fame 179
Hoerner, Joe 112
Hoffman, David E. 27
Homestead-Miami Speedway 179
Horton, Willie 162
Houston Astros 39, 79–80, 82–83, 96–98, 103, 106–107, 118, 124, 164, 172
Houston Colt .45s 49, 56, 73
Hoz, de la Miguel Angel "Mike" 34, 36–37, 60
Hubbell, Carl 85
Hunt, Ron 50
Hunter, Jim "Catfish" 132, 138, 141, 153
Hurd, Tom 25
Hurdle, Clint 170
Hutchinson, Fred 39–41, 68
Hutton, Tommy 179

Iglesia del Carmelo 21
Institute of Sports, Physical Education and Recreation aka INDER 30
Inter-American Series 29, 35, 37, 39, 43
International League 13–14, 16, 22–25, 34, 42, 48
Iorg, Garth 177
Israel, Elbert "Al" 12
Izquierdo, Enrique "Hank" 25
Izquierdo, Hank (Mrs.) 26

Jack Russell Stadium 94
Jack Tar Hotel (Clearwater, FL) 94
Jack Tar Hotel (NJ) 26
Jackson, Al 67
Jackson, Grant 86, 109, 153
Jackson, Larry 87, 91, 93, 96
Jackson, Reggie 121, 136, 140, 158–159
Jacksonville Braves 12
Jacobson, Steve 144
Jaster, Larry 88
Javier, Julian 48, 115

Index 203

Jenkins, Delores Jackson 94–95
Jenkins, Ferguson 44, 84, 86, 88, 93–94, 108
Jersey City Jerseys 25, 30, 32
Joe Robbie Stadium 171
Johnson, Alex 58, 64, 66, 87
Johnson, Bob 118
Johnson, Davey 170
Johnson, Deron 66, 138
Johnson, Jerry 112
Johnson, Lou 105
Johnson, Walter 106
Jones, Willie 109–110
Joyner, Wally 167

Kansas City Athletics 116, 134
Kansas City Packers 128
Kansas City Royals 116–159, 161, 166, 172
Kansas City Royals Hall of Fame 166
The Kansas City Star 163
The Kansas City Times 124
Kasko, Eddie 40
Kauffman, Ewing 121, 127–128, 131
Kauffman, Ewing (Mrs.) 121
Kauffman Stadium 180
Keane, Johhny 64, 82
Kennedy, Bob 163–164
Kennedy, Robert F. 106
Kenworthy, Duke 128
Kerr, Christie 179
Killebrew, Harmon 38, 121, 142, 145, 147
Kiner, Ralph 51
King, Dr. Martin Luther 103
Kirkpatrick, Ed 130
Kiwanis Club of Miami 171
Klein, Chuck 110
Knoop, Bobby 122
Knowles, Darold 127
Koufax, Sandy 41, 49, 52, 54, 69, 80–82, 84–85, 91–92
Kritzer, Cy 23
Kuhn, Bowie 110

Lachemann, Marcel 168
Lachemann, Rene 169, 171
La Guaira Tiburones (Sharks) 100, 118, 123
Lane, Marvin 140
Lanier, Hal 97
Lara Cardinales (Cardinals) 101, 118
Lau, Charlie 142, 146, 163
Lawsen, Earl 39
Laxton, Bill 102
LeFlore, Ron 161
Leiter, Al 174
Lemon, Bob 117, 119–120, 127–128

Leon, Eddie 138
Leonard, Dennis 145–146, 149, 153, 155, 158–159
Lewis, Allen 50
Leyland, Jim 173–174
Linz, Phil 87
Lisk, Delphine 26
Littell, Mark 149, 153–154, 159
Llanos, Armando 8
Loaiza, Esteban 177
Lock, Don 105
Lolich, Mickey 125
López, Al 82
Loria, Jeffrey 180
Los Angeles Angels 30
Los Angeles Dodgers 40–41, 45–47, 49, 52, 56–57, 65, 67, 69, 71, 80–82, 84–86, 90–92, 97, 103–104, 106, 133, 145, 167, 171
Los Angeles Herald-Examiner 63
Los Angeles Times 168, 181
Louisville Colonels 27
Lowrey, Harry "Peanuts" 78
Luciano, Ron 145
Luna, Major José David 130
Lyle, Albert "Sparky" 158–159

MacDonald, Bill 31–32
Macon Dodgers 12
Maduro, Jorge 18
Maduro, Roberto "Bobby" 9–11, 14, 21, 23, 27, 29–30, 32, 93, 137
Magallanes Navegantes (Navigators) 100, 118, 162
Mahaffey, Art 44, 48, 55, 57, 59, 72, 87
Maloney, Jim 68
Mantilla, Félix 12, **89**
Mantle, Mickey 80
Manuel, Charlie 107
Marianao Tigres (Tigers) 20
Marichal, Juan 72, 82–83, **89**, 97, 138, 166
Maris, Roger 45, *111*
Marlboro Smokers 20, 35
Marquez, Miguel 45
Martin, Billy 158, 169
Martínez, Buck 139, 144, 153, 176–177
Mauch, Gene 16–17, 42–47, 52–73, 77–79, 81–90, 94–98, 102, 104–107, 112, 152, **164**–168
May, Carlos 123
May, Dave 133
May, Jerry 119
May, Rudy 120
Mayagüez Indios (Indians) 34, 36–37, 42–43, 77, 87

Mayberry, John 124–125, 128–129, 131–135, 137, 142–143, 148–149, 153–154, 158
Mays, Willie 54, 74, 80, 82–83, 97–98, 125
Mazeroski, Bill 107
McCarver, Tim 65, 112
McClendon, Lloyd 173
McClure, Doug 154
McDaniel Lindy 137
McGraw, Tug 127
McGwire, Mark 168
McKean, Jim 168
McKeon, Jack 128, 130, 132, 134, 138–139, 141–142, 145–146
McLain, Denny 76–77
McLish, Cal 47, 78
McNally, Dave 113
McNamara, John 169
McRae, Hal 129–130, 137, 140–144, 148, 151–152, 155, 158, 171
Mejías, Román 34, 77
Melton, Bill 148
Memorial Stadium 125
Mendez, Armando 177–178
Mendoza, Cristobál "Minnie" 11
Mesa Community College 172
Messersmith, Andy 113
Metro, Charlie 120
Metropolitan Stadium 82, 89, 133
Mexican League 140, 166
Miami Marlins (IL) 15, 31
Miami Marlins (MLB) 179–181
Miami Sports Hall of Fame 179
Miami Stadium 24
Michael, Gene 172
Michalak, Chris 176
Mikoyan, Anastas 20
Miller, Marvin 131, 136
Miller, Paul 10, 27
Milwaukee Braves 10, 45, 53, 58, 60–62, 70–72, 84–85
Milwaukee Brewers 116–117, 133, 139, 144, 154, 166
Milwaukee County Stadium 139, 145
Minneapolis Millers 17, 19, 33, 42
Minnesota Twins 29, 33–34, 118–119, 121, 133, 137, 142–143, 146, 151–152
Miñoso, Orestes "Minnie" 10, 28, 33
Money, Don 102–104, 109
Montañez, Willie 113
Monteagudo, Aurelio 100
Montelone, Rick 168
Montreal Expos 112
Montreal Royals 15
Moore, Donnie 167

Morejón, Danny 17–18, 25, 34
Morgan, Joe 80, 126, 134, 161
Moss, Les 165
Municipal Stadium (Cleveland) 117
Municipal Stadium (Kansas City) 116, 119–120, 123–125, 127–128, 131, 135, 148–149
Munson, Thurman 140, 148
Murcer, Bobby 121
Murphy, Bob 51
Murray, Jim 181
Muser, Tony 170
Myatt, George 78, 112

Namath, Joe 108
National League 40, 49–50, 54, 57, 60, 63–66, 68, 85, 87, 89, 92, 95–96, 98, 102, 109–110, 116, 126–127, 129, 133, 140–141, 145, 160, 165, 169, 171, 175–176
Navarro, Luis 26
Nelson, Dave 147
Nelson, Roger 128–129
Nen, Jendy 181
Nen, Rob 181
Nettles, Craig 144–145, 153, 158
New York Giants 113
New York Jets 108
New York Mets 39, 45, 49–51, 53, 62, 66–69, 71, 85–87, 95–96, 107, 112, 118, 127, 157, 171, 173–176, 178
New York Yankees 67–68, 76, 79, 82, 87, 121, 130, 132, 137, 144, 148, 150, 153–154, 156, 158- 160, 163, 169, 172, 176, 178
Nicaraguan Winter League 33
Niekro, Phil 82, 148
Nixon, Richard 129
Northern Autumn League 33, 36
Northern League 10–11
Nunn, Howie 25

Oakland-Alameda County Coliseum 138, 150
Oakland A's 38, 120–122, 124–125, 127, 132, 134–136, 138–141, 145–146, 150–151, 155, 168, 173
Obregón, Teodoro 11
Offerdahl, John 179
Oldis, Bob 78
Olean Oilers 10
Olerud, John 177
Oliva, Tony 33–34, 74, **89**, 121, 165, 172, 177
Oliver, Al 147
Oliver, Bob 124

Oliver, Gene 96, 102
Omaha Royals 128
Orange Bowl 179
Ordoñez, Rey 175, 177
Orta, Jorge 145
Osteen, Claude 96, 106
Otero, Pepito 8
Otero, Reggie (Mrs.) 42
Otero, Regino "Reggie" 10, 34–35, 39–40, 100–101
Otis, Amos 38, 116, 118, 120–121, 123, 126–128, 130, 132–134, 143–144, 147–148, 150, 166
O'Toole, Jim 57, 59
Owens, Jim 42

Pacheco, Antonio "Tony" 10, 118
Pacific Coast League 17, 59, 104
Padilla, José 10–11
Palmeiro, Rafael 175
Panama-Nicaragua Winter League 34–35
Pappas, Milt 82
Parker Field 24
Parra, Daniel 10
Pascual, Camilo 34
Patek, Freddie 119–120, 123–124, 127–128, 132, 134, 137–141, 143–144, 148, 151, 157, 159, 177
Pattin, Marty 146, 149, 155, 158
Paul, Gabe 9, 25, 26
Peña, Orlando 25, 32, 34
Peña, Orlando (Mrs.) 26
Pequeño, Alfredo 20
Pérez, Atanasio "Tony" 31, 93, 148, 171–173, 177, 180
Perry, Gaylord 80
Peterson, Fritz 146
Philadelphia Athletics 119
The Philadelphia Bulletin 73
The Philadelphia Inquirer 50, 73
Philadelphia Phillies 33, 35, 40, 42–45, 47–112, 115, 119, 150, 156, 161, 173
Phillips, Adolfo 58, 61, 75, 87–88
Piña, Horacio 134
Piniella, Lou 115, 126, 128, 130, 134, 137, 159
Pinson, Vada 40–41, 58, 66, 147
Pittsburgh Pirates 42, 48, 52, 54, 64–65, 68, 81, 90–92, 102, 107, 119, 128–129, 147, 162, 174
Pizarro, Juan 77, 86, 165
Plumb, Lt. Commander Joseph C. 131
Polo Grounds 45
Ponce Leones (Lions) 35, 42, 123
PONY League 10

Port, Mike 166, 168
Porter, Darrell 154
Posada, Leo 34
Post, Wally 41
Powell, Bill 12
Power, Vic (Pellot) 66, 71, 75, 128, 147
Puente de Jovenes Profesionales Cubanos 171
Puerto Rican Winter League 32, 36–37, 42, 76
Purkey, Bob 41

Queen, Mel 120
Quinn, John 35, 42, 47, 58, 70–71, 73, 87, 97, 102, 106, 113
Quintana, Luis "Yiky" 178
Quirk, Jaime 154

Rader, Doug 148
Ramírez, Rafael "Felo" 178, 181
Ramos, Pedro 29–30, 34
Randle, Lenny 124
Randolph, Willie 153, 159, 172
Rapiños de Occidente (Western Raptors) 35
Rapp, Vern 123
Reedy, Fleming 12
Reese, Rich 132
Rende, Sal 173
Reyes, Napoleón "Nap" 10, 26–27, 32, 34
Reynolds, Bob 137
Reynosa Oilers 33
Ricciardi, J.P. 176
Rice, Jim 132
Richmond Virginians 14, 17, 24
Rico, Fred 116, 119
Ripken, Cal, Sr. 169
Rivas Solay, Estela 7
Rivers, Mickey 159, 172
Roarke, Mike 160
Robert F. Kennedy Stadium 117
Roberts, Robin 91, 109
Robinson, Brooks 138, 166
Robinson, Frank 40, 57, 66, 121, 132, 145
Robinson, Jackie 113
Rochester Red Wings 15–16, 21–22, 25
Rodríguez, Armando 139
Rodríguez-Mayoral, Luis 147
Rodríguez Olmo, Luis 35, 42–43
Roebuck, Ed 58, 60, 67
Rojas, Candida Rosa (Boullón García): as mother 38, 43–45, 84, 114–115, 151, 181; as baseball wife 181; courtship/engagement and marriage to Cookie *16*, 20–21, 31, *170*; interaction with players' wives (Jersey City 26; Kansas

Index

City 150–151; Philadelphia 75); learning to drive 42; perfume mishap 121
Rojas, José Luis 179
Rojas, Miguel Angel "Mike" 44, 84, 104, *154*, 156–157, 162, 172–173, 181
Rojas, Octavio Luis "Tab" 38, 43, 84, 104, 114, 119, 126, 142, 151, *154*, 157
Rojas, Octavio Victor "Cookie": All-Star Games 82, *89*, 121, 125–127, 133–134; amateur baseball 8; as broadcaster 178–180; childhood 8; with the Cincinnati Reds 37–42; with the Cuban Sugar Kings 13–*22*, 23–30; defending all nine positions 97; hitting streak, longest 105; with the Kansas City Royals 116–130, *131*–159; as major league coach 160–165, 171–177; as major league manager *164*, 166–169; minor/winter leagues' player 9–32, 35–*36*, 37, 42–43, 76–77, 93, 100–101, 117–118, 128–129; parents 7–8; with the Philadelphia Phillies 44–112; with the St. Louis Cardinals *111*–115; as scout 165, 169; winter league manager 86–87, 136–137, 162, 165–166
Rojas, Roberto Arturo "Bobby" 114, *154*, 157, 165, 181
Rojas, Roxana 7
Rojas, Tyler 101
Rojas, Victor Manuel 101, *154*, 156, 165, 167–168, 179, 181
Rojas Muñiz, Octavio Gregorio 7
Roosevelt, Franklin D. 7
Roosevelt Stadium 24, 26, 32
Rosa Cubana (baseball team) 8
Rose, Pete 43, 57, 134, 161
Roseboro, John 41, 52, 81, 92
Rothchild, Larry 174
Royals Stadium 130–135, 137–143, 146, 155–156, 179
Rudi, Joe 148, 156
Ruíz, Giraldo "Chico" 34, 39, 43, 57–58, 69–70, 72
Ryan, Mike 102, 105
Ryan, Nolan 129–130, 132, 143

Sadeki, Ray 64, 67
St. Louis Cardinals 32, 42, 48, 51–54, 58–59, 62, 64–70, 74, 76, 82, 84, 87–88, 91–92, 98, 104–105, 109, 111–113, 115, 118
Samuel, Amado 50
San Diego Padres (MLB) 164
San Diego Padres (PCL) 104, 107, 109
San Francisco Giants 49, 52, 56, 58–59, 66–67, 72, 80, 82–83, 86, 89–92, 96–97, 102–103, 107, 133, 138, 173, 175
San Juan Senadores (Senators) 33–34, 36, 42
Sánchez, Raúl 17–18, 25–26
Santo, Ron 53
Santurce Cangrejeros (Crabbers) 32, 37, 39, 42–43, 76–77, 93
Savannah Indians 12
Savannah Redlegs 11–13, 40
Sawyer, Eddie 94
Schaal, Paul 124–125
Scheinblum, Richie 126, 128–129
Schofield, Dick 48, 92
Schultz, Barney 64, 69
Scott, George 139
Seattle Mariners 155
Seaver, Tom 133
Seguí, Diego 34, 100–101
Seitz, Peter 113
Seminick, Andy 109
Shannon, Mike 62
Shantz, Bobby 60, 71
Shaughnessy, Frank 14, 16–17, 21, 23–24
Shaw, Jim 80
Shea Stadium 51, 53, 85, 144
Sheets (Mrs.) 156
Shlaes, Amity 7
Shoemaker, Willie 97
Short, Chris 45, 52–54, 57, 59, 62, 66–67, 80–81, 85, 87–88, 91, 93, 95, 103–104, 108–109
Showalter, Buck 172
Sierra, Rubén 171
Simmons, Curt 64, 68, 88
Simpson, Wayne 129–130
Sims, Duke 132
Sisler, Dick 57, 68
Sixto Escobar Stadium 37, 42
Skinner, Bob 107–110, 112
Smith, Reggie 116
Smith, Willie 108
Society of American Baseball *Research Journal* 72
Soderholm-Diffate, Bryan 72
Solaita, Tony 143, 149
South Atlantic (Sally) League 11, 40, 172
Spahn, Warren 60
Splittorff, Paul 130, 132, 134–135, 137–138, 141, 146, 149, 153, 155, 158–159, 166
The Sporting News 24, 122, 124–125, 134, 136, 163
Stallard, Tracy 45
Staub, Rusty 98

Steevens, Morrie 57
Stengel, Casey 86
Stennett, Renaldo "Rennie" 172
Stephenson, John 51, 130
Stoneham, Bill 126
Striker, Raúl, Jr. 178
Stuart, Dick 78, 81–83, 87
Stubing, Moose 168
Suárez, Miguel 175
Sutter, Bruce 163
Swift, Bob 77

Tabasco Olmecas (Olmecs) 166
Tallis, Cedric 118–119, 128–129
Tampa Bay Devil Rays 175, 177
Tanana, Frank 151
Tanner, Chuck 169
Tartabull, José 100, 177
Taylor, Antonio Nemesio "Tony" 10, 30, 33, 44, 48–50, 55, 66, 70, 75, 78–81, 84, 89, 95, 99, 115
Taylor, Hawk 50
Tenace, Gene 132
Terry Park 123, 154
Texas Rangers 101, 124–125, 127–130, 146–147, 149, 154, 175
Thomas, Frank 69, 71, 83
Thompson, Mike 122
Three Rivers Stadium 140
Tiant, Luis 30, 33, 36–37, 100, 120, 166, 177
Tiefenauer, Bobby 25
Tiger Stadium 121, 132
Tokyo Dome 175
Torborg, Jeff 106
Toronto Blue Jays 173, 176–177, 179
Toronto Maple Leafs 15, 22, 27
Toros del Este 166, 180
Torre, Frank 60
Torre, Joe 58, 59
Torres, Félix 25, 76
Torrez, Mike 158–159
Tosca, Carlos 173, 176–177
Tovar, César 118, 123
Tower Theater 31
Triandos, Gus 47, 50, 63, 83
Tropical Park 33
Trujillo, José Manuel "Manny" 160–161
Truman Sports Complex 123
Tsitouris, John 57, 68
Tucson Cowboys 12
Tufts, Bob 165
Tulner, Charles 11

Ueberroth, Peter 167
Uecker, Bob 87, 96

University of Alabama 114
University of Michigan 21
University Stadium 100, 118
Upshaw, Cecil 98

Valdés, Hernan 28
Valdespino, Hilario "Sandy" 34, 177
Valencia Industriales (Industrialists) 35, 43, 100
Valentine, Bobby 170, 174–175
Van Hyning, Thomas E. 33, 35–37, 93
Van Raalte, Ron 163
Vargo, Ed 60
Veale, Bob 91
Vedado Tennis Club 2
Venezuelan Baseball Hall of Fame 11
Venezuelan Winter League 100–101, 118, 123, 128–129, 136
Ventura, Robin 177
Versalles, Zoilo 30, 33, *89*
Virdon, Bill 169

Waitkus, Eddie 109–110
Waltz, Rich 179
The Washington Post 27
Washington Senators 122, 129
Watson, Bob 118
Watt, Eddie 100
Wausau Lumberjacks 11
Weaver, Earl 121, 126, 138
Weill, Roberto A. 180
Wellman, Bob 12
West Palm Beach Sun Chiefs 9, 11, 39
Weymer, Lee 84
Whitaker, Lou 38
White, Bill 52, 62, 87, 91, 94–95, 102–103
White, Frank (Kansas City Royals) 137, 141, 146–149, 155, 157, 165
White, Frank (Macon Dodgers) 12
Widmar, Al 78
Wieand, Ted 15
Williams, Billy 126, 148, 165
Williams, Dick 133, 140, 169
Williams, Jimy 169
Wiltbank, Benny 162
Windle, Dick 35
Wine, Bobby 48–49, 51, 55, 66, 71, 74, 78–79, 89, 95
Wise, Rick 51, 53, 78, 95, 112
Wohlford, Jim 143, 154
Wood, Wilbur 124, 126, 137, 148
Wright, Clyde 139
Wrigley Field 45, 81, 94, 105, 108–109, 163
Wulf, Steve 69

Yankee Stadium 68, 131, 133, 148, 153, 158–159, 178
Yastrzemski, Carl 19
Yeager, Steve 172

Zabala, Faustino 118
Zobrist, Ben 101
Zulia Águilas (Eagles) 123, 128–129, 136, 137
Zygner, Sam 31

www.ingramcontent.com/pod-product-compliance
Ingram Content Group UK Ltd.
Pitfield, Milton Keynes, MK11 3LW, UK
UKHW042000140426
5217IPUK00015B/907